Hang Gliding Spectacular

Fantastic Flying Stories

From The Hearts Of Those Who Live The Dream

Edited By
Jim (Sky Dog) Palmieri
Maggie Palmieri
Bob (Sky Dog) Grant

Illustrated By
Jules Makk

Great Flying Stories By Great Pilots
SKY DOG PUBLICATIONS
www.skydog.net

Hang Gliding Spectacular

Library of Congress Control Number: 2001119017
ISBN: 0-9715642-0-5

Printed in the United States by:
Morris Publishing
3212 East Highway 30
Kearney, NE 68847
1-800-650-7888

What Others Are Saying About This Book

I have been in the sport of hang gliding for just over a year and I gave up a morning of flying just to finish reading this book. The flying stories were so good; in my mind I often became the pilot in the story. Besides being fun to read, many of the stories have hidden gems allowing me to learn from other pilot's experiences. *A new student*

As an instructor, I am continuously being asked what it is like to fly up high or in the mountains or cross-country. Now I will tell my students to read this book. The stories in *Hang Gliding Spectacular* are so revealing as to what hang gliding is about, I highly recommend all pilots, new or old and at any level to read this book. *An instructor*

As a Tug Pilot, I get to see many pilots with all flying abilities from all over the world. Each pilot I tow is the product of many flying experiences, some good and some pretty scary. This book reflects the pilots I get to tow. I highly recommend this book to any person who has any interest in hang gliding. What you read is what you get! *A Tug pilot*

My husband has been flying since 1972 and our lives revolve around hang gliding. I have enough stories to fill a book myself. I gave my husband the review copy of *Hang Gliding Spectacular* and he read the whole book at a single sitting, interrupting me so many times just to listen to him read from a portion of an article. This book is a MUST for any pilot who lives and loves hang gliding. *A wife and sometimes driver*

As an author of many hang gliding articles in various international hang gliding magazines, I find this book absolutely interesting. I commend the editors for taking the time to put together this great collection of hang gliding stories. These flying stories are the BEST the international hang gliding community has to offer. *Author and hang gliding pilot*

About the Cover Photographer

MARK VAUGHN
Hangtographer

**Both a professional photographer
and hang glider pilot, Mark joins
his two loves to bring us images
that just wont quit.**

ANY PHOTO OF MARK VAUGHN'S
YOU SEE IS AVAILABLE FOR
PURCHASE AS A CLOCK OR PRINTED
PHOTOGRAPH.

**Usage Rights Also Available
For Editorial And AdvertisingPurposes**

PLEASE FEEL FREE TO INQUIRE
ABOUT YOUR PARTICULAR NEEDS
BY CONTACTING
MARK VAUGHN

MARK'S PHOTOGRAPHY
marksphotography@aol.com
508-877-8545
56 FLORISSANT AVENUE
FRAMINGHAM, MA 01701

This Book
HANG GLIDING SPECTACULAR

Is named in honor of the world-famous
ANNUAL HANG GLIDING SPECTACULAR
AND KITTY HAWK AIR GAMES

The Hang Gliding Spectacular
Is The Oldest Continuous Hang Gliding
Competition
In The World

Under the excellent direction and mentorship of John Harris,

The Hang Gliding Spectacular
is always held during the 3rd weekend of May.

Airsports Expo
Skydiving ⋏ Paragliding ⋏ Ultralights
Dune competitions
Demonstrations
Aero-tow Competition
Street Dance and Awards Ceremony

For information contact:
Kitty Hawk Kites
P.O. Box 1839
Nags Head, NC 27959
Call: 1-800-334-4777 or 1-877-FLY-THIS (359-8447)
email: **events@kittyhawk.com** or **bruce@kittyhawk.com**

Table of Contents

Outrunning the Dogcatcher

Old Dogs New Tricks

<u>The Sky Dog Howls</u>

The Wandering Dog

Warning-Disclaimer

Dedication

HANG GLIDING SPECTACULAR

Is Dedicated to the Memory of

Michael "Hollywood" Champlin
September 9, 1958 to June 16, 1999

Winds of Passion

Denise Lindquist

A breeze on my cheek, a gentle caress.
A taste of things to come.
This excites me beyond compare.
I stand at the edge, waiting for you.
Take me to new heights of joy and passion.
Lips trembling, eyes glazed with fire.
I look forward to our joining, my first time with you.
Ready now, I run into your arms, and you lift me up.
Let us share this moment,
this dance, this magic in the air.
Oh glorious wind, embrace me!!
I wish to learn more of you.
To taste this sweet joy of flight.

A Dedication to Michael Champlin

They Called Me *Hollywood*
Tiki Mashy

Michael Champlin Speaks ...

June 16, 1999, Hobbs, New Mexico. The day looked great, but the lack of wind made it far from a world record day, and since I'm swinging for homeruns everyday, flying for distance today would be pointless. However, I was still excited about flying today. I told Tiki that maybe JB would let me fly his Millennium in thermal conditions this afternoon. She smiled and gave me the thumbs up. Minutes later JB came up to me and said, "Hey Hollywood, you wanna fly my glider today?"

"Heck, yeah!" I

I'd flown JB's glider a couple times before in Hobbs in smooth conditions. The flights were pretty much unremarkable. My only concern then was landing. The pitch on the Mill seemed to be more responsive then what I was use to on my flex wing, and that in particular concerned me. I told Tiki that I was afraid of pulling back too hard on the stick, but didn't let on to JB the depth of my unease. A couple of weeks previous, two guys came to Hobbs with Millenniums. One had expressed that he was afraid to fly slow on landing, fearing he might accidentally spin it. Hearing that made me wonder how prone the Millennium was to spinning. Would it give me any warning or would it just happen? Boy, that really got me thinking. I don't know, after flying the Mill a couple of times, I had pretty much decided that it was probably not the glider for me, but I'd give it every chance to prove me wrong, though. I knew I was better suited for the Exxtasy or the Atos, but deep down I ached for the performance of the Millennium. Anyway, this thermalling flight would be the deciding factor.

Tiki towed me up to about 2,000 feet, no problem. JB was standing by on the radio. I radioed to JB and Tiki that everything was fine, but that I'd signal them when I was going to land by saying, "Foam the runway! " Never having had any stick time, I seem to soar comfortably over the airport. Then after about two hours the call of nature started knocking on my bladder. I radioed to JB for some direction on how to relieve myself in this contraption. He jokingly replied, "Just do a loop." Well, considering the fact that landing the Mill was not my strong suit, I weighed my two options carefully and felt it would be slightly less stressful to land. When I approached the L.Z. I was so stinkin' high, I radioed to JB, "What do you think about me trying a spin?" He nonchalantly replied, "Okay," and talked me through it. I executed it perfectly. I radioed back, "Wow, that was easy, this thing gives you lots of warning before it happens." I was still plenty high and decided to do one more to be sure I understood the characteristics. Nice execution, no problem. Then JB radioed, "Hey, Tiki said she didn't see the full spin, she wants you to do it one more time." I replied, "Okay..."

[End of transmission]

They called me "Hollywood," but not because I'm flashy or anything like that. My hang gliding buddy, Hungary Joe, gave me the nickname for two reasons; first because there were too many Michael's in Los Angeles, and second because I had a successful career as an actor, doing commercials, movies, episodic television and stage.

When I graduated from college with a degree in forestry, I found little to no work in my chosen field, so I started my own business in South Florida, then eventually stumbled into acting. My business was booming and the revenue from my acting jobs was abundant. Life was good.

Yet life, my life, my existence, my wild embrace of the martial arts fueled my craving for wanting to understand more about my own existence. Why I am here and what is my true purpose? Corny as it may sound, it wasn't until I took that first hang gliding flight in 1992 that all my wild roads converged in the purest form of flight. Was this my destiny? Believe me, I'd ventured down numerous risky avenues like skydiving, motorcycles, advanced scuba diving, trick jet ski riding, rock climbing, competitive kayaking, competitive kickboxing (heck, I held two black belts, in Karate and Judo—I idolized Bruce Lee and his teachings). Talk about a wild road for kicks, I dove off a high bridge in my hometown and cracked my sternum in half, but none of this stuff challenged my energy like flying. Oh yeah, I knew early on I'd always live my life in high gear, because anything less would be a waste.

How ironic. Hang gliding saved my life. And as the years passed I relished in all I was learning from books, magazines, hang glider pilots, sailplane pilots, etc. I was a giant magnet in the fast lane reeling in every bit of information that came my way. I tenaciously queried my peers with tedious and sometimes complex questions, but gladly shared my findings with anyone patient enough listen.

But it wasn't until my first 200-mile flight in 1995 that I realized that an "average Joe," like me, could do something noteworthy in this sport and perhaps be able to inspire others. If I were to describe my flights over the past four years I'd say (no bragging intended): I racked up between 2,500 to 3,000 cross-country miles each season (a season is approximately 2 months); of that 13 flights were between 200-248 miles; 38 flights between 150-185 miles; and a countless number of flights between 100-145 miles. Along the way I set the Florida state record twice and won the Wings of Rogallo contest two years in a row with a cumulative score of over 600 miles.

Believe me, I didn't think I was a great pilot. I was just a pilot full of tenacity, tremendously focused, throw anal retentive and egghead in the mix and you've pretty much pegged my flying.

But the real joy didn't come in setting the state record or racking up three or four 200-milers in a season, nope. What excited me the most was the thought of giving back to the flying community what I had learned and drawn from each of those flights. I could never keep silent about my flying techniques or weather information or even simply what does or doesn't work.

I sought out knowledge passionately and happily shared it with those who were interested. Perhaps this was my purpose—to seek and obtain the knowledge and then give it back.

Anyway, I'll leave you with this, I've always tipped my hat to those who came before me and given a leg up to those who'd need it. So, next time you're soaring up there amongst the puffy cumies, look closely, you'll probably see me there, tipping my hat to you. You folks gave me your time, insight, patience, laughter and inspiration and I thank you. Yes, this was my destiny and I can only hope that in my life I have given as much inspiration to others as I have received.

Oh, scribbled on a piece of paper in my wallet I carried around this inspirational note, which I tried to live up to:

"The key to immortality is first living a life worth remembering."

See ya up there.

Michael Hollywood Champlin
September 9, 1958 to June 16, 1999

Additional Comments by Tiki Mashy:

Thank you, Michael, for teaching me that going far is the challenge and enjoying the ride is the reward. So many pilots inspired "Hollywood" that I can't begin to name names, but I know he would want to send his thanks to a handful of people who made him feel special during his early days of hang gliding. Special thanks must go to Curt Graham, Malcolm Jones, Joe Greblo, Don Quackenbus,h and Matt Spinelli. I apologize if I have forgotten anyone. Michael appreciated everyone he met, no matter how briefly.

Editorial Comments

On the Dedication of Hang Gliding Spectacular to Michael 'HOLLYWOOD' Champlin

Jim (Sky Dog) Palmieri

Two years have passed and it is still difficult to think, let alone write, about the passing of a friend, Michael 'Hollywood' Champlin.

We pass through this world interacting with a myriad of acquaintances, we will make many friends, but we will contact just a very few special people. I do not know how to explain this, either as a scientist or as a pilot, or even as a parent.   There is just a unique bond that exists when someone special is befriended.   In the world of Hang Gliding I have two, Betty Pfeiffer and Michael Champlin.

While putting together this book and reading all the special stories about all those special flights from so many special pilots, my mind kept returning to the thoughts of Michael Champlin. The subtitle of this book states...

From The Hearts Of Those Who Live The Dream. If there was any one pilot I know who lived the dream, it was Michael Champlin. So many of the stories in this book were made possible because of the influences Michael has had on the hang gliding community. More importantly, many of the most important flights in our sport are now the result of preparation for or competition in the ***Michael Champlin World XC Challenge*** (See footnote). After reading so many of the contributors' articles, it became obvious to me that this book had to be dedicated to Michael Champlin and there was no better person to write the dedication to Michael Champlin than Tiki Mashy. Within minutes I was on the phone to Tiki and got her to agree to write it once the 2001 Wallaby Open (April 22-28) was over.

Early Monday morning, May7th at 12:30 am, I could not sleep thinking about Michael Champlin and the dedication of this book to him, so I got out of bed and went into our computer room (which doubles as our hang gliding memorabilia room) and began to write. No sooner was I on the computer than I received this email and the dedication of ***Hang Gliding Spectacular*** to Michael Champlin from Tiki Mashy. She wrote... **"Jim, Use this if you want. I wrote it about 6 months after Hollywood died. Wow, this is probably the**

I received this email and the dedication of *Hang Gliding Spectacular* to Michael Champlin from Tiki Mashy. She wrote… **"Jim, Use this if you want. I wrote it about 6 months after Hollywood died. Wow, this is probably the first time I've said, "died" instead of "accident." There's still that painful lump in my throat"**.

I stared at her email and found the words painful, making it impossible for me to even read what she had written. My heart opened up just trying to imagine the pain she must have felt when Michael died and what she must be feeling having to relive the tragic moments just to prepare the dedication for *Hang Gliding Spectacular*. I am glad she did. Tiki, I will always be thankful to you.

I first met Michael in December 1996, almost a year before Maggie and I had finished writing *Sky Adventures, Stories Of Our Heritage*. We had just arrived at Wallaby Ranch, outside of Orlando, Florida, from Roanoke, Virginia. I remember the day as clearly as if it had just happened today. Maggie and I were sitting at a picnic table, just outside of the office. The mid-morning sun was warm and the day was gentle. A pilot walked up to us and introduced himself as Michael Champlin. He was quite good-looking and quite physically fit and his voice was quite gentle. He said to us that he had heard that we were writing a book about the history of hang gliding. We mentioned that we were in the process of compiling over 100 articles from 100 pilots who had submitted for the book. Michael pulled out a checkbook and began to write a check saying he wanted to buy a copy. Michael said to just send him a copy whenever it was done. He wrote out a check for $20.00 and then said to us…"What you are doing is a great thing for the hang gliding community. I want to support you." Then he walked away. This was the first check we had received, and Michael's book was the very first book we mailed out. This was Michael Champlin, gentle, honest, trusting, caring and supportive. Throughout that week I spent much time just talking to Michael. He was such an interesting person and such a knowledgeable pilot. I followed his flying progress, setting the Florida State XC Record during the spring of 1997. As the Wallaby web page records: *Mike "Hollywood" Champlin - The Florida State and Wallaby Ranch Record was broken on April 5, 1997. Wallaby Ranch to Lake City, Florida: 147 miles (235km thanks RZ) by Mike "Hollywood" Champlin. Mike did the flight on a Moyes SX 4 he rented from Wallaby. Mike earned $250 for breaking the Florida Record from Wallaby. Mike Barber, Davis Straub also flew over 100 miles from Wallaby on the same day.*

The memory Of Michael Champlin is frozen in my mind forever.

On Thursday, June 17, 1999, I received the following email from Davis Straub as part of his famous, **The OZ Report**:

From: Tontar1@aol.com

Date: Thu, 17 Jun 1999 10:26:33 EDT

Subject: fwd: fatality (OZ Report)

To: cbccnews@kurious.org, nwpg@listbot.com, NWPGLIDE@kurious.org

The Oz Report

Our friend dies.

We are all in shock.

As I write this late on Wednesday night I'm just a zombie. I've been crying all afternoon and I keep crying. Michael "Hollywood" Champlin has died flying.

This morning we were just seven happy hang glider pilots ready for a day of fun flying at Hobbs, NM on a light wind day that promised good lift and triangle tasks. All of us were flying together and had known each other in various ways. It was great to be altogether here and experiencing what nature provided.

Tonight everything is different. We don't have a purchase on why we are here.

This morning Michael decided to fly John Borton's Millennium, just to fool around and learn about this different glider. He had already flown it a few times in the evening to 2,000' on a previous day when we didn't fly during the day.

Michael and Tiki have been here in Hobbs ready to set world records. Michael has been extremely focused on setting the Class I hang gliding distance record, flying often at Hobbs and in Wyoming. Tiki set the women's record here last year (since passed by Tova Heaney). I'm here because Michael convinced me that Hobbs could be a wonderful place to fly.

Michael launched John's Millennium around noon from the northeast-running runway, and got up quickly. The rest of us (Mike Barber, Patty Cameron, Ramy Yanetz, and myself) towed up, worked our way up in well-formed lift to 5,000' AGL and headed north to Lovington against an 8 mph headwind to do a triangle.

Michael continued to fly the Millennium over the airport for over an hour. He was on the radio with John Borton, who was providing casual instruction. Michael decided that he wanted to try to do some spins.

Michael completed two spins successfully. He then attempted another spin. To come out of the spin he pushed the stick forward, which aims the nose of the glider at the ground. He entered a high-speed dive - a very high-speed dive. The Millennium will recover from a spin if you just let go of the stick as soon as you go into a spin. You can speed its recovery by pushing the stick forward. You don't need to push it all the way forward, and it is not a good idea to go into a dive to recover from a spin.

The glider came out of the dive, presumably because Michael eased off on the stick. It was now going very fast, most likely beyond VNE. The glider climbed going straight up and then the wings folded back. There was no attempt to deploy the parachute in spite of the high altitude of the glider.

A review of the wreckage by John Borton, showed that the pin that Holds the two wings together at the nose had been bent and the safety ring on the pin was missing, likely sheared off in flight after the pin was bent. Once the latch came off the pin, the wings folded. After the wings folded back, the glider dove nose first into the ground from 4-5,000'.

Our utmost sympathies go to Tiki and John's family. We want our friend back desperately.

Michael was a very conservative pilot and a very analytical one as well. He taught me quite a bit about weather forecasting and we had numerous discussions about speed to fly, etc. I got to fly with him a number of times on long flights and really enjoyed the experience. Many people on the hang gliding mailing list have enjoyed his contributions.

Michael has many friends in Florida and at the Wallaby Ranch where he set the Florida state record. His life has been hang gliding. Hang gliding is the richer for it.

I wish my friends would quit dying. It really scares me.

Davis Straub

I could not believe my eyes. I was sitting at the computer in the classroom where I teach and just stared at the computer for the next hour. I do not remember the rest of the day. I was numbed by this bad news. Maybe weeks later, I called Tiki to tell he how sorry I was. I told her how Michael had bought the very first **Sky Adventures, *Stories Of Our Heritage*** book. She talked, telling me stories about Michael. I don't remember much of what she told me because just hearing them saddened me. Tiki's voice was broken as was her heart, I am sure. Then Tiki told me a story about Michael and her, which I shall never forget.

Tiki said that Michael would read to her from **Sky Adventures, *Stories Of Our Heritage*** while she would cook dinner or after dinner was over. Tiki said he enjoyed reading the book to her and she enjoyed having him read to her. It shocked me that Michael Champlin, who had given me such a special gift—a gift of trust and support—derived pleasure form that very book we had sent him. This one incident alone made the years of work on this book worthwhile.

Maybe, as you read some of the great stories in **Hang Gliding Spectacular, *Fantastic Stories From The Hearts Of Those Who Live The Dream***, you will think of Michael Champlin. You may be new to Hang Gliding, or maybe you are one of the contributors, or maybe even have shared the sky with Michael Champlin. Whatever your connection, the sport of Hang Gliding has been made better because of Michael. As you enjoy the many flying stories, know in your heart that Michael is there with you.

Respectfully Submitted,

Jim (Sky Dog) Palmieri

May 7th, 2001

[The Michael Champlin World XC Challenge is a yearlong cross-country contest designed to allow pilots from every region and soaring craft the opportunity to compete against one another. There is no entry fee or pre-registration requirements. The Challenge is open to sailplanes, hang gliders, foot-launch rigid wings and paragliders; Visit the Web Site at: http://www.hanggliding.org/

Acknowledgements

The editors of *Hang Gliding Spectacular* wish to thank all the contributors from all corners of the world for their willingness to share their most amazing flights and experiences with the rest of the flying community. It is not often that a pilot is willing to take the time and effort necessary to put their experiences, whether good or bad, into writing. Many of the stories in this book are about fun flights and several are about near or potentially tragic experiences. We can learn from all of them. We sincerely thank all contributors for sharing these experiences with us. A special thanks to Mark Laferriere for his friendship over the years; one of his many paintings graces the back cover. In addition, we thanks all our friends and colleagues on the Internet Hang Gliding Forum for their dedication and respect of the sport and their positive influences over the past eight years for without them, this book would not have been possible. Finally, our heartfelt appreciation to Erica Lipps for her help in proofing the final draft.

FOREWORD

Notes From The Editors

Hang gliding so shapes the lives of pilots with experiences few people get the chance to live. If there is a common thread to all these experiences by all the pilots who fly, whether instructor, new student or seasoned veteran, it is the myriad of stories, which get told in the LZ or the neighborhood pub. Sometimes, I have seen a new pilot with less than 3 hours total airtime experience his first thermal flight to cloud base at Wallaby Ranch tell his story around the dinner table with seasoned pilots listen quietly yet captivated because they can relive the excitement exuded by the new pilot. Flying Stories are the *entry fee* into the brotherhood and sisterhood of hang gliding. And always, one story will lead to another and to another...and so both the tradition and heritage of our sport is maintained.

I don't know the reason for the attraction pilots have for the experiences pilots have through shared stories. Maybe it reflects back to the days of primitive man sitting around the campfire at the end of the day reliving the exploits of the great hunt they just returned from. Maybe it is a way that pilots can learn from others who are more experienced or who have had experiences in different environments or different flying situations. Maybe it is just the creative nature of the human mind to relive and maybe even restructure the great events of the day. Many of the flying stories in this book are quite serious and probably extremely accurate and probably just as many if not more have that *creative spin* which ultimately becomes the *tall tale*. Why flying stories hold the excitement for so many probably reflects all the above reasons and half a dozen more. No matter what the reason, the flying story makes up the very fabric of our flying culture. These stories will be passed down from instructor to student, from club mate to club mate and from pilot to pilot. Many of these stories are like thermals, taking on a life of their own, growing in size and magnitude while others will be lost as rapidly as they formed. The purpose of this book, Hang Gliding Spectacular, is to capture some of these stories in print before they are lost forever. Hopefully, this book can act as a portal or window into some of the flying experiences of some of the best contemporary pilots we have within our dwindling hang gliding community.

The sport of hang gliding has changed rapidly from a community of pilots flying different versions of flexi-winged hang gliders to pilots flying very high performance, high efficiency topless hang gliders approaching rigid winged sailplanes. The potential for efficient cross-country flying has increased greatly as reflected by the number of pilots covering great distances on weekends or in the open competitions held in the United States and around the world. The newly evolving aspect of out sport carries with it its own newly developing culture, with its own unique flying stories. Many of these contemporary stories are reflected on the pages of this book. In addition, there has been a movement to combine the best of technological advancements with the development of a higher performance and safer flying entry-level single surface glider. Many older flying sites which were no longer accessible to the higher performance longer LZ requiring hang gliders are now being rediscovered by pilots flying the Wills Wing Falcon, Aeros Target, Airborne Fun or any of the new entry level gliders. Combining these advancements with the development of Aero-towing and safer and more readily available instruction, especially at the Aero-tow flight parks, and one can see how rapidly the sport is evolving in different directions. Hopefully *Hang Gliding Spectacular* has captured all the aspects of the changing sport and its newly formed yet changing culture.

The editors have taken on the task of publishing this book to capture some of the lore of the sport. Sky Dog Publications has previously brought you two books, SKY ADVENTURES, *Fantasies Of free Flight*, a 265 page book of 36 flying stories and SKY ADVENTURES, *Stories Of Our Heritage*, a 500 page book with 115 stories by 100 different pilots focused on the flights and experiences reflecting, our heritage during the early days of the sport of hang gliding. Because of popular demand by pilots and by the USHGA for SKY ADVENTURES, *Fantasies Of Free Flight* and for another book dealing with just fun flying stories, we have put together another book for you. We hope you enjoy reading the articles, stories and the humor reflected in Jules Makk's illustrations. We have kept the book to a size, which can easily fit into a harness or briefcase so that you may enjoy it whenever you need your *Flying Fix*. In addition, we have included a CD, filled with photographs and autobiographies of the contributors, many photographs of hang gliders and a few short videos of hang gliders flying. These can be used at your computer for pure enjoyment when you are not able to fly. The photos can also be used to supplement your computer screen saver or used as computer wallpaper.

As a final word, the editors of Sky Dog Publications recommend that you take the time to record in writing, your memorable and maybe not so memorable flights. They may become an article or part of a chapter in a future Sky Dog Publications book, but they certainly will become a memorable part of your flying career, to be enjoyed by you or by family or pilot friends at some future time.

The stories in this book are just a fraction of what is out there and just a small part of what we so love about out sport of Hang Gliding. Please enjoy!

Jim (Sky Dog) Palmieri

Maggie Palmieri

Bob (Sky Dog) Grant

Jules (Sky Out) Makk

skydogpublishing@home.com

Sky Dog Publications

6511 Deepwoods Drive

Roanoke, Virginia 24018-7645

540-772-4262

http://www.skydog.net

Puppy
Love

The Beginner

Jim Ryan

Here's my story; it's short and sweet. I had gone through three months of grueling training, 90 flights down a 40-foot hill. My take-offs and landings were like butter: fast, smooth, and second nature. With no site near my home for high flights, I went to Point of the Mountain, Utah, to earn my Hang II. They drilled me for a week, since I had to learn how to turn the glider. Carrying that glider up that hill in the mid-summer heat, over and over—ugh! Finally I earned the coveted Hang II. I went around to the north side, a 300-foot bench with a 1000-foot mountain behind it. The wind was ultra smooth at 18 mph. I jumped off, benched up and was at 1000+ feet for two hours! My longest flight until that time was under one minute! Since I was light on the glider, I was the highest pilot on the ridge. There were fifteen gliders beneath me the whole time. When I landed, other pilots asked me how I liked it, and all I could do was make gurgling sounds, "Ga, ga!"

My First Thermal Flight

John Wiseman

It was the end of August back in 1999, and I was in a tough position. My wife had recently started a new job. My son Scott's summer camp was over, and school would not start for another week. I decided to take the week off. We could go to the pool, work on the house, and best of all, maybe do some flying. I had been down to Highland Aerosports in Ridgely, MD, once before, so I thought we could drive down and try out my new camera mount.

Monday morning we got a relatively late start, not arriving at the airpark until 12:30. To save some time, I grabbed a single chocolate-covered donut and ate it in the car, fully expecting to have a nice picnic lunch with Scott after we arrived in Ridgely. When we got there, the owners, Chad and Sunny, greeted me with, "It looks good." I had just gotten my H2 the previous April, and I had little idea what "good" meant. I had done some basic ridge soaring, but I had never flown in thermals, so I really didn't know what to expect. However, I did not want to miss "good", so I set up my trusty Falcon, spending a little extra time positioning my camera. I hurried to put the glider on the cart and get in line, making my big mistake for the day—not eating lunch before the flight. But then again, my previous tows were all 10-minute sleds. It was 1:15, but I figured I'd be right back for a quick bite anyway.

My launch from the cart was smooth and uneventful, then at about 400 feet the tow plane suddenly jumped up. The tow plane at Highland is a turbocharged Dragonfly, but for a moment I thought that Chad had ignited an auxiliary solid fuel rocket booster or something. I could not believe how fast he rose, so I quickly pushed way out to keep up. I caught up to him just in time to have him sink down, just as far and just as fast. Now this was requiring some serious concentration on my part. Up to this point it was all pitch correction, albeit much stronger ones than I had ever needed before. Around 1000 feet the first roll disturbances hit us. I could see the plane's wings dip very quickly, with Chad's quick reactions straightening things out rapidly. I knew that I would hit that same turbulence within 2 to 3 seconds, but I was ready for it. After riding this invisible air roller coaster for about 4 minutes, Chad waved me off. I pulled the release and tucked away my bridle. It was very hot and humid, and I was sweating like crazy after that tow. I zipped my harness only about halfway to allow some air to circulate around my legs. By the time I got settled, I had lost about 300 feet. I felt a slight shuddering of my wing; I was about to find out what they meant when they had said, "It looks good."

I was gliding past the north end of the runway over one of those huge, circular irrigated fields that are so prevalent in the eastern part of Maryland. All of a sudden I felt both of my wings shake slightly, then smoothly lift upwards, like a giant umbrella that the wind had suddenly caught. At the same time, the wind speed picked up, and I felt a sudden increase in humidity. Adding to the sensory overload, my vario started beeping at a fairly quick rate, quicker than I had ever heard before without being attached to a tow plane! I glanced at the vario; I was now at 2200 feet, and rising.

My instructor and observer, Jeff Harper, was not here guiding me on the radio, and there was no one in else sight. I was on my own. OK, what did Jeff tell me in past conversations? What did all those books that I had read tell me to do in these situations? Turn!

And turn I did. I don't think I had ever done more than 2 consecutive 360's in a glider before, as I never had a reason to. But now was the time. Another glance at the vario; 400 fpm up, up towards a large cloud that I could see beyond the nose of my glider. I tried to hold my turning radius constant. At 2800 feet I felt the wings shake and heard my vario go silent; I had lost the core of the thermal. I remembered that when I had initially entered the thermal, both wings rose symmetrically. I figured that I must have entered it straight on and that I was circling out towards one side of the thermal. As such, I went back to where I thought the core should have been. I was totally amazed to find that I was now going back up, again at 400 fpm. Approaching 3000 feet, I set that as my mental goal. I peaked out at 2950 feet, what a disappointment not to make that magically round number! I tried to find the thermal again, but could only maintain zero sink for the next few minutes.

Going on a glide, I continued around the northwest corner of the airport. I got to the next circular field, where my left wing rose quickly, and the rest of the sensory perception freight train hit me solidly, just like in the last thermal. This time I was ready. Turn left! Push out! I must have gotten into this thermal more solidly, because I started going up smoothly, but much more quickly than before. This was only my second thermal, but I could tell the difference in strength right away. The vario's yell got my attention, and I glanced over at it to see that I was going up at a rate of about 600 fpm. I could tell that I was climbing fast; my vario was beeping faster than my racing heartbeat! I started this climb from 2500 feet, and quite quickly passed my goal of 3000 feet. At 3200 feet, the vario's beep died down and I was just maintaining altitude. I lost a little altitude trying to find the thermal, and finally did. I continued up to my maximum altitude of 3350 feet, where I was able to stay for five minutes.

In all the excitement, I had forgotten my keel-mounted camera, so I snapped off a couple of pictures while at my maximum altitude. Much to my amusement, I had shared the thermal with a clear plastic sandwich bag that had been swept up from who-knows-where. It wasn't quite as romantic as the soaring-with-eagles stories that I had heard from my friends, but it was a start. My inanimate flying partner reminded me that I was hungry, and my lack of food was now seriously starting to catch up to me. I had been flying for 30 minutes; almost double my previous best. I was happy with the length of the flight and with my altitude gain, including 800 feet in one continuous climb. But I wasn't happy with the quickly forming thermal erupting in my stomach. All that circling, and the bouncing up and down entering and leaving thermals, had left my body with a single mission—eject the chocolate donut.

It was certainly a big mistake not eating lunch before I launched, as I am hardly ever affected this way, but it was too late to worry about it now. I decided to land and go have that long-awaited meal. I pulled in the bar, rapidly losing about 900 feet, when those now familiar indications of lift pounced on me again. I had hit another thermal, just when I was trying to get down! I flew fast and straight towards the field, but gained another 300 feet without trying. I was starting to feel better, and it was a good thing, because I hit one more thermal, getting back up to 2500 feet, before I was able to pull in and glide back to the landing zone. I had been in the air for 40 minutes. With conditions the way they were, I could probably have doubled that had I felt better. As it was, I had a hard time trying to lose altitude to land.

I went to the cooler to look for food and water for me and Scott, who greeted me with a surprised, "Where were you all this time?" Seems I wasn't the only one who thought hang gliding consisted primarily of 10-minute sled rides. While eating, I noticed that the windsock was rapidly changing directions, indicating strong thermal activity throughout the field. I decided that conditions were becoming too strong for my experience level, especially for the tow up and the landing, so I decided to just watch and relax for the rest of the afternoon; I was already quite happy with what I had accomplished.

That evening I transferred the barograph plot from my vario to my PC and printed a copy. I could graphically see the flight details, like the exact spot where I remembered losing a thermal and then picking it back up again. Along with the photos I had taken, it was a neat souvenir for my bulletin board.

I spent the rest of my vacation week on a mental high, having experienced for the first time true thermal flying, and having accomplished the flight without any outside assistance. So now, when I hear pilots say, "It looks good", I know what they mean and I'm ready to go, especially now that I've modified my pre-flight checklist to include decent food and water.

Soaring, The Forgotten Dream

Mark (The Shark) Jones

Almost everyone has had the dream sometime in their life, where they just walk into to the sky on imaginary wings. I think it is a dream common to everyone at some point in his or her life. For me it was a rather scary, unrealistic childhood dream. Maybe, for an instant, I thought it would be nice to actually do it; but the thought was quickly discarded since it is, well, physically impossible. Then one day an experience rekindled that old, forgotten flame.

When I was hired at an industrial controls company in February of 1999, I was told a little traveling was involved. A little, I assumed, would be around the city, or maybe the state. After settling in and getting things up and running, I began traveling to further and further destinations every week; 200 miles here, 400 there... even 550 miles. Soon I was two and three states away, sometimes almost half a continent from home. Inevitably, the day came when it would cost less to fly than it would to drive. I had no idea what to expect on a plane since I'd never flown before, but the media had done a pretty good job of scaring us into believing we have a 50/50 chance of making it out alive. Would I risk dying for my job?

Statistically, we hear that flying on commercial airlines is safer than driving, but I've always been the extra-defensive, careful type and can boast (knock-on-wood) a zero-accident record. But a private plane is a different matter. I was going to trust my life with another person driving. I would have no control. Not that I'm a control freak, but when it comes down to my life on the line, I'd rather have some control, if you know what I mean.

The company I was to visit was located in Altavista, Virginia. They also owned a sister plant in Columbus, Ohio, and their company plane would be at the Columbus airport on Wednesday morning at 7 am. I was to meet them there and hitch a flight to Altavista with other contractors and clients already scheduled to fly that day.

After several hours of driving in the wee hours of the morning, I arrived at the Columbus airport with absolutely no time to spare. An accident and construction had delayed me to the point of mild panic. I couldn't find the hangar; the directions were wrong; I'd never been to an airport! The 45-pound travel case full of tools and computer parts was weighing heavily on my shoulder as I ran from hangar to hangar. Of course, it was the one all the way to the end.

So there I was, panting like a bulldog, sweating bullets, half in a panic, worried about flying, fearful of meeting my client on time, and I've just made it with 28 seconds to spare. God, the things I put myself through for this job!

A thin, stately man dressed in the finest business suit I'd ever seen stood up and introduced himself as my contact, the CEO of the multi-billion-dollar pharmaceutical company. The CEO! I had done a relatively good job of keeping my calm and cool look to this point, between gulps of air; but I think he could tell that I was just a little bit nervous. He stated that we would be flying together on his private plane to Altavista.

Great. Just flippin' great. First flight ever, I'm late, pulled something in my shoulder, soaked two paper towels with sweat from my forehead, and now I have to fly with the owner of the company? It can't possibly get any worse...

Whoops! Never say that! As we headed towards the tarmac I overheard the pilots talking about "still learning" something. GREAT, I thought, a student driver. We crammed nine people, plus cargo, into the seven-seater turboprop. Perhaps he was purposefully pushing my displeasure buttons, or perhaps this was my punishment for being late, but the CEO motioned for me to sit in front of him in the backwards-facing seat! Not wanting to disappoint this man or disgrace my company further, I agreed with a half-hearted smile, a very counterfeit smile.

He tried some meager attempts at loosening me up, but I wasn't very cooperative. There was only one thing on my mind at that point—watching the door close. Probably bored by this time, he picked up The Wall Street Journal and started scanning his stocks. I thought it would be prudent to also grab a newspaper and "read" as well.

We taxied out to a staging area where the pilots tested the props and engines. I felt both reassured and apprehensive. Why did they need testing in the first place, was something wrong? We moved onto the runway and a few seconds later started accelerating, fast enough to make the rental sports car I had driven to the airport seem like a VW bus stuck in the mud.

The shimmy and shake of the wheels on the pavement was similar to driving a motorcycle across a metal drawbridge. We shimmied and shook a little while longer until we reached takeoff speed. Suddenly, only a short distance down the huge expanse of runway, the shimmying abruptly stopped as we bounced up and jiggled around a little bit. There were still remnants of tip vortices from other, much larger craft banging us around. I wasn't the only one looking concerned at this point. Several others were a little green around the gills. "Oh, please be safe, " I thought, "Today is just not my day..."

Then came a bizarre calmness. Wow, look out there... the ground is getting smaller! As we left the airport the air became much smoother. Fear and suspense were quickly replaced with awe. I watched, more and more amazed with each passing second. We just flew though a cloud! It gave us a bump too. I always thought plane rides were glass-smooth; it looked that way from the ground. In actuality, it's a lot like a car, but with some really strange g-forces thrown in to quickly disorient the newcomer.

Soon we were above cloudbase and between two huge cumulous clouds; the view was awesome. Such a huge expanse reduced us to but a speck in the massiveness of it all. The autopilot had been disengaged as was evident from the non-perfect controls and I assumed some training was going on in the cockpit. They performed progressively tighter and tighter rolls until we were maxed out in a rather tight bank, and we all looked at the ground through the opposite window. I thought I could feel a little slip going on, but wasn't sure. Perhaps it was a spiral dive. But that didn't break my fixation with the window at all. The experience wasn't nearly as bad as I was thinking it would be. I liked it!

Then we broke the cloud-top barrier and the ground became a sea of white puffy snow. What a sight that was!

As I looked dreamily at the disappearing ground from this great height, something very fuzzy came back to me. Something I couldn't quite place. Was it a recollection? A feeling? Oh, wait, it was a dream!

I remembered then, I wanted to fly once, a long, long time ago.

What happened to that dream all these years? If only I'd known it could be real. If only I'd known it could be like this!

I needed to be out there in the air, on it... in it. Not in a pressurized sardine can again. No... I needed wings of my own.

As a kid I'd seen my father's friend flying an ultralight trike, and he just loved that thing. It had looked like so much fun! I remembered him now. He would buzz past the house every once-in-a-while and wave. I recalled his joy and excitement.

Right then I determined that flying was in my blood. It was inescapable. My father had liked to fly as well, but he never pursued it. I determined that I would.

So after this epiphany, the wind gods came to me. They permeated my thoughts and dreams and frequently reminded me of my newfound loyalty. I posted pictures of gliders in my cubicle at work to honor them, but it wasn't enough. They told me great stories of wind and sun on faces unknown and flying in circles wing-to-wing with feathered friends. I wanted to learn about hang gliding, and began a search for all the information I could muster about flying. The wind gods in turn whispered secrets of the boundless freedoms that free flight harbored, and added that it was the ultimate gift a mortal could receive. I agreed, and set out to make that dream a reality.

It took very little time to realize that I was serious about free flight. I wanted to sprout wings and soar.

The rest, as they say, is history.

Now that I've had the pleasure of starting my lessons, I've learned something one of the greatest men in history dreamed about his entire life, but never had the ability to experience firsthand: "Once you experience free flight, you will forever walk the earth with one eye skyward- for there you have been, and there it is you long to return." - *Leonardo DaVinci.*

I indeed have one eye skyward. You were right, friend.

Part Bird and Part Pilot

John Stokes

My father exposed me to flight at about four years of age. He was always taking me to the local airport in Meridian, Mississippi, where we watched planes takeoff and land. He also bought me a variety of flying model planes including rubber band and gas-powered models. My first attempt at personal "flight" occurred at the age of four or five. At the time, there was a television show called *Ripcord*. On this show, the heroes skydived and parachuted to rescue the lady in distress or to foil a bank robbery. I thought this was the coolest thing! When the guys were free-falling with their arms extended, they looked like birds to me. This all looked pretty easy. The parachute container looked like one of my mom's purses. The parachute looked like a bed sheet to me. I had these items at hand! I also had a large sweetgum tree in my backyard that provided a lofty perch from which to launch, do my freefall, and deploy my parachute. The plan was simple enough... get my mom's purse, stuff a sheet into it, climb the tree, jump off a limb, then, as I was free-falling, reach into the purse, pull out the sheet, hold on and float to Earth. Easy enough. I got the purse, sheet and my best gripping *tenny shoes*, climbed the tree and jumped out! I was introduced to three things that day... Gravity, Sudden Deceleration, and my Guardian Angel. Not two seconds after I jumped, I hit a limb with some net-like branches. This promptly knocked the breath out of me and gave me a wake up call with reality. Flight would have to come in a different way.

My first exposure to hang gliding came in 1974 while attending Memphis State while burning off some time in the university library. I saw an article in *Reader's Digest*, "The Flyingest Flying". This article described people in California flying off hills attached to giant kites. I had always dreamed of flying and took a few flights in small planes, but it didn't really feel like the flying did in my dreams. The flying described in the article sounded more like the dream flying I was hoping to attain. I finished the article with a hunger to know more about hang gliding. Luckily, I happened across some "Ground Skimmer" magazines in the library and I devoured these at a sitting. I didn't know it, but Memphis State's Aerospace Program had a fledgling hang gliding club. I saw some ads in the magazine for hang glider kits. The closest source for one was located in Nashville through a company called Cloudman Glidercraft. They offered ready to fly models, too, but they were about $100 more. I sent away for some info and within a few days, I had a brochure. A 16-foot standard Rogallo kit cost $350. I saved my money and in the Spring of 1975, I bought my first hang glider. I had never seen a hang glider before, let alone put one together, but the construction was pretty simple and it had all the essential tools, including a nico-press. (I had to cut the wires and put thimbles on). The thing did eventually fly, but not until I was directed to a hill with sufficient slope and height.

A pilot named Rick Boggan from Memphis was responsible for getting me in the air. The 16-foot standard I built was taking quite a beating on the shallow slopes. I was trying to launch a 4:1 (at best) glider off an 8:1 sloped hill. Also, the manual that came with the glider described the launching method as one would launch from a seated position. I had a simple, super uncomfortable blueballs-prone harness, so the recommended manual launch position didn't jive with my harness. The control bar had some matching, yet graceful curves molded into the downtubes that weren't there when I first assembled the glider. I was working at a gas station at the time and went to wash the mud off the sail. As I finished washing the sail, a fellow in a white VW bug did a u-turn in front of the station. This artist, hippie looking guy got out and wandered up to my glider and said, "Is this your kite, Man?" I said, "Yeah". "What happened to your control bar?" When he asked this, I knew he had some knowledge of hang gliding. I told him I had been trying to fly it but couldn't get off the ground. He introduced himself and said he was a pilot and had been flying for six months. He was an expert in my eyes.   He recommended a hill where he guaranteed I would get off the ground. Two days later, I met Rick at the hill and sure enough, I flew and it felt just like it did in my dreams! Rick was a natural pilot and helped pioneer many sites in our region. He later quit the sport after one of his friends was killed at Petit Jean Mountain in Arkansas. Rick, however, is one of those pilots that could quickly return to flying because of simple, natural ability. I owe Rick much and he is probably responsible for me being a hang glider pilot today.

My most memorable flight was with Osceola, a one-winged Bald eagle. He has made me look at the world thought a different set of eyes. I try to envision what flying was to him before he was shot. He had not flown in over thirteen years. Obviously, I cannot see the detail or have the range that he has with his incredible vision. All of this time, ground bound, he watched hawks and eagle as they soared overhead. We aerotowed to 2000 feet and released over Lookout Mountain. As soon as we released, a pair of red-tailed hawk passed under us. Osceola watched these birds until they flew out of sight. On the way home, I thought about that moment and got a little choked up! How he must miss flying and all the freedom he had. I am currently writing a book about this experience and hope to have it ready later in the year.

The second most memorable flight I had was at Sheba Crater in Arizona. Butch Pritchett, a West Tennessee pilot, and I had trudged our gliders through the loose cinders up to the bench takeoff. To make things worse, we watched as the locals drove to the top. We set up and launched into the smooth glass-off, benched our way up and stayed above everyone who launched off the top. The view was incredible! Looking down at the lava flows from both Merriam and Sheba craters was pretty neat, and seeing the Colorado River gorge and the Painted Desert from the air was awe-inspiring. The wildness of the area made me feel insignificant, and if a pterodactyl had flown by, I wouldn't have been surprised! To end a perfect flight, Butch and I had great landings, and as we broke our gliders down, we heard coyotes in the distance. Nice end to a great day.

Another memorable flight I had was at Mt. Magazine in Arkansas in 1980. Three of us from Memphis, Joey Mannon, John Christof and I had gone to get in a soaring flight. I was flying an Olympus 160 and was a little light for it, but launched into about a 15 M.P.H. wind. I got away okay and Joey took off next. He had to wait for a lull as the winds were increasing. We soared together for about 15 to 20 minutes, waiting for Christof to launch. He didn't have a wire crew and was attempting to find a lighter cycle. Finally, we saw him turn his glider away from launch. He had given up. The wind speed had increased to 35 M.P.H.! I noticed that I had the bar about to my waist, and then to my knees, and I wasn't going forward! In fact, I kept watching a rock outcropping below me that was slowly moving forward! I was losing ground and the sun was starting to get low in the sky. There we were in the classic situation of being up and not able to get down. Joey and I had an aerial conversation on what we could possibly do. Our plan was to try to make it to the end of the mountain and hope for the best. There was no full moon that night, so staying up was not a very enticing option. I said a whispered prayer for help in this situation and it was answered! About ten minutes before sunset, the wind just suddenly diminished! We were both able to penetrate out to the landing field and landed safely, but what a nail biter that was!

Barking
At The Moon

The Magical One

Francois Dussault

I am from Thetford Mines, a small mining town about 2 hours from Montreal, Quebec. Our flying season ends early because of the extreme cold of the winter months. I had purchased a new Sensor 610F-2, a 150 with flaps, from Bob Trampenau and took it to our local site for its maiden voyage. I had owned a Sensor 152 earlier and was aware of its flight characteristics, but had never flown a glider with flaps.

My two flying buddies and best friends, Marc Laferriere and Daniel Fortin, joined me. Our local site is a small 800-foot mountain with a wooden ramp and trees just feet below the ramp. Although the wind was light (0-5 MPH) I thought I could make a safe launch in the very cold (5° F), dense air. At least I hoped I could.

I waited 15 minutes on the ramp for a small breeze before I launched. I had a very aggressive run and became safely airborne; I resigned myself to a sled run in the cold winter air. But, to my amazement, I went up over launch in air that was virtually still. Every time I looked at the windsock, it was motionless. I have been soaring this ridge since 1989 and my 215-pound hook-in weight always required a minimum of 10 MPH wind to soar the ridge. To my amazement, I was 150 feet over launch, without wind. Marc and Daniel were yelling, *"Where is the engine"?* I then realized that the one significant difference from my old glider was Bob Trampenau's unique flap system that he had designed for the Sensor.

I was very cold and after a mere 15 minutes of soaring and decided to head to the LZ. With VG pulled tight, my glider was like a sailplane. On final approach, I released and lowered the flap system. The glider remained responsive and stable, yet landed like a single-surface floater.

I want to thank Bob Trampenau and Seedwings of California for having created this magical glider for me. I have always enjoyed hang gliding but now I am truly in love.

Full Circle Flying

Shane Moreland

I suppose it started for all of us with a dream in one form or another. For me the dream of flying today is as strong as it was when I was a kid.

I remember the dream of flying over the field in front of our house. I remember the feeling. The smell. The butterflies. Hang gliding information was hard to come by in the mid 70's in the mountains of West Virginia. Library books from such authors as Dan Poynter made me realize the dream could come true. I would look at the diagrams and pictures. I would check out that book many times. I finally traced the glider diagram onto a piece of paper that would become plans for my first hang glider. I had no idea that a few miles away in the West Virginia mountains real pilots were flying real hang gliders.

I didn't have bamboo. But I did have plastic sheeting. I found some long straight sassafras saplings that I whittled down to four pieces for the airframe. Once I put it all together with some twine and tape, it was ready for flight. My brother, Micah, helped as I sat on a sled on a snow packed hill with the glider held above my head. No control frame, I just held onto the crossbar. As he pushed me I gained speed. The plastic and sassafras contraption tried to lift off and it did. It flipped back and broke into pieces. There had to be a better way.

I soon witnessed hang gliding as pilots flew off Knobly Mountain outside of Cumberland, Maryland. They would soar the ridge and land at the fairgrounds across from the Potomac River. I could watch this from my porch in West Virginia. What an excitement to see these guys fly, actually fly and soar! I couldn't afford one of those, but I knew I would someday fly a real hang glider.

When I moved to Oklahoma after getting married, the dream hit again. I even bought an army surplus parachute for my sail. Here we go again. While researching and planning to build another failure, I noticed a hang glider for sale in the paper. A real hang glider for $250.00! It was a Cirrus 2 with a few plastic battens in each side. There were supposed to be deflexors on the leading edges, but they were missing. I didn't care. It had a sail, an airframe, a harness and a motorcycle helmet. I was ready. So my wonderfully patient wife, Lucia, helped me set it up on the red soil of Western Oklahoma. I had some real flights. Just hill hopping, but my feet were off the ground; for at least 15 seconds and I was flying!

I sold the glider for what I paid for it when we moved to Florida. After all Florida had no hills and no hang gliding in 1985. Did it? The dream went into hibernation for the next 14 years.

Nine (9) children later we moved to the beautiful Blue Ridge Mountains of Virginia. While mowing grass one day, my kids pointed out hang gliders flying the ridge above our house. Little did I know when we bought an old farmhouse in Montvale that it was just below what is probably the best West-facing launch in Virginia. I quickly piled the kids into the truck and raced up the road to where the pilots were landing. Some of the best pilots in the state were landing; Greg Mick, Rich Lawrence, Nelson Lewis and John Lane. They saw the excitement in my eyes and began to offer information on learning to fly. Actually, I think they really saw a driver. After all, how many guys with nine children learn to fly hang gliders? I finally got wonderful training from Steve Wendt at Blue Sky near Richmond. He's an absolutely dynamic teacher. Local pilot Vic Ingraham let me use his Wills Wing Falcon many times to practice on the training hill between lessons. After getting my Hang 2 from Steve on the training hills and platform towing, I was ready for the mountains. The mountain pilots in Virginia are a possessive bunch. They want their launch and landing sites preserved and they'll make a new pilot absolutely accountable and keep a short leash on him until he's ready. I could pick up the phone at any time and get good advice from any of them. Jim Palmieri, John Lane, Greg Mick and Vic Ingraham were overflowing with advice.

I flew from the West Facing Montvale launch many times. I flew cross-country a few times. I had realized my dream. Or did I? I made it a goal to fly down the valley a few miles, fly over my house and land in the field in front of it. This was the real dream. Then one day, the conditions and the glider were just right.

I had just bought an Airborne Shark 144. After a day on the training hill and one sled run from Montvale I was ready to get this glider soaring. One Sunday in March the forecast was for 270-degree winds at 12mph—perfect for Montvale. After church and a quick lunch I coaxed my friend Kenny Palmer to take me to launch. Kenny's family owns the launch. He says he's never been tempted to fly a hang glider, but man does he love mountain biking. Something about going 35 mph down the side of a mountain with no road on a bike gives him a thrill. My daughter, 13 year old Lael, agreed to be part of my wire crew. A couple of my other kids wanted to go as well. When we got to launch, conditions were perfect. I set the glider up, preflighted and did a thorough hang check. Every time I step up to the 1700' AGL launch I get butterflies. Lael and Kenny each grabbed a side wire. They've been a good wire crew in the past with my old Airwave Magic IV. The Shark, however, is a whole different glider. It ground handles so well. The wind was consistent at about 12mph. So, I did need a wire crew on the 20-foot-long ramp. Things looked and felt good. Once the wing felt balanced and loaded I gave the two commands: "My Glider! CLEAR!" I was up. I shot straight up about 50 feet above the ramp. It was wonderful for me, but better for Kenny. He's only seen me do no wind launches from there. Run like crazy off the end of the ramp, dive below launch to pick up speed and get out of the slot. He hates to see me dive like that. But, this time was a thrill for him and for me. I maneuvered back and forth along the ridge in front of launch in some choppy air until I got about 300′ over. Then it smoothed out. I looked down to see Kenny and the kids watching and waving. I finally topped out at 1100′ over launch. I could see the LZ and Lucia parked there. She was waiting there to videotape my approach and landing. She usually witnesses a sled run as well. After a half-hour in the air, I saw her pull away in our van and head down the valley to our house. Kenny and the kids below were stretched out on the ramp getting a Sunday afternoon sunning. I thought, *"Today is the day! I'm going to fly home!"* Just the thought gave me a lump in my throat.

After an hour, I proceeded south along the ridge. But the mountain turns more northwest down the valley. I got about a mile away from launch and started to lose altitude. Rats! I then headed back up the ridge and got up to 1200′ over. Then, I spotted them. Hawks out in the valley in a thermal. Could I get to the thermal and get home that way? Should I leave the safety and lift of the ridge? Why not? There are bailout fields all along the way, and I know all the farmers who own the property! I headed out and got to the middle of the valley and lost *NO* altitude. I made my way to the hawks and their well-marked thermal. They are masters! I circled a few times and gained a few hundred feet. I then headed down the valley with the ridge far off to my left. I was doing even better in the thermals than I had on the ridge. Leaving the ridge was the best thing I did. That's the thing about hang gliding that I really enjoy; I'm always learning something. As I flew over our neighboring farmers' homes and fields, I felt so comfortable. I really enjoyed the ride. Probably for the first time in hang gliding, I just laid back and just enjoyed the scenery. I could see Smith Mountain Lake to the Southeast, Roanoke to the South, Hogback Mountain near Lexington to the North, and my house not too far away. As I flew down the valley, I spotted one bailout field after another. I pulled the VG on and headed straight home. Our house got closer and closer. When I realized I was actually going to make it, I was pumped! A couple of the kids were out in the yard. I was a thousand feet over them. I yelled down to get their attention. What a site: more kids running outside, my wife waving, our two dogs jumping and barking. And the whole time I'm in some very buoyant air. I circled several times, checking wind direction and picking a spot to land on the hill in front of our house. The kids were great. They've learned how to give wind direction to flying pilots. It was perfect. Looking down on it all and flying a beautifully handling glider nearly put me in a trance. The 25-year-old dream instantly came to life.

I made a final pass over the house and nearby walnut tree. Plenty of clearance on my final glide. I pulled in to get good speed since I was landing slightly up hill. I flared the glider and sat it down. I unhooked, got out from under the glider, and looked back. I had done it. Just seconds before I was soaring above my house, just the way I've seen hawks do so many times. Soon my kids and a few friends joined me on the hill. It was fitting that the Sky

Dog, Jim Palmieri, just happened to be coming for a visit. He joined me on the hill for a perfect sun-setting celebration.

So the dream is alive. But the real thing is better. The sights, the sounds, the smells all added up for an incredible experience. The Bible says, "Delight yourself in the Lord and He will give you the desires of your heart." He certainly did this day!

It was risky ... a gamble ... but it paid off !

Hometown Champions and Hometown Sites

Adam Parer

My hometown has some excellent coastal sites that provide very challenging and satisfying flying. From late spring to early autumn this coastal strip on the East Coast of Australia offers outstanding days for soaring. Flying over the beaches between the regularly spaced headlands, landing, taking-off, flying from one cliff to the next; this type of gliding allows any pilot to hone all of his basic skills. The following flight is taken straight from my logbook and illustrates one of these typical days.

3rd March 2001

Airborne Climax 13

East-southeasterly light-10kts

22 landings

5.5 hours

Launch site; Strezleki

The air was very smooth at first although the lift was fairly light. I had been soaring Strezleki for 30 minutes and then started some aerobatics; 360's, then chandelles. Did several speed runs while no one was around, the climax is feeling really nice.

I headed south along the ridge to The Monument and did some aerobatics. Topped out with as much height as possible and headed south to Merewether, scraping through around the swimming pool. Passed the Old Clubhouse with about 30 feet.

Topped out at Merewether, gained as much height as possible, did some aerobatics, and then did a speed run to Merewether take-off. Did 4 top landings and then did 3 landings half way up the face. Took off, got as much height as possible and headed south for The Gun Club. Maybe 15 feet above the saltbush just before the ridgeline starts.

Worked the front face of the Gun Club then jumped back into the first bowl. Soared the first bowl then jumped straight into the third bowl. Headed back to Merewether, then kept going north back towards Strezleki. Stopped off half-way to Strezleki and landed at Dixon Park. Did 3 landings.

Took off, headed north to Strezleki and kept on going into Newcastle Beach. Soared the hospital and headed in towards the harbor, getting lift off the Esplanade and the Holiday Inn. Got to Fort Scratchley and landed there. Had a toilet stop, then took off again. Headed back to Strezleki and did some aerobatics. Headed back to Dixon Park and did 9 landings/take-off.

Took off and headed straight to Merewether, just got through. Turned around and did another 2 top landings at Dixon Park. Packed up and went with the crew up to the pub.

I think the quality of pilots who come from this area speaks a lot for the quality of the local sites in Newcastle. Rick Duncan is a previous world champion. Shane and Russell Duncan are prime examples, but the hang gliding community in general is of a very high standard. Neva Bull, Phil Beck, Conrad Loten and Tasch Macellan are other accomplished competition pilots. Phenomenal aerobatics can be seen from pilots such as Wayne Collinson who has spawned a generation of impressive aerobatics pilots including Michael Cotts and Todd Wilkins.

Flying to Wayne's Party

John Hamelin and Tim Locke

Several of the Connecticut pilots flew Talcott Mountain today. Mostly because today was also the day for Wayne's Backyard Blue's Bash. Ellenville, NY was out as a flying site because it was too far to drive; anyway, we would never get back in time for the Wayne's party. But he'd have no respect for us if we didn't fly somewhere, being it was such a soarable day, so Talcott Mountain it was.

At launch all the local pilots decided that the goal for the day, of course, just had to be Wayne's house. Most pilots sunk out in their attempts to clear the ARSA airspace that borders Talcott Mountain. My trusty Exxtacy made it easier. Tim Locke made it too in his new Topless Sensor. What a way to arrive! Tim and I landed (burning off a couple of thousand feet) in a field just over the tree line of his backyard. But not before hooting like a stadium flyer to the mix of pilot and non-pilots guests below. My wife, Mo, and the rest of the gang showed up later.

It was a 16 mile flight, but it could just as well been a 160 miles for the excitement that we had. The highest Tim and I got was 6000' agl, but getting out from there under the ARSA was a trick. The best way I can describe the flight is through the words of Tim Locke:

Saturday presented a pilot's dilemma. Do we go flying or do we go to Wayne's party. The only solution was to fly to the party.

We were psyched! We played around with our cell phones and GPS units, which amused the *wuffos* on Talcott Mountain. There is nothing that will sharpen one's XC senses like knowing that there is a keg of Honey Brown Beer at the end of the day's goal. John Hamelin showed his Exxtacy who was the boss and spanked that EXXtacy relentlessly to get to the party on time. Dan Jester and I teamed up and streaked south to clear the airspace restriction and boomed up from there. We had our chase team of Rick, Bridget, and Sharon in hot pursuit. It's easy to get your friends to follow you when you are headed for a party. I flew directly over the goofy-looking Department of Motor Vehicles in Wethersfield and waited in line for the next available thermal. The next task was to find our goal. The GPS did me little good since I had not programmed the coordinates to Wayne's house. But my good *jabber-jawed* friend Wayne spotted me and talked me down from 4000 ft. This is how the radio transmission went.

Wayne: Do you see the pink volleyball net?

Tim: No.

Wayne: Do you see the swimming pool?

Tim: Which of three dozen?

Wayne: Can you see this?

With that, Wayne set off a smoke bomb; it turned out to be a dud! I got radio controlled close enough to see a stream of partygoers heading into the field next to the bash. Within minutes of landing they had my glider bagged and were carrying my *diver* back to the party like Bushmen returning to the fire with the trophy. John is right; it is not the length of the flight but the quality. Dan and John; thanks for being great wingmen.

XC Dreams Come True: June 17, 1999

Dan Shell

It was an epic day. One that would live around campfires on mountains across the region for years to come. Likely the telling wouldn't even be much embellished. When you're hang gliding, you don't have to tell fish stories. The conditions looked promising, but we'd all seen promising days where the ambitious talk on launch ended pretty promptly in the LZ.

Everyone was set up by noon with the forecast NW 10 to 15. John Lawton had been by flying his (RC) Zaggy but was convinced that the day would be blown out for hang gliders. Velocity dropped by midafternoon, however, and he was set up in time to get off with the gaggle. I was last to launch and considered bagging it as velocity increased steadily for an abridged eternity. The wind eventually quieted for a few seconds, though, so Katie Dunn and Ryan Harlow assisted me off.

It was immediately apparent that we were working a strong north cross. This confined workable ridge lift to the north face and made for a wild ride low. It also drifted the thermals closer to parallel with the valley allowing us to work the lift higher within reach of the valley. By the time I'd found something to get me off the ridge John Lawton reported reaching the powerlines at Centerpoint. Steve Lee was crossing the first gap south. Curly Dunn was working another core just to my north as we climbed to around 2000 over. When that topped out he turned upwind toward launch. I followed, but with my inferior glide I stood still and sank in that direction. Downwind worked much better.

It sounded like Mark Furst was out front with Steve Lee not far behind. John was climbing somewhere in the vicinity of the first gap. I was behind at Cordell's but running downwind. Crossing the powerlines with less than 500 feet, I began to measure the glide to Dale's in this tailwind. It looked just possible. It was about then that I was surprised to hear Steve report setting up approach at Dale's. It was comforting and disheartening at once, as I knew he'd be there if I made it, but it must have been some hefty sink up ahead to put him on the ground. Slowing down seemed prudent. A good thermal in the middle of the gap eased my dilemma all the way to 3000 over and across the gap.

From here I could see Kathy working low but far downrange. I asked her if what she had was worth running for and assumed she was too busy climbing to answer. When my lift slowed I dove for her thermal. In no time we were both on the trees near Suck Creek. Trolling the ridge in the negligible ridge lift, Kathy made the first turn. I flew through the same area and we were soon looking across that thermal eye to eye and spinning fast into the sky.

By now Kenny Sandifer and John Lawton were somewhere above us between Suck Creek and Inman Point, where Mark Furst was struggling valiantly on the ridge. Mark eventually landed there with Bill Colvin. Steve was being retrieved at Dale's by hang driver extroadinaire, Ryan Harlow. As I climbed to cloudbase at about 4200 over I was astonished to see Bruce Hibbard fly by waving within a few dozen feet. When we saw him make a sinky dash for The Point (Lookout) across Raccoon Mountain, Kathy, Kenny, and I decided to try the Big Daddy's Sand Mountain route. Nevertheless, as we got farther south and The Point got closer, Kathy too was sure she had it on a glide and went for it. Kenny and I continued across the river toward Big Daddy's, zero sinking or losing slowly.

A more recently discovered and safer route to Lookout than the one taken in my previously documented attempt (XC Dreams and Nightmares), it requires flying along the river at Nickajack Lake, a much wider water crossing, but affords plentiful LZs across Sand Mountain once on the other side. The first good field on the opposite bank is near a truck stop/gas station/fireworks store called "Big Daddy's".

With that field easily in reach, Kenny advised flying more southerly toward some fields on top of Sand Mountain. When we arrived there I only had 1800 feet left and announced I would be landing on top of Sand Mountain. John replied, "What? Are you on final approach from 1800 feet? Keep going!" I was persuaded to drift over a couple of more fields. The second one had the thermal that really didn't get us back out, but allowed a drift within reach of and then a run for fields in the Lookout Valley.

Kenny was now higher and out front. Somehow John was behind us but very high. Steve was already in the Lookout Valley looking for Kathy. She and Bruce Hibbard had landed up the valley near Wildwood, GA. As I told Steve I wouldn't be landing on top, a flash from the interstate caught my eye. He was hitting me with a signal mirror from his van window as they drove under me, simultaneously advising me I had the Lookout Mountain Flight Park LZ made. He said, "Keep going!", but I couldn't even see it. I knew it was there because launch was visible beyond and this was obviously New England (GA, near Trenton) in which I was about to land among large hay bales. The LZ, my ten year XC goal, was just beyond the tops of the foothills.

I prayed for one thermal to get over those hills. God is good. It wasn't strong. Not fast. Just enough. I gained less than 200 feet and crossed the tops of the hills within counting distance of the leaves. There was even enough room for a downwind, base, and final, but absolutely no altitude burning was necessary. Kenny arrived high enough to soar Lookout while I kissed the ground, but he eventually landed there too. John Lawton arrived shortly thereafter and climbed out again, continuing on course. I told him he shouldn't be having this much fun seeing how it was "blown out!" He eventually landed near Fox Mountain about 15 miles north of Fort Payne. Congratulations John!

Kenny and I had plenty of time to celebrate in the Lookout LZ as Ryan, Steve, Bruce, and Kathy continued down the valley to retrieve John. Of course the celebration continued for the entire hour-long ride home, as we relived every thermal and low save. This flight represented fulfillment of a long held dream for me and I still enjoy reliving it, but just beyond Lookout is open XC country with plenty of fields, several small airports, and ridges of diminishing size all the way to Atlanta. I think the rainbow undersurface of my Sport would look great in a sunset shot of the skyline...

Mt. Magazine and Samantha

Mark Poustinchian

For many years, local pilots in Arkansas have been talking about the unreachable 100-mile flight in Arkansas. On June 7 1998, the first 100-miler finally became reality - Ed. (This article was published in November 1998 issue of Hang Gliding Magazine)

What made this flight so great was the fact that it took place on a day that was far from perfect. The thermal index was showing 4,500' MSL for the thermal tops and a high-pressure day with 5-10 mph southeast winds. The sky was mostly blue and there were a few thin clouds, which appeared for a few minutes but started falling apart as soon as they began to form. The forecast high was for the mid-70's. The night before, it was unseasonably cool and the temperatures dropped into the mid-50's. My girlfriend, Samantha, who last year drove almost 2,000 miles chasing me on X-C flights, suggested that I should give it my best and try to go as far as I could. She has been a great supporter, and without her I would not have been able to fly as much or go as far as I have.

We arrived at Mt. Magazine and started to get ready for what appeared to be a very questionable day. At the same time the few thin clouds that were periodically popping disappeared, and it started to look very blue.

A few weeks prior, I was very fortunate to have had the opportunity to fly, thermal and go X-C with the best X-C pilot in the world, Larry Tudor. I remember him saying, "The sun is shining, it must be good." Larry started to fly in Arkansas last year and has done great out here. I have learned a lot by watching him and realizing that long flights are a real possibility here if you just do it the right way.

A couple of weeks before, at Mt. Nebo, Larry and I were climbing together on Laminar ST's during an X-C flight. The difference between his flight and mine was that he flew 60 miles, but after working my rear off for several hours in marginal conditions over the flats, I ended up at only 32 miles. I took my usual route over the valley and flatlands and the friendly, green landing areas. However, Larry decided to stay high over the mountains and high ground, far from the landing zones and green fields. I realized that for all these years I had been doing it wrong, and was not giving my glider enough credit for its glide capability and performance. I also realized that I had been flying very conservatively and paying the price for it with short and difficult flights, which could have been a lot longer and easier. It is amazing how much you can learn from an expert! It also makes you realize that you are not as good as you think you are. That is one of the things that makes this sport so great; there is always so much room for improvement, and the learning never stops.

Trying To Stay Alive

Terry Spencers

Steve Kinsley, Doug Wakefield, and I met at the LZ today at 12:30, piled onto Doug's car and headed to launch. Bob Radcliff and Gary Cambell arrived as we were setting up. Bob said that it had been early Autumn since his last good flight, and Gary hasn't flown at all since he broke his hand in five places while unloading his glider. Doug was ready for an XC, Steve was ready for whatever, and I was just hoping for a good landing.

My last flight was 2 weeks ago when I did the "down tube boogie." Doug launched first and got up right away. I moved into the slot next and was surprised to hear that Doug was only a couple hundred over. I executed one of my worst launches in recent memory. Immediately I felt uncomfortable flying; I needed to settle in and fly the glider. Unlike Doug, I didn't go right up; I was finding no lift and was beginning to think that I was doomed to another sled ride. With a little scratching, I got above the ridge. Doug, still only a couple hundred to the good, was headed to the north finger. I saw a "haze dome" forming to the south and headed that way. As I passed in front of launch with only a couple hundred, Steve was sliding into the slot. I thought that he might wait after seeing our performance, but he didn't.

Now with the three of us in the air it was XC time! The "haze dome" had taken me to 5,000 feet msl. while Steve and Doug still appeared to be struggling at the north finger. When I pulled out of the thermal and headed towards them, I lost a thousand and found that they were doing fine. Initially, I thought that we were going to go the north point and then heading south, but Steve was heading south right away. I pointed south and tried to get into his wake! I had the benefit of having more altitude than Steve. It's nice to feel safe! Doug stayed around launch while Steve and I went south. Steve plowed along, while I stopped here and there to turn in weak thermals to maintain altitude. Steve's confidence was unflappable. He must have had the bar to his knees! I could judge his speed by his crab angle. He had opened up some distance on me, and was at least a quarter mile in front. I knew that when he slowed down that I could do a couple turns when I reached that area! Ironically, we ended up at the south bowl at the same altitude. We boated around sniffing for lift. I blundered into something trashy and started to go to work! Steve found something nearby that seemed to be another core of the same thermal. I was having one hell of a time trying to center in the lift. Steve did a couple of turns and pressed on.

We were very close to the gap, and I was in a rocket ship thermal. I decided to stay put and watch Steve. I've seen his gap-crossing technique, and it's pretty ballsy; I'd prefer to cross with more altitude. While Steve ran to the next bowl (the ugliest one), I was hanging onto the control bar for dear life. I had the bar to my waist and was climbing at 1000-1400fpm. The longer I watched Steve struggling low, the more determined I was to hang on and ride it all the way to the top. I got to about 6500ft. and could see gliders below the ridge back at launch. Steve was now in survival mode, valiantly working all the little knobs and trying to hang on until something happened; it never did. Steve performed an impressive landing as I flew over, headed for the gap. A wuffo was walking out to Steve almost immediately. Because we didn't have radio contact, I did some high-banked turns hoping that Steve would see me and know that I had crossed the gap. Steve didn't see me but the wuffo did! He told Steve that I was "this big," with his fingers pinched together! Cool!

As I began to cross the gap to Short Mountain I hit the sink that seems to be typical there; I was starting to have doubts. Short is a scary place to be if you're low. I've only been down Short three other times and been low all three times. It's a "butt puckering" experience! Landing zones are a LONG way off! Fright turns to relief when you know that you can make a tiny downhill LZ, even if there is a power line across the middle of it! My thoughts were about Steve and why he sank out. Steve being on the ground was a BIG blow to my confidence; the ridge must not have been working even though there was wind on the ponds. I suppressed the urge to chicken out and pressed on. I had lost 3000 feet in the first mile down Short. With the Bar to my waist and a tight VG, I screamed down the ridge, aiming for the rock slides that I felt sure would be working! Bingo! Half way down the mountain I was in a thermal and headed back to five grand! I pealed out before I topped out and went on glide, skipping a few rockslides and going for one a little further. Again I was climbing to five grand and back on glide. I reached the last good slide before the point, I needed to get a good one there to continue south. If not, I'd be landing in Mount Jackson for the forth time. All the thermal generators seemed to be working and this one was no different. I was climbing with very little drift. This turned out to be crucial, because I had 6500 feet leaving Short. Wow!

There is one thing worse than being on Short and that's being on Kern Mountain! Kern is lower than Short, shallower than Short, and it's ever further out to the LZs. The ridge has *got* to be working to go back there! I made my decision quickly. There was no way, *no way*, that I was going back there! Instead, I flew straight off the peak. I got as small and pointy as I could and went on glide for some chicken barns and silos. There were a number of brown fields upwind, and I was hoping that I could intercept something coming off those fields. I must have gone about four miles and was down to 2500-3000 feet. I was scoping out LZs and working very light lift. The wind direction had switched; with the bar pushed all the way out, I was drifting towards some rockslides on the southern end of Kern. The landing zones are closer there, but it is still intimidating. I figured that since I was in lift (even if it was light) and headed for the rockslides, I should be all right! As it turned out, the slides and the thermal combined to give me 3-400 up. Whew! I was relieved when I got back to 4500 feet. I figured that I'd better take what I had and jump the gap at Rt. 211.

I encountered very strong sink and a bit of a venturi. I was eyeing those small fields again. With the wind now crossing from the north, I was below the ridge when I reached the other side. It was pretty scary, but I would have never gone back to the Ridge if there weren't lots of rocks, facing directly into the wind at that. A cloud shadow had passed earlier and they had been cooking for sometime. I was confident that they'd be working, and they were!

I got some very strong lift from those rocks and got back to 6500 feet. The drift was a little stronger, so I reluctantly left before topping out. Big Mountain looks like an easy cruise, with LZs close by. Ironically, I never even thought about them, I was too high to worry. I just pushed on while planning strategy for the next ridge. I crossed a small gap and got to another cooker. While turning, I was looking at Grubbs Knob. It appeared that past the knob, the mountain turns toward the South. I figured that with a north cross, the lift might be nonexistent. I was in a pretty good thermal and planned to top out. This one got stronger and stronger. I got to about 6800 feet and thought that I could break my personal best. Just then it started to wane. I eked past 7000 feet, looking for at least 7200 feet (my best), pushing out as much as I dared. I either rediscovered the core or it turned back on, but either way, I was screaming! I blew by 7200 feet and headed for 8 grand. Just short of 8000ft. it started to sputter. I was so close that I felt like snapping the bar out and kissing 8000 before whip stalling! Suddenly, just like before, I was back screaming again at 1000 fpm. I was just under 9000 feet when I lost it.

With that kind of altitude and only a couple miles from Massanutten Peak, I figured that it was "over the back" time. I flew all the way across Page Valley and still had 6000 feet. I was looking at the Blue Ridge and Skyline Drive and was completely out of ideas. There was no place to go to get to the ridge, all these little mountains in front were creating rotor. I had the altitude to reach the Blue Ridge, but there was no way that I was going to risk landing in a steep downhill LZ and get rotored on the way in, too. Forget that! Instead, I headed for the best-looking thermal generator I could find. I had 5000 feet and no lift. I hung out in survival mode trying to stay alive... I didn't.

I had picked a landing zone and was monitoring two conflicting wind indicators. Luckily the LZ would allow me to land in either direction. Someone was driving down the road as I turned on base. I headed right for him. I banked steeply on final to make sure he saw me, figuring that he might see me slam in and come looking for survivors. I got a little rotor and a little gradient. The glider kept going and going and going. I had misjudged the wind direction, after all, but it was a perfect landing. The glider yawed 45 degrees just before I snapped a full flare. No steps, WOW! What a flight.

Steve arrived just as I was zipping up my bag; you just can't beat that.

This Tug Pilot's Dream Come True

Rick Agudelo.

Well, I did it. I got to fly tug in all five days of the Flytec Championships. I came here to Quest Air in November of 2000 a Hang-2 pilot with a mission to learn as much about flying as I could. Boy did I come to the right place. Not only the home of the Dragon Fly but the home of Bobby and Connie Bailey, two brilliant minds in the world of hang gliding; Bo Haagwood, the national hang gliding champion; Russell Brown, Campbell Bowen, Jim Prahl; the list goes on. While I was working on my Hang-4 I started to learn how to fly the Dragon Fly under the guidance of Bo Haagwood and finished my training with Jim and Russell. They trained me with the intention of having me available as a backup pilot during the competition in April.

When comp day came I was ready. I was a Hang-4 pilot, I had my ATP from the U.S.H.G.A., and pilot rating from the U.S.U.A. During my stay here I had impressed the Quest crew with my cooking skills and had been asked to cook for the masses during the competition. So, along with Connie and Riley we organized dinner and breakfast for the seven days of competition. The day would start with the arming of the coffee urns and bringing out the fruit, breads, and cereal in order to be ready for the hungry crowd of pilots. Shortly after cleaning up it was off to the pilots meeting, and then out to pre-flight the tug that I would be flying.

Holy shit, I had arrived here five months ago as a Hang-2 pilot with only two different flying sights under my belt. Now, after intense training with the best Dragon Fly pilots in the world, I was about to tow up the top hang gliding pilots on the planet. I parked my plane in line next to the staging area and sat in the shade of my wing for a few deep, calming breaths of air. It didn't work, but it was a worth a try. We got the signal to wind up the engines and we were off. Before I knew it, I was one thousand feet up with a hang glider pilot attached to my towrope. To my right was a 582 tug climbing out of the field with me. Up ahead there were six more tugs. While keeping one eye on the mirror, one eye on the gauges, and a third eye making sure we didn't collide with anyone, I could see a gaggle beyond the fleet of tugs. Not just any gaggle, but what looked like a dust devil that had picking up about ninety hang gliders and was swirling them up to the sky like a bunch of dried leaves. It was a most magnificent sight.

The pilot behind me pinned off, and as I turned back toward the field I was amazed to see two tugs coming at me, and two more climbing out of the field. Hang gliders were scattered all over the sky, either on approach or climbing out towards the gaggle. I put myself into a sixty-five mile an hour dive toward the field and timed my decent so that I could get to the field and land as soon as possible. I cleared my final turn and timed it so that I landed just seconds after the 912 in front of me touched down. We have to make short field landings and hit the mark, so slipping into ground effect and straightening out at the last minute is all part of the arial ballet. Sometimes I would do a one-wheel landing and turn to get in front of the next glider, ready to do it all over again. The ground crew, hot on their toes, would finish a safety check and wind me up. I would be off again, with another tug landing close behind me to fill the gap.

Before I knew it, it was all over. We had done one hundred and twenty launches in less than fifty minutes—with no injuries. I stepped out of the plane with adrenalin dripping from my tongue. I could hardly wait for the next day, to do it all over again. An older man walked over to me and said, "I worked on an aircraft carrier in WWII and I have never seen anything like this before in my life."

The next day didn't seem as intense. In fact at one point we were so organized and flying heads up that I swear I could hear *The Blue Danube Waltz* as we continued our aerial ballet. We got better; one hundred and two pilots towed up in less than forty-seven minutes. I've never seen, let alone been part of, such a well organized towing system in my life. I consider myself privileged to have been an integral part of such an amazing accomplishment. Thank you Quest Air and all those who helped guide and prepare me, for such an awesome experience.

My Most Memorable Flights

Tiki Mashy

Summer 1982 - my second night flight: I launched my hang glider, in pitch darkness, off Crestline (3,500ft. in the San Bernardino mountains in Southern California); there was but a sliver of a moon. My landing area lay five miles away. I could barely see it. Having a great time, I soared awhile above my launch point in darkness, and then leisurely headed out to land. As I reached my landing area I was devastated to find that a cloudbank had moved in between me and the ground, blanketing everything in white. Scared and without options, I banked the glider up and started spiraling down, praying the whole time that the blanket of whiteness did not go all the way to the ground (because if it did I knew I would probably impact the ground headfirst at a high rate of speed.) Luckily I popped out of the cloud at about 300 feet, my heart pounding in my ears. My friends were waiting with baited breath and their headlights turned on—lighting my runway. "This is my last night flight." (Or so I vowed at the time.)

August 1984 - my last night flight: There was a full moon when I launched into the canyon off the back side of Kagel Mountain (2,500 ft. in the San Gabriel mountains - Los Angeles, CA), however it was too dark to see the canyon floor. I flew around the mountain and out to the landing area. I reached the landing area and started setting up my approach. Everything was going well, but when I turned onto final I saw a glider just below me. I was terrified. If that glider didn't get out of my way, I was going to crash into the top of him. I started yelling feverishly to the pilot below me, warning him that I was just above him and yelling to get out of the way because I was descending quickly. There was no response. Recognizing impending disaster, I took evasive action. But he seemed to be flying the same course I was. I had little time now as the ground was approaching rapidly. I kept yelling and pleading to the pilot below that we were on a collision course, "Get outta the way!" Again, there was no response. Finally I realized we were doomed and that a collision was imminent; I was going to crash into the top of this guy's glider, and it was probably going to hurt. Top wires, kingpost, Oh No!!

Just before impact I braced for a hard landing by letting go of the glider and getting into a fetal position, covering my head. To my surprise, I impacted the ground. Oh, my God, what happened to the glider? I stood up, a bit dazed, and dusted myself off. I actually felt okay, nothing broken. Wow, I'd dodged a bullet that time.

Okay, now I'm pissed, I'd give that guy a good tongue-lashing. What an idiot. Just then I heard tons of laughter as my friends surrounded me. Much to my embarrassment, they informed me that the idiot pilot below me, the one I'd been dodging and screaming at, was in fact my own SHADOW! Aaaugh! How absolutely embarrassing! I have never again flown at night.

The Kagel flight was Hollywood's favorite story to tell about me. He didn't witness it, but he told the story so well that everyone always got a kick out of it. I was always embarrassed—everytime he told it.

Jules

©skyout
Jules Makk 2001

Outrunning

The

Dogcatcher

Aw, 'Chute

Mark Grubbs

There are a few aviation stories concerning pilots who, through no fault of their own, find themselves dealing with a statistical rarity in turbulence or equipment failure that results in serious injury or death to the pilot.

This is not one of those stories.

This is a story of how a pilot's complacency during a dangerous maneuver resulted in a menacing, life or death situation, and how the pilot magically, lucked his way out of it.

Monday, February 16, 1987 (President's Day) showed promise for good thermal conditions. Andy Piziali's soaring forecast predicted a good lapse rate and thermals to 5,200 feet MSL. After adding the "Piziali Factor" to Andy's numbers, Russ and Tammy Douglas, Bob Trumbly, Wayne Ashby, Andy and I made our way up Mount Diablo. After a crowded, difficult set-up at the new North launch, we all uneventfully launched into light thermal conditions. My Magic III and I immediately barged our way into a beautiful thermal that Russ had just found above Ransome Point, and the five of us spent the next hour or so working wide, 300 to 500 FPM thermals to a maximum of 4,000 feet MSL.

Both the quality and quantity of thermal lift improved as the day wore on, but it was getting late (4:30 PM), so I decided to be polite for a change and plan for a landing. Leaving Eagle Peak at approximately 3,000 feet MSL, I cruised over the buoyant Mitchell Canyon Road landing area. I continued up the road, hoping to catch a glimpse of the parking conditions at the nearby pizza parlor. When I was above the road entrance to the rock quarry, I headed back to the LZ. At 2,000 feet MSL, over the LZ, I began a series of what I had planned to be mild (90 degree) wingovers, despite comical requests over the radio for a loop.

I dived to gain airspeed, pitched up, and rolled into two successive maneuvers, which I felt were conservative in terms of airspeed and bank angle. Now, diving out of the second one, I pitch the nose up a little early, but roll to the right slightly anyway, because I'm afraid of doing a whipstall. It's going to be a little slow over the top, but no worse than any other slow one that I've done. I'm at the top, banked over about 90 degrees, but it's REEEEL SLLOW. I'm prepared for the slip...

A little bump, as if a light thermal is pitching the tail up and sideways...

WHAM! The base tube is ripped out of my hands and I crash into the keel. I don't have time to look at the placard on the keel, even though it's right next to me, but I'm sure that a glance at the numbers would verify that I've suddenly exceeded my Magic's pitch, roll and load limits. The outside of the performance envelope: well, here it is, the sonofabitch, and *it doesn't want to stretch!*

The sail does stretch, however, as excessive loads bend the inboard ribs around the crossbar. I'm caught in two uncontrollable inertial frames of reference as my glider relieves itself of all aerodynamic responsibilities. I begin to feel the jerking, angular acceleration of a tumble, along with the intense awareness that the ground is rapidly on its way up here to slap me in the face!

It's time to pull out some life insurance.

Rotational forces pin my head to the keel. I have to stretch my neck muscles to look down at the red deployment handle. In the background I can see the green grass and blue sky chasing each other around my feet. Too much sightseeing at this point won't do me any good. I hear ripped sailcloth rustling in the spinning airflow. It feels like we're starting another rotation, blue sky below me. I grab the handle, pull it down and throw the parachute container over my head like a Frisbee. I try to grab the bridle so I can yank the bastard back in if it doesn't open, but I'm violently snapped into a prone, slightly head up attitude as the 'chute opens with a distant sounding "THWOCK!" I try to climb into the control frame to cushion my impact; but I CAN'T FIND THE CONTROL FRAME! ! Jeezuz, the tumble has broken the control frame! I grab what 's left of a down tube and try to haul myself upright so my legs will take the impact...

...No idea how much time I've got left. Got my feet below me now. Quick glimpse of parachute above. It works! Where will I land? Descending faster than expected. Good, no power lines. Hey, there's one of those logs lying in the grass. I wonder if...

...THUD! WHOMP! The glider's nose hits the ground a fraction of a second before I do, and my legs absorb the remaining momentum, an impact equivalent to jumping off the roof of a one-story house. I'm lying on top of a crumpled heap of dacron and aluminum, vaguely aware that a crowd is running towards me .

Bob is the first to reach me. "Wow, are you all right?"

Tough question. I have to think for a second. No immediate pain; I run a personal diagnostic check. Spectacles, testicles, watch, wallet...

"Yeah, I'm okay!"

I'm assisted in unhooking from the wreckage, and Andy disconnects the parachute bridle from my harness and begins folding my parachute into a neat little package. A crowd of kids is walking towards, the one in front is carrying a bright, silver object—my deployment bag!

As I slowly walked away from the wreckage, a few visual, sobering details of the tumble became apparent.

Along with the predictable broken leading edges, there was an enormous tear in the sail, which began at the trailing edge, near the keel pocket, and continued chord-wise up the sail and stopped just past the upper/lower surface seam. The keel had broken at the forward end of the sleeve, but the Ashby Speed Rail had remained intact. Fortunately, my High Energy Sports cocoon, with its integral skydiving harness, appeared undamaged. (Sometime later, I decided that the sail had ripped because a sharp aluminum tube protruding from the boot of my harness had poked through the overstressed trailing edge when I fell onto the sail.)

It took a few minutes for me to notice another bizarre detail; the control frame was completely intact. I was unable to find the control frame after deploying the 'chute because I had been forced through the ripped sail during the tumble. During the descent, I had grabbed the kingpost, not a down tube, to get upright.

Meanwhile, Russ and Bob discovered more testimony to the violent forces that my glider and I had just experienced. A washout strut assembly, with its sheared retaining bolt, had arrowed down 1,200 feet and buried itself six inches into the hard dirt.

Eventually, we got the remains of my glider into its cover bag and onto Russ and Tammy's truck.

It's difficult and embarrassing to admit that the destruction of my faithful wing was totally due to pilot error. I made the decision to do aerobatics, even though wind conditions in the LZ were indicating possible turbulence from broken thermals. I made the decision to roll into a maneuver without adequate airspeed, and to remain complacent when I entered a high-banked stall. I chose to maintain a light grip on the basetube, instead of "white-knuckling" the bar and pulling it to my knees.

The results of those bad decisions include the following: A strong sense of personal loss (me and my Magic had flown lots of miles together), a damaged (but repairable) ego, and a colossal respect for the dangers of improperly executed aerobatics.

The following day, hoping that news of my deployment had not yet spread, I telephoned Wally Anderson at Chandelle to inform him that the quality of his 'chute packing skills had been proved for a second time.

"Hey Wally", I said, "I think it's time to have my 'chute repacked."

"Well, if it's been a while since you've opened it up, you might want to air it out a little bit."

"No problem Wally, it's been aired out."

Cloud Racing

Larry Fleming

Looking out across the Owens Valley from Paiute launch at the snow capped, jagged peaks of the Sierra Nevada Mountains always leaves me a little breathless. They seem so close until you look way down at the valley floor and spot the green oasis of Bishop, California surrounded by the brownish desert and the tiny matchbox sized trucks, loaded with pilots and gliders winding up the "road" to launch. It is then that one realizes the grand size of this valley where the big air can churn up extreme conditions in an eye-blink, where pilots' decisions can lead to long distance flights across starkly beautiful mountains and valleys; landings beside hot streams, cold rivers, or shade trees; long walks, waits, or nights in the wastelands; or death. "Fly not too close to the sun, nor too low near the water," Daedilus said to his son Icarus when he put on his wings. I was about to start an adventure, like Icarus', which would teach me the lesson of those words first hand.

Some days it seems that no matter how focused you become or how quickly you try to move in preparation for a flight, stuff happens which keeps you dragging around on top of the hill, trying to get ready to fly. That summer day in July was my turn to roam around on top of the Paiute Launch in the Owens Valley. The delays were especially maddening because my group of flying buddies and I (we call ourselves the Tarantulas) had just spent a very wet week of our vacation getting soaked while watching the rain run down off our weeping, sagging tents and today was very possibly our last and only flying day. I was the last to leave the ground to race north, listening to my fellow Tarantulas' radio reports about how far ahead they were and about how far behind they were going to leave me!

My "friends" love to "motivate" one another. My launch had been good and the air was fantastic. I had soon reached an altitude that allowed me to start my glide towards Nevada. Cruising along in the high desert air, while crossing wide, gaping, glider-eating canyons, and watching the 15,000-foot peaks pass along side is exhilarating. Somewhere around the twenty-mile mark at Benton, I noticed the sky clouding over behind me, shutting off the lift. I also saw sheets of rain falling back from where I had recently launched. A black and gray sky streaked and obscured White Mountain peak behind me. There were cloudbursts dumping long threads of rain all the way back as far as

I could see. The valley floor, lapping up into the mountain range, was totally shaded and I strongly suspected the ground winds there would be treacherous. "Looks like there's no going back on an out and return flight today," I remember thinking. The sky ahead was also clouding up. I was concerned about being caught between two powerful gust fronts. Ahead looked better than behind, so onward and upward! My fellow Tarantulas had long ago turned east towards Coaldale and Tonopah, leaving me to trail far behind, and I wanted to follow, but the ground there was darkly shadowed over for many miles. The door to the east was closing fast and I was on the wrong side of it. My suspicions were soon confirmed when I heard radio cries to our lead chase truck, asking for retrieve and calling out the locations of grounded pilots who had been at the tail end of the pack.

The northern route was filled with blue sky and fresh, puffy clouds lining up towards the wide-open Nevada ranges. I had to race the gust fronts behind me and pass through a rapidly over-developing area in front to reach the clean air. The door would not be open long. I decided to glide to the leading edge of the cloud-street and continue north, splitting away from my group, but first I needed to pass directly below a massive buildup of cumulus clouds that had begun to dump two enormous columns of rain!

Approaching the blackish, gray mess over Basalt at 14,000 feet gave me several minutes to ponder my best path through the obstacle course of rain and cloud. There were two columns of moisture, just plunging from the jagged bottom of the cloud, falling maybe seven thousand feet down to the hot, dry air below and then simply disappearing, vanishing into thin air. So this is what virga looks like. It was a unique perspective, looking down at those inverted columns and up at the black, falling sky. Not wanting to fall into sinking air, I chose to fly up the middle, between the massive storms. "Virga to the left, virga to the right, I'm going up the middle. Look for me on the road to Mina," I radioed to the #2 chase truck.

The lift became buoyant, sweet and strong. Then, suddenly, it became very strong! I began to compare my climb angle with my progress forward and quickly realized at 16,000 feet that it was not a question of *if* the huge, black monster of a cloud was going to swallow me, but rather *when!*

There was no way I could push out to the front, into the clear, blue air and I was too far along to retreat. I was totally screwed, either way. Yep, I was going in! At 17,000 feet cloud base appeared to be just a kingpost away. The pitch-black bottom seemed to be dome shaped. The edges swirled and curled around, appearing to lazily fall off from the sides only to rapidly suck back into the evil creature. It was alive, hungry and anything underneath was its food; moisture, dropped gloves, picnic tables, or hang-gliders. The monster didn't seem to be too choosey.

Many thoughts passed rapidly through my mind. Words such as "frozen," "dead," "stupid," "glider-ripping-monster," and "holy shit" were spewing out of my brain. It was definitely time to look at options. "CUT

LOOSE AND THROW THE 'CHUTE," were my first panicked thoughts. After weighing the possibility that I would need to freefall several thousand feet before deployment or risk being sucked into the cloud with a billowing, wallowing, jellyfish-like contraption instead of a stable gliding machine, I decided throwing the 'chute should beway down on my list of options. The thought of abandoning and losing my sweetheart Xtralite 137 also made me think twice. I considered deploying my drag 'chute to increase the sink rate, but some quick, sweaty math told me the overpowering lift would still pull me into the cloud's innards.

As the cold, heartless wisps enveloped me around 17,000 feet and the ground began to disappear, I prayed for sink. And then the thought came to me! *The virga was sinking!* If I could just steer my pointy little nose into that falling column, I could ride the elevator down. It would have to happen quickly. The ground kept wisping away, whiting out and reappearing, as my world became murkier and blurrier. I needed to set a course and travel for a while in the correct direction before I became totally disoriented and mind-twisted by the freezing, foggy mist.

Just as the lights went out and the world turned dark, I found myself plunging from the darkness of the cloud into the top of the freezing verge-column. It was like being poured out of a milk bottle into the kitchen sink. The variometer read down and I wondered about the effect of water soaking my sail. Would the machine still fly stabile? I never found out because, instead of falling water, I had falling snow. There was a thin thread of white powdery stuff on my base tube, gloves, side wires, sunglasses, and leading edge. "Hello, chase, I'm down to 15,000 and icing up."

"Yeah, right. It's 115 degrees on the desert floor. Tell us another one. We need the laughs," they said.

While it seemed a lifetime to me, it really didn't take that long to plunge out of danger and into the blue air. I found myself below the leading edge of a cloud-street, leading far away to the north. The brilliant, white puffy pathway split the sky into two parts: mean, dark, and nasty behind and blue, happy air out front. It was a simple matter to just boat along, under the front edge of the divide, singing a happy song as the State of Nevada rolled slowly below. The glider felt as if it was powered and I felt as if I were the sky-god of the day, gazing down upon my kingdom.

I had gambled and won. I was not to be the boy who flew too high and fell to earth, but rather the pilot who had challenged the monster and cleverly escaped. I was the hero, the cloud racer!

I probably could have pumped myself up and tried for more miles. But to tell the truth, I was tired, breathless, overjoyed to be safe and happy to be landing at Luning next to my friends and my ride back to camp. The sun was dropping lower and the day was about over anyway, I rationalized. After a fast, light-wind landing right beside my chase crew, I packed up the glider and we headed back to Bishop to rejoin the other Tarantulas who had been scattered between Basalt and Tonopah. Our group rejoined each other much later in Bishop to tell our various tales. We would have arrived later still had our driver not discovered that a "massage parlor" that appeared out of nowhere around Mina didn't really feature massages. We had quite a laugh about that during our adventure-filled story-time at dinner with the other Tarantulas. Sharing the fun and high spirits with good friends helps turn hang gliding into a life-style instead of just another sport; it becomes play. Sometimes, however, we find ourselves in situations, which may turn playtime into a survival challenge. Although running from and chasing clouds can lead to many interesting adventures, Daedilus' conservative advice is still appropriate today. Best wishes and good luck to any other cloud racers out there.

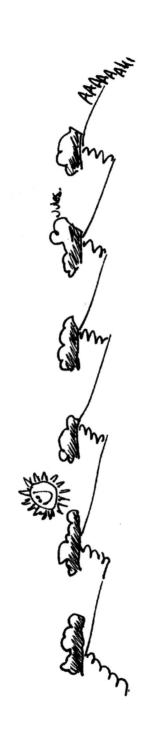

Death and Taxes

Chad O. Koester

Sunday, April 15, 2001

The Craters are volcanic cinder hills in northern Arizona, northeast of Flagstaff and south of the famous Monument Valley. Merriam Crater has a launch near 6,800 msl and the landing zone is near 5,600 msl. Running in veins from Merriam are old lava flows with pretty nasty rocks, but outside of those veins are open grazing ranges with cattle and antelope roaming virtually free. The tops of the craters have many areas that are tiny lava rocks that get in everything. In places, you can set up your glider to find your basetube has sunk into the rocks an inch or two.

While working with students in the morning at a position about midway up the hill, I had watched Mick fly overhead in an uneventful sled ride. After finishing with the students, it was time to head up the hill to get in a little airtime for myself. Midday conditions from the top of the hill looked extremely mild. Hazy and blah, the sky had not changed a bit since Mick's earlier flight. Mike, a new transplant from Kansas City, was flying my Sport 167. He had gotten low near the knoll in front and had a nice save (without a vario I might add) and was getting up. Mick had launched, boated around near launch then saw Mike getting up and went to join him. I was up next with the Fusion. I launched into a nice cycle and got very little, so I headed straight for the knoll to get under Mike and Mick. I bubbled around for a while thinking I was about to get embarrassed and sink out while vario-less Mike had gotten up. Finally I locked into a core and got up to 7,500, then worked around, not climbing much, and sinking down several times. Mike landed, and I kept flying a bit while drifting southeast. Within 15 minutes I had climbed above Mick and was now seeing a southwest drift. The thermals were getting a little stronger in climb and a bit stronger in turbulence. Finally, Mick sunk out. I had drifted over Merriam almost straight toward Flagstaff for a little less than a mile. With a student on the ground waiting, and my bare hands freezing at 11,500' I decide an hour flight was sufficient. I should land and get other things done.

As I glided back toward the LZ, having already sunk back down to 9,500, I began to climb again while flying in straight lines. The next thing I knew, I was back to 11,500 and my hands were again feeling the cold. I started searching for sink (does this sound weird to you?) and found there was very little of it. After a long, sustained session of circling in what little sink I did find, it finally became lift, just like everything else. I flew straight from the Merriam LZ toward the Sheba LZ (a neighboring Crater) only to regain the 2,500 ft I had managed to lose by the time I traveled a quarter mile. The drift was constantly changing and becoming more prominent; this was a convergence. Butterflies, recently escaped their pods, riddled the air at altitude. At one point, I met up with a hawk and gave myself a momentary diversion by chasing him around. I don't think that he appreciated it much as he made several evasive turns and flips. He then folded his wings and dove away. I was jealous of his fine VG system. I continued for forty minutes; the lower I managed to get, never below 8,500 msl, the more turbulent the conditions.

Flying with speed through lift to find sink, I hit big lift—1,200 fpm. I pulled a quick 180 trying to keep away from the lift. I slipped my turn intentionally, thus gaining quite a bit of air speed. Just as I was easing the bar out to relieve the speed, thus starting to pitch up, I hit another big up. I'm not sure how big, as there was no time to look. It was pitching me hard enough that I thought the only way to recover was to pull a hard wang out of it.

POP! Something in my harness gave way, startling me. I thought in an instant, "I'm over-stressing something, pull in to keep from breaking the thing!" I pulled in only to find myself in a total vertical stall. Scary quiet. Then a quick increase in a low tone as airspeed picked up. I held on to the basetube for everything I could. As the glider began to tail slide, a very violent pitch-over ripped the bar out of my hands.

All I could see were blurs of basetube and other glider parts violently moving about me as I tumbled over and over like a rag-doll. I tried to grab my parachute, but couldn't. The tumbles stopped after five or six full revolutions as the glider went into a dive. I quickly looked to find my 'chute handle, ripped it off my chest, and looked for the open spot. I threw the 'chute and watched the deployment bag explode off the 'chute while the 'chute itself remained wadded up and began drifting up and in toward the wreckage. I grabbed the bridle and gave one yank and saw the excess reeling back out again quickly and thought, "Let go before you get you arm ripped off!" The 'chute opened with the sweetest pop you have ever heard!

Now I was under canopy, but still at the bottom of the wreckage and upside down. I climbed into the wreckage, managed to get it to flip over and grabbed my hook knife. Upon getting in the control frame, I realized that one downtube was broken and realized that it would not provide much protection on impact. I began climbing up the keel to get as high as I could. I saw the bridle scraping back and forth on my rear wires and was thankful for plastic coating. I climbed until my hands were at the haul back position, one above, one below. The parachute was occasionally surging forward and back (I think the wing was stealing air from the chute some) and I was descending toward a barbed wire fence with metal poles along the road up to Merriam. As I looked around I could see my truck already in route, leaving a nice dust plume on the way.

Just as I was about to hit, I made sure my legs were slightly bent. The nose hit and then the good downtube hit and took most of the impact. I quickly grabbed the bridle with my hook knife ready in case the parachute began to drag me, but I knew that help was already close. Within 15-20 seconds of impact, Mike was there to wad up the chute.

They pulled the glider off of me and looked me over for injuries that I might not yet feel. Fortunately, my injuries totaled one cable burn on a finger from sliding down the haul back cable on impact, one bruise on one shin from the base tube being ripped out of my hands, and one bruise on one shoulder from taking out the downtube in the tumbles.

Surveying the glider, the right leading edge had failed. Initially, I thought this breaking was what brought the glider out of the tumble into the dive, but further inspection of the damage suggests it broke during the first tumble or two, which might explain why it was so violent and why I was thrown through a downtube. The failure on my harness turned out to be the pitch adjuster line. Further inspection indicated that one of those little rocks from launch had become lodged in the adjuster cleat. I realized later that the bruise on my left shoulder was from the *right* downtube.

I feel fortunate that my instruction was such that I was never allowed to fly solo without being taught to deploy a chute, and I had practiced deployment many times. My instructor, the late Rob Richardson, was very insistent on this matter, not that I argued, and I am grateful for the quality of preparedness he instilled in me. Several days after the accident, I realized not only had his training saved me, but that it was his personal parachute that had saved me. I had bought it from his estate to replace another 'chute sometime after his death. THANKS ROB!

There were so many variables that could have changed the outcome that I count myself extremely lucky. Uncoated wire could have cut my bridle; I could have landed in an old nasty lava flow, or that barbed-wire fence; an older style 'chute could have resulted in broken legs. The saying goes, "The only two things that are certain are death and taxes." On this day I went home and filed for an extension, thus avoiding both!

If I had to do it all over again I would have performed a better preflight of the harness; once realizing the convergence got more turbulent at lower altitudes, I would have either just rode it out for an hour or two or picked a direction and kept going until I flew out of it. When asked how I got tumbled I reply, "I did not get tumbled, I tumbled". It was my own actions that resulted in the vertical stall – Pilot Error!

Deployment

Mark Lukey

My record is still intact. I didn't throw it, or have to throw it...

The ground crew says I was 500 to 600 feet AGL. I was climbing on static tow in my suprone harness (a SupAir Evolution PG harness) with a chest-pack-mounted reserve using a Hewitt tow bridle and a WW spreader bar. During the process of wriggling up into the seat I heard and felt a *pop!* in the vicinity of my chest. I looked down to see 25' of HG parachute bridle paying out below me. I hit the release line, and pulled in, then felt a large tug as my Quantum 440 drogue chute opened very smoothly at about 25 to 30 mph. Then, because that's a really huge drogue chute, it quickly became the main factor in the equation, turning into a reserve parachute.

"Well, I guess that's it for flying today," I thought to myself. Then I thought about the irrigation ditch with deep water in it, and quickly located my hook knife.

Something was pinning my head to the left riser of the spreader bar, preventing me from trying to steer the glider away from the ditch. In the supine harness I had some steering available with my feet, and I tried to use it, though rather ineffectively under the circumstance. Simultaneously I was trying to free my head. I wasn't sure exactly what was caught under the right side of my helmet (it turned out to be the reserve bridle strap), but I wanted to be in the control triangle badly enough, instead of pinned by the neck, that I was willing to ditch the helmet about 50 feet above the deck. I got in the triangle quickly, and collapsed with the glider as it wafted gently into its little hole in the ground. Actually, the impact wasn't bad at all. Would have been exciting in a tree or onto rocks, I suppose—or the ditch, which I missed by about 50 feet—but this was a soft, flat, corn field with foot-high plants.

I got the radio working and let the ground crew know that I was OK, then eventually managed to get free of the harness and towing bridle. I was tied in there pretty good. If the wind had been blowing harder, I'd have had to start cutting line. Surrounded by good friends, we picked up poor Marsha, my beloved hang glider, and carried her off the field. In order to locate the harness more easily, I stuck the aft 4' of keel upright in the ground. As we were folding her up (she went into the bag, so I at least get a point for that), I sent Little

Mark out into the field to retrieve the harness and radio, guided by the keel/post. He said later that it reminded him of the scene from *Brave Heart* where the sword is left standing in the field as a challenge icon. You bet.

I suppose some of the more analytical readers are wondering what caused the release. Me too. I think I know. The lower portion of a static tow Hewitt bridle connects to a hook in the vicinity of the belly button. That hook is held in place by a bellyband running from one side of the waist to the other, tying in at some convenient pair of points on the harness. My bellyband had been tied to the bottom of the spreader bar risers; it was probably too short. On my previous suprone static tow flight, I wasn't happy with how the bellyband stretched around the reserve chest pack. I suspect that on this flight the bellyband was above the deployment handle, and that as I pushed myself up into the seat, the bellyband scraped the handle downward hard enough to pull the pins. I don't have any other theories at this time.

XC stats:
2 minutes.
400 yards.
1 point claimed for getting it all back in the bag.

Glennies Creek

Adam Parer

The first time I went cross-country hang gliding was after 90 hours of coastal flying. The site, called Glennies Creek, is a 1080' hill with a very large lake at its base and the drive to launch requires a 4x4 to negotiate the slow winding track. It was a cool autumn day, the sky was clear with just a hint of cloud formation to the west.

Eight of us arrived at the site in two cars. I was starting to feel that eager edginess I get when a flight is coming up. I was also feeling a little nervous, as the setting was completely unfamiliar to the coastal sites I had only recently learned to fly. As we drove around the edge of the lake I noticed that the wind was calm; the surface of the lake looked like a mirror. There was absolute silence throughout the whole valley, apart from the noise of our cars as we made our way along the winding track up to take-off.

As we pulled up to the top of the hill it was blowing quite strongly from the west, the perfect direction. Everyone was quickly out of the cars and setting up. But by the time I had checked out my glider the wind was even stronger and a number of the advanced pilots decided they would wait to see if the conditions improved. I did not have any instruments; more importantly, I had not purchased a parachute yet. I was told to "take it easy." The more experienced in our group reassured us it was still safe to fly, although the air might be a bit bumpy.

Having been given the OK I was off in a flash in my Gyro 160 Mk II. The lift was phenomenal. I had never flown so high before, and soon I was looking back at the hill amazed at how tiny my friends and the two 4x4's appeared from the air. I quickly started to use the height to do some aerobatics. I was in absolute bliss having so much height to carry out continuous chandelles, multiple 360's, wingovers or any other maneuver I felt like doing. The relatively small coastal sites near my home had never provided such altitude in which I could do maneuver after maneuver and I continued on like this for over half an hour.

I was spiraling through a series of very steep 360's, completely relaxed, concentrating on the keeping the bank right when I noticed the mountains in the foreground were not rising in my field of view but were doing the opposite, I was climbing. I was way out upwind of the ridge so I knew this should not have been happening, especially when doing maneuvers that use up so much height so quickly. I looked around and noticed the sky had changed since taking-off. The clouds were now covering half the sky, and although they were still so far above me I was shocked by the detail of the cloud base. Dropping into coastal mode I immediately leveled out and penetrated further away and upwind of the ridge. This always results in loosing height, on the coast anyway.

I kept my eyes glued on the mountains to the west, and to my horror I was still going up. I eased on more speed, something that normally results in the Gyro dropping really fast, but not this time. I added more speed and felt the familiar increase in billow as the outboard leading edges started to flex. But a glance upwards to cloudbase left me with a heavy weight in my stomach, as the well-defined base was now a seething, rolling mass drawing me closer by the second. I focused on the mountains upwind and with maximum possible speed headed out over the lake, still climbing!

The updraft into the clouds had a strong grip on the Gyro and I could only imagine the fate that awaited me above cloudbase. The fear consumed me, but I did not panic. While I did everything conceivable to loose altitude I remembered having experienced this exact same fear before. It came to me in a flash as I recalled a serious wipeout in the surf when aged 12. Anyone who has been a keen surfer and done it for long enough will know the feeling of coming close to drowning and this was identical to what I was experiencing now. I had stumbled into the path of one of natures most powerful and fundamental processes, and I had to get out of its way. I was learning first hand what it was like to get sucked into a cloud.

I was spinning the glider, spiraling, pulling on speed, and finally praying to find a way out of the imminent fate that awaited me. I had the glider at full speed and as I looked out along the right leading edge I noticed the slightest 'S' bend, a mild flex inward from the nose to the cross-bar junction, and then a flex back toward the tip, the billow was extreme. The keel wire from the king post was rattling its shackle where it attached to the keel. My fear went up another level as I contemplated the possibility the Gyro might not stay together long enough for me to get out of this when, with my gaze firmly fixed on the mountains ahead, my ascent slowed. "This is working," I thought to myself. So I kept on, just praying my climb would slow, and eventually I leveled out.

With my heart in my mouth I plummeted out of the sky as quickly as I could. By the time I set up my landing I knew I had survived with only eight lives left, but that was good enough for me. I landed right next to the lake's edge in absolutely calm conditions. I crawled out of my harness and sat next to my glider. Looking at the wing I noticed the leading edges were straight once again, the 'S' bend was gone and immediately I felt total respect for the Gyro and how it got me through the whole experience in one piece.

As I sat there I looked across the lake and everything looked sharper, the colors brighter. The smell of the grass and the water, the total silence of the valley, everything, was more intense. I looked up at the sky to see the benign appearance of the clouds. But looking harder I could just make out the boiling motion of its edges; they weren't fooling me.

My friends came down in the cars and said, "Wow you were so high; how was the flight?" They were unaware that I nearly became an unwilling part of a cumie. Try as I may I could not convey to them the seriousness of what had just happened. We packed the glider, loaded up, and made our way home. Everyone was talking, the radio was on, and everything was 'normal' again. But for me I had just regained a healthy respect for nature and its ability to catch any one of us off-guard.

Groundhog Tumbles

Grant (Groundhog) Hoag

On Monday July 5th I launched with ten other pilots from Horseshoe Meadows in the Owens Valley. With light conditions and a ceiling below 14,000 feet, many people stopped flying near Big Pine. I was behind many other pilots, so I finally left the Sierra Nevada Range for the Inyo Mountains nearly five hours after launching. There was gentle lift in the valley while crossing to Black Mountain, and I climbed up the west face as it baked in the late afternoon sun. I rose over the top of the west ridge and dove north for what I hoped to be the afternoon glass-off near Flynn's.

In southeast winds there exists a convergence zone north-northeast of Black Mountain. There the prevailing winds and expanding air from Owens Valley meet and mix. This area is known to have gusts of turbulence as well as strong lift. If you can fly through this big air, the slightly less hostile Inyo foothills beckon to the North.

Flying straight north through that zone at 9,000 feet, an unexpected gust rolled my Moyes CSX almost 90 degrees. As I pulled in to dive out of it, a second gust hit, inverting the glider. My feet against the undersurface, the glider stalled as if at the top of a failed loop; then it backslid and snapped around, breaking my grip. In the ensuing tumble I was wrapped over the keel with my Wills Wing Z-5 harness suspension lines caught in the wing pullback latch. The left shoulder of the harness ripped open when I slammed into the keel, bending two of the three spreader bars in the harness.

I found myself a rear-seat passenger in the now upright and intact glider. It was mushing along in a stall with me entangled in the keel pullback clasp at the trailing edge. I looked around and saw that I was several thousand feet above the foothills, and the glider was pointing generally west. It looked like I had a few moments, so I radioed a Mayday and my location to Powerline Mike, who was drinking beer at Klondike Lake at the end of his flight. I repeated my location, and after a moment's hesitation to reflect on the enormity of what was next, I threw my chute.

The opening parachute twisted the glider around. I struggled without success to move higher onto the glider. The canyon walls rushed up, and I was delighted to see a steep rocky hillside with few boulders instead of cliffs. I closed my eyes and relaxed for impact.

The shock was lessened by a strong wind up the canyon, which slowed the descent rate of my recently repacked 12-year-old High Energy Sports parachute. Once on the ground, however, the parachute threatened to drag me across the canyon and over a cliff, so I pulled in the billowing chute bridle and grabbed enough suspension lines to deflate it. It took 30 minutes to get out of the harness, call to Mike to say I was OK, and to vector him close enough to see me on the hillside. I folded the Moyes CSX , and found that neither the crossbar nor the leading edges had broken in the tumble and impact. Then I started hiking down into a canyon where Mike said the Black Mountain Road was located. Although I had started flying with a full Camelback of water, after the five hour flight there was little left. Suffice it to say that I was very dehydrated and overheated when Mike and Ilona found me carrying the harness down the hill. Mike and I then went back for the glider, and we returned by flashlight. Mike and Ilona had to be back in Las Vegas by the next morning, so by the time they left me in Lone Pine I was one tired and beat up dude. But I was alive.

Hang I, Icarus II

Tracy Tillman

In a galaxy far, far away, after a dark and stormy night, I learned to hang glide:

In 1976 or 1977 (I'm not sure of the date—maybe due to losing too many brain cells during that time period in my youth) I had taken hang gliding lessons from Boris Popov at Northern Sun in Minneapolis/St. Paul on a Sun standard rogallo wing.

I went back for a second weekend of more advanced rigid wing lessons on an Icarus II. We didn't use a harness; we just hung from the armpits. I had a great time, and flew well. I was especially impressed with the glider.

It was also a real hoot for the students to watch one particular student. After every launch he just jumped out of the hang cage, causing the Icarus II to do a huge loop in the wind, over the tops of our heads, and crash on its nose behind us. KA-BAM!

He jumped three or four times in a row. Boris, understandably, was getting more and more pissed off. It was amazing how high the glider would get at the top of each loop, and how loud the crash was. We were all laughing hysterically, literally rolling on the ground—except for Boris. With each loop and KA-BAM! Boris' face would get redder, and the veins in his forehead would stand out. I thought his head might pop off. Finally, he wouldn't let the guy fly any more. Incredibly, the glider wasn't (visibly) damaged, and we kept flying it for the rest of the day.

I loved that glider and had to have one. It flew so much better than the rogallo wing, which probably had a 4:1 glide. I heard that Dudley Mead (remember him?) wanted to sell an Icaraus II that was under construction, so I drove my relatively new '76 Camaro down to Dayton, Ohio to see it. I bought the glider on the spot, with a 20'x4'x3' transportation box Dudley had constructed. We tied it all on top of my Camaro. The box seemed to be about twice as big as the car.

Halfway home I encountered a big headwind; the lid blew off of the box and one wing folded over in two in the wind. Damn. Then, while driving through Rochester, MN in the middle of the night, the car's tranny quit shifting. I was able to make it to a Sears garage, and waited for them to open.

They eyed me suspiciously, but hoisted the car on the rack and fixed it, with the box still on top.

Soon after getting home, I repaired and completed the construction of the glider, and went back to the same site in Minneapolis where I learned to fly with Boris. The site was a hill at a garbage dump with a stinky slough at the bottom (probably toxic).

My new glider flew great. Too great. On the first flight, I hit some lift, and just kept on gliding and gliding and gliding, hundreds of feet further than on my previous flights. I saw the edge of the slough pass beneath me, feeling wonderful and bird-like...

My feet skimmed the surface of the muck and I landed smack in the middle. Nice thing about the Icarus II; it floats. I hung on to the hang cage by my armpits, and tried to swim the glider to the edge, until it got hung up on something. I had to let go of the hang cage and try to touch bottom in order to move the glider to get it out. I dropped down into the dirty, smelly, scummy garbage water and my feet sunk down into the slimy bottom until my nose was just at the water level. YUCK. What a smell.

I eventually got out, and my buddies helped me pack up to leave. We had about a 2-hour drive back home to Mankato, with me wet and stinking up the car real bad.

That's my one and only water landing. The fever, nausea, headaches, and red spots and dots went away after a few weeks, although, my car never did smell right after that.

I put a lot of time on the Icarus II, even going motorized. I've got some great old pictures; I'm hanging by my armpits and my huge flared '70s pant legs are flapping in the wind. One of my old flying buddies, Larry Smith, still has that old Icarus of mine and is still flying a beautifully-built motorized Easy Riser up there in Minnesota.

The Icarus and Easy Riser were strong, fun gliders, but were very sensitive in pitch. After inverting and tumbling an Easy Riser, I got one of those new-fangled hand-tossed parachutes. Meanwhile, as a result of his own "interesting" experiences, Boris developed the ballistic recovery system and started the very successful BRS company.

Still, those gliders were fun to fly, and had great performance at the time. I wonder how they would aerotow.

The Inverted Flare

EJ Steele

It was well in to the afternoon of a long, late summer day. So it was a bit surprising that Debbie (the local wind-talker) was reporting 20mph winds from the north-northwest. Yet, as soon as I lay the ringer down, my partner in crime was calling me ("Double-D" they call him. A definitive meaning for which has not yet been established. I think it stands for "Darkness-Dave" or something like that; but that's another story). He too had Debbie's number. When we rendezvoused at the LZ and saw that it was just he and I, the romance of launching the backside grew much, much stronger.

An optimistic drive up was rewarded by the presence of exactly what Debbie had promised. The climb to launch is a good 300 feet in altitude from the road; but we hardly felt the weight of our gear as we raced to setup. As we tore through baton pockets and leg loops, we kept taunting each other with visions of grandeur; "Oh man, this is going to be great. All to ourselves!" Desirous-Dave would push.

I would raise him one; "Let's get real high, wait 'til dusk, and land on the beach!"

I should have learned something by the short duration of his flight spent in front of launch. A steady 15mph North wind usually generates adequate lift to soar the backside; this evening it was twenty, straight in our faces! He made one pass away from the gap (the escape 180° back over the road that leads to the base of launch, and to the "retrievable" side), climbing out all the way. But, in a dramatic fashion, the return pass was nothing but a desperate attempt to get through the gap with safe altitude. He went from a comfortable 100 feet over launch (~400 feet above the gap) to thanking God we didn't park the truck any further out in the road.

The sky was developing into a blossoming sunset, and the thought of soaring in it was too inviting to think that I would be treated in the same manner as my counter-part. I remember when Daddy-Dave's son (my wire-assist by default) nervously shouted over the wind noise; "You don't have to do this, ya know!"

I just cracked a cocky, but confident smile over my shoulder, and said; "Oh yes I do. This is perfect Brotherhood!"

Moments later, I found my cycle. It easily pulled me up and away from launch as I climbed into my harness, and began to feel that wonderful thrill of flight. It was only for a few moments that pre-launch anxiety escaped my thought, and then things got weird. Suddenly, it was if I flew into a large vacuum bubble. The glider just stopped flying.

Naturally, the glider dropped to regain air speed; I tried feverously to help it (push out, pull in, left, right, push out). I was traversing the hillside, barely above the trees. Finally, I felt this huge kick in the ass, like the wind had dramatically switched direction. (Interestingly though, my wingman reported that as I fell into the hands of Mother-Nature, the wind at launch continued to come straight in at 20mph.) Screaming toward the treetops in front of me, I must have reached 75mph within a second or two before I decided it was the best time to push out. Unfortunately, my timing was off, and I clipped my right wing; which repeated the whole effort to regain airspeed. Now, not only was I lacking airspeed, I was yawing like all get out, and was so far down in to the canyon that the rotor was having it's way with me. The glider was picked up by the left wing and thrust in to a cartwheel (so that I did simultaneous 180° roll and 90° pitch maneuvers in fractions of a second). I could no longer fight it. I was straight up and down, nose pointed towards the earth, top surface facing back toward launch!

Amazingly it didn't take much to figure out the best course of action. I could see the ground rushing up at me, and thought; 'I can't go in face first. That'll hurt like hell.' Nope. I was going to have to land it on it's back! So, in the last few seconds before impact, I clinched the bar and rammed it down (or, I guess in this case, up?) to my ankles.

The glider went over! Very coordinated I might add. The motion was so abrupt that the top surface "flared" into the air and gently set me down on the treetops. The glider continued to rotate over until I was upside-right again, and came to rest in the trees about 15 feet off the ground. I was certain that I hadn't been knocked out. In fact, in the days to follow, I never found any cuts, bruises, or whiplash; I didn't even experience a rash from all the poison oak I swam through to get out of there.) In my temporary state of shock, I found myself giggling, as I dangled there, calling to my comrade on the radio.

It was so late in the day I had to leave my kite on the hillside for the night. The following day, at the crack of dawn, I hiked up to launch to retrieve my gear. I kept hiking further and further away from launch to get a view down into the canyon. Finally, from a neighboring spine, there it was. Oh-my-God! It really happened. Nothing drives home the reality of it all than to see your baby pinned to the hillside, way down in some canyon you're absolutely *sure* you'd never survive the ride in to.

When I hiked back to launch, and down to the glider, I sat for a spell and took in my surroundings. This was the small portion of earth afforded to me in a time of great need. I don't know how I made the instinctive decision to "flare" upside-down, or who works the buttons upstairs; but I realized then, mine is some semi-charmed kind of life!

Windy Cliff Launch, Pickle Butte Idaho

Kevin Frost

I don't know if this is my best story. But it sure has a heck of a punch line. I screw up and almost get a buddy killed; he ends up a hero; but no good deed goes unpunished.

It was back in the spring of 93, I was a new H4 flying a Formula. Spring came to western Idaho after a long cold winter, and in the middle of the week we found ourselves with a bright sunny day and enough wind to make a trip to Pickle Butte, our small NW facing ridge soaring site. So my brother DJ, Rich (the Kalbasoar) Kalbus and I all scheme to play hooky for the day and enjoy the beautiful flying weather.

We hit the ridge and checked out the mannequin head-on-a-stick next to launch. Her hair of gold was flowing in at slightly west-of-perfect wind. We decided to try the seldom-used center launch, which faces the wind a bit better. It was used less often because it was just a big flat rock that stuck out from the cliff with nowhere for the nose man to go except to quickly flatten himself out and let the pilot launch over the top of him.

I didn't want to be that guy, and I didn't want to have to launch all perched out on that rock in gusts with only one wireman. So I selfishly raced to set up first, stuffing battens like a dirty bastard. No challenge against the ever finicky Rich who just barely had his battens carefully polished and spread under his wing like fine silverware at a king's table about the time I asked him to grab my nose and walk me out.

It was a bit gusty and I had a little trouble trying to keep the wings level as we inched out to the edge of the ledge. We rode out a couple gust cycles. When the wind died a little I quickly yelled clear and timed my lunge as I normally did on main launch, not allowing Rich time to fully duck down against the rock.

Looking straight ahead I gave a mighty leap and charged right into Rich. And the world went into that slow-time mode that often happens in these situations. And I'm thinking, "Ok, I'm screwed. DJ has let go of my sidewire; I'm on the edge of a cliff plowed into this brick wall of a noseman; and in about a second something really bad is going to happen. A wing is going to lift and I'm going to cartwheel."

Then I'm flying, no if's or but's. I'm totally ok.

Rich had immediately realized my predicament, grabbed my control bar, ducked and rolled away from me while pushing the bar up and out.

I'm still in slow-time just a few feet from launch, helicoptering up and out and I look between my legs and see Rich roll off the edge.

"OH, SHIT!!!"

I look up to check for a level horizon then look back down and Rich is rolling and bouncing off sharp-edged boulders just below launch. I keep quickly looking up and then back down, and Rich keeps falling and bouncing in underwater-slow-motion-dream-time. And I'm thinking, "This is really going to be bad".

Rich comes to a rest, perhaps 20' down on a pile of sharp rocks and I'm thinking that he is dead or badly injured.

It's fast time again and I'm just sick. I pull in the bar and start buzzing my poor broken friend. I get as low as I can to assess his situation and I'm imagining all the horrible things that could have come of a fall like that. Is his spine shattered? If he lives will he spend the rest of his life controlling a wheel chair with his tongue? Does he have a head injury? Will I be visiting his wasting husk of a body in a nursing home for the next 20 years?

And it's all my fault!!!!

It's all my fault, and I'm personally responsible for single-handily destroying the life of my friend.

I continue buzzing him with my heart in my throat, self-loathing filling my soul. And then a small miracle, he moved a little! A sign of life! Then a major miracle. As I watch from the air, bar stuffed and buzzing him as low as I dare get, and as my little brother and a concerned wuffo with his two little daughters look on, Rich crawls several feet over to a little snowdrift, pulls down his pants and sits down in the snow!!

I keep buzzing Rich and feel a little better. Then Rich looks up at me and sees me worriedly buzzing him and gives me a big 'thumbs up'!!

I was elated, my heart soared, and I soared. I let out on the control bar and climbed into a sunny blue sky. I started breathing again and noticed that it was the most beautiful spring day ever. I soared the length of the ridge basking in redemption. And as I passed Rich I kind of did a small wingover and dipped my wing to him. And he again gave me hearty thumbs up! I continued running the ridge, and every time I passed Rich sitting bare assed in the snow, I dipped my wing and he raised his arm for a big thumbs up salute!

Later my brother and Rich both confirmed…   that wasn't his thumb.

Lookout Mountain Here We Come

Daniel Redick

It was a warm day in December 1975. Winter starts late in Tennessee. *Sweata' weatha'*, the locals called it, but for us Canucks it was warm.

Three adolescents in their thirties (Bob Grant, Ben Moore and myself) had driven all night to reach the fabled ridges of Lookout Mountain. We lodged in one of those roadside motels that the new Interstate had by-passed, leaving it destitute for business and now owned by hippies and occupied by glider pilots, most of whom paid their rent with indentured servitude.

We didn't have instruments like those sissy sailplane pilots. We didn't *need* instruments. We were hang glider pilots. We could soar like the eagles! The fact that we couldn't *afford* instruments was beside the point; we had variometers for ears and lodestones for brains! Look out, Lookout Mountain, here we come; we're pumped with adrenalin and ready for action.

A dozen or so pilots were congregating at a favorite launch site. The grand vista of the valley below enhanced the euphoria and the tales that were being told were taller than the surrounding hills. We were waiting for an approaching cold front to swing the wind into the face of the cliff. During the wait, I was approached by an old gaffer (he reminded me of farmer Yasgur from Woodstock, but that's another story). He told me that he farmed a few acres in a clearing just behind the ridge and that, on occasion, hang glider pilots landed on his property. It seemed to me that the rotor atop this ridge would make that a dangerous venture, but then some people are foolish enough to try anything. No wonder this sport is getting a bad reputation, I thought to myself.

Plastic ribbon tied to branches overhanging the cliff soon started rippling upwards. An empty cigarette pack tossed over, came back up and over our heads. It's time to launch!

Like giant butterflies morphing from chrysalides, our brightly colored wings were being spread. Spectators were gathering to behold the great event. Oh, how envious they must be, I thought.

The first glider was launched and the pilot let out a loud "yahooo" as the wind over his wing lifted him skyward. Cheers and "aahs" rose from the crowd. (Well, okay, a half-dozen people isn't a crowd, but that's how I remember it.) Everyone who wanted to soar that day did soar. The band of lift was long, wide, and strong.

I remember when I was a child, lying on my back in a pasture field watching in awe as hawks circled above, effortlessly riding on the warm rising air. I dreamt of joining them one day. That day had arrived. A curious hawk was soaring beside me. It was ethereal bliss. I had realized my childhood dream. I circled and played in the rising wind, crisscrossing paths with my fellow fliers above and below.

Hours passed and I was alerted back to reality by the numbing cold in my hands. The wind had been getting stronger as well as colder. Things on the ground were definitely looking smaller; my crab angle was increasing. It was time to come down.

I faced my glider into the wind, and pushed the control bar almost down to my knees. Forward progress is never very apparent at altitudes, so as I bided my time trying to ignore the cold, my eyes were drawn to the shabby tin roofs of some farm buildings in a clearing behind the ridge. The words of the old farmer echoed in my ears; "sometimes they land in my field". Time passed. Could I even be sure that I was making *any* forward progress? Temptation increased. If I turned downwind I would be there in a flash. If others had done it, why couldn't I? Maybe the danger of 'the notorious rotor behind the ridge' was just a myth. I yielded to temptation and turned downwind. Wow, we're boogyin' now, I said to myself, as that clearing behind the ridge quickly approached. All was going great until...

Have you ever watched a leaf on a windy autumn day? Watched how it tumbles and swirls in the turbulent air? Well, that best describes the way that I now found myself being tossed about. My life *did not* flash before my eyes, but I was sure it was over, none the less!

I now believe in miracles, because about fifty feet above the ground directly over the far end of the clearing, my glider righted itself and was flying me to my intended target. I made my approach flying back towards the ridge, expecting to land into the wind. Not so! Here in the lee both the wind and me were going in the same direction. It was not a pretty landing, but I wasn't complaining.

This should have been the end of my story but much to my horror I looked up to see several of my fellow fliers following my lead. I was sure that somebody was going to buy it. Fortunately however, the sun was setting and the wind let up a bit, allowing most to make an uneventful landing. But not Bob Grant. Oh no, *he* has to make his approach flying over one of those shabby tin roofed outbuildings. Did he clear the roof? Not a chance! But he did land on his feet, both of which went right through, leaving him stuck there with his legs dangling inside the building. Bob was unscathed, but a little red faced as he apologized to the owner for damaging the roof.

The old farmer would accept no compensation. Instead, he invited us into his humble abode, offered us moonshine, and probed us for tales of other adventures.

Post Script: Contrary to the way that I told this story to my friends twenty-five years ago, I now humbly confess that the skilful maneuvers about which I bragged were a complete lie. I was solely at the mercy of the wind.

Fusion 1 Splashes Down

Mark Vaughn

It was a crapshoot, but it paid off.

Rob Jacobs, Tom Lanning (AKA Sparky), Jon Szarek, Jon Musto, Jim Collella (AKA Fusion Jim) & I were all on top of Morningside's 450 foot agl launch, Thursday afternoon, waiting for the right moment to jump. I just happen to be the lucky one on deck that launched into a boomer strait to cloud base.

Once there, I was met with white streaks of flying snow & ice. OUCH! That stuff stings doing 30.

Reaching 7,312 ft msl (cloud base) I headed off toward the town of Newport flying from familiar LZ to familiar LZ. While in route, I fly into the Rotor of Mt Ascutney, about 7miles up wind; I'm now pushed down to about 5k and getting tossed around like a floating ice cube in a blender. *Houston, we have a Problem!*

Turning north to escape *Blender Alley*, I finally fly my way free of this continuous hammering. Now over the Valley between Claremont and Newport, I hit another boomer, which lifts me back to snow & ice. I head off toward Mt Sunapee flying over the Newport golf course under a cloud street, at times exceeding sixty mph ground speed. Pure cloud suck avoidance. I can hear the ice striking the shell of my helmet.

Reaching Mount Sunapee and just past the *forbidden field*, I'm faced with a decision. Do I venture off crosswind towards Route 89 and Warner or stay with the stronger tail winds and maintain my current southeast heading?

Just under 7k and seeing Pats Peak in the distance, I decide to continue to the southeast. WRONG DECISION! Not thinking about my rotor encounter at Mt. Ascutney, I fly right into the rotor of Mt Sunapee. I try to fly out of it but there is no place to go. I'm sinking at over 1,000 fpm and there's no familiar LZ in sight. All possible LZ's are covered in white and I don't dare chance an ice covered lake or pond landing as I might break through. Every open area I see is blanketed with white when viewed from 5000 ft. Bradford is just a couple miles ahead and it is my only sure chance for a safe landing area.

So with a tightening of the VG, I head toward Bradford. Once there and still sinking like a stone, I find it's mostly under water. GRRRRRRR! I'm now at about 3K and working on a landing plan. I descend to 1000 ft and can see small islands in the flooded field, which tells me the water is at least shallow. (A GOOD THING)

I start to see wind lines on the water, which fortunately are perpendicular to the longest landable dry spot. I get down to 300ft with harness open and drogue chute in hand. I enter my downwind-leg and reach my base-leg turnpoint at the treetops at the end of the field, (or should I say pond?) I turn onto final and deploy the drogue chute. Stuffing the bar to create MAX Drag (BAD IDEA!) I monitor my glide. Approaching the end of my intended LZ, I pass over three islands. Oh no I'm getting too slow wait wait, 5 more feet! DAMN! I need to flare...

Splash, Whack, Crash, Berbal Berbal, *&%%$#%$@&! Only 5 feet short of *Terra Firma*! The *winter rust* is thicker than I thought. It'll be back to the training hill for some spring spot landing practice. Now soaked from the waist and elbows down (the water is freezing cold and it don't taste so great either) I drag my soggy butt to shore and start to break down. SQUISH, SQUISH, SQUISH. Luckily the sun's still out and I'm wearing my black non-cotton Thermax clothing, so I'm not too uncomfortably cold. I use my cell phone, which remained dry, thank God, to contact my dedicated limo driver, Rob Jacobs. (ROB, You Da Man). I tell him what happened and I can just feel he's doing all he can, not to burst out loud in laughter. He stops to pick me up a HOT! cup of Dunkin Donuts coffee. He even remembers the sugar. He then delivers it to the Bradford LZ, which from this day forward shall be known as the BRADFORD SEA PORT. The intense razzing now begins. Rob shows up just shaking his head in what I perceive as disbelief. In reality he's amazed that I went so far, so fast, from just a 450ft hill.

Rob, thanks again for picking me up and delivering the Joe. Hey, I think we have the making for a GREAT! Dunkin Donuts commercial.

My instruments, harness and parachute were soaked. After drying out my Flytec revealed that my strongest climb was over 1,600 fpm. All I know is that my vario was pegged.

I was up for an hour and fifteen minutes and reached 7312ft off a 450ft hill. Unofficially I flew 22 miles, although I still need a GPS fix on the pond to confirm that. For my *next flight* off a 450-foot hill, I promise I will have a flotation device.

Menstriecrash

Roy Garden

It started off as a modest expedition to a site we had heard of but never flown, just a couple hours drive from where we live. Two hours hang driving with Mr. Smith, much bollix being talked about the potential to fly xc back home. As if; it's 100 odd miles and nobody we know has flown 100 klicks, never mind 100 miles.

So we eventually got to the site, right above a town called Menstrie in Scotland and overlooking the Wallace Memorial; it's about 1800' top to bottom with a 15 mile ridge run.

The first fly in the ointment was that there's only one road to take off and its exclusive use belongs to a *paraplunging* instructor. After much time wasting we found this *paraplunger* and got ourselves a lift to the take-off. He relieved us of £3.50, each, for the privilege. We had spent so much time looking for this *paraplunger* that we had neglected to look for any LZs. But hey, it's Scotland and you can land pretty much anywhere.

The view at the top is excellent, looking down over the heart of Scotland and on towards Edinburgh. There are lush green farmland, LZs everywhere, some with cattle, some with freshly cut fields, very few trees and right below us the town of Menstrie.

It was blowing 15-20 straight on with little cumies a couple of grand over take-off with no wave to be seen anywhere and looked just perfect. I ran around like mad getting rigged before the weather took a turn for the worse. Rigged, harness on, eh, hold on…

"*Mr. Paraplunging Instructor*, where do you land?" (It's always best to find out if any of the locals are inclined to take umbrage at you landing in their fields in the event of a sledder.)

"In the town square," said *Mr. Paraplunger*.

"It looks a bit small from up here."

"No no, it's fine, we get hang gliders landing there all the time."

Oh well, he is an instructor, thought I; he must know what he is talking about.

I had an uneventful take off and a really nice flight, getting 1500 to 2000 over and having fun. After about 40 minutes I decided that I wasn't, after all, going to make 100 miles that day. The next best thing would be a pint of the local hostelry's finest cold ale while sitting in the sun down below.

I proceeded to burn off three and a bit thousand feet to get closer to Menstrie. I thought I'd take a better look at the town square to see if this *paraplunger* was talking bollix after all. Amazing how much easier it is to core sink than to core lift.

When I got to 1000 over the town I thought that the LZ still looked small. Downwind had trees all along it with no gaps. The left-hand side consisted of a row of houses (as you would expect in a town). The right hand side consisted of a row of houses (as you would expect in a town). Upwind side had a medium sized sports center with a road, the main highway for the area, running behind it. Across the road was a pub with a beer garden.

The air I was in was pretty neutral, 2000 down, so I thought I'd loose another couple of hundred, get down to 800 and look again. Meanwhile I was looking for alternate LZs. There were LOADS of them just outside the town, within ¾ of a mile in any direction. Even the upwind LZs were within range.

Sink, sink, sink. As I looked down, the thoughts running through the head consisted of, "It's too small," (The LZ, honest). But there's beer; the fields would be MUCH, better but there's no beer.

This somehow got into a bit of a feedback loop in my head

Safe LZ but no BEER!

Challenging LZ with BEER!

Safe LZ but no BEER!

By the time I was 300 over and having a really good look, sanity kicked in and it was obvious that it was WAY too small—about ½ the size of a football pitch with 40-foot-high obstacles in the form of houses and trees on all sides. By then I was too low to run away to a good LZ.

Bugger, bugger, bugger. What was it that *paraplunging* dimwit said to me?

"No, no, it's fine, we get hang gliders landing there all the time"

I did a perfect approach over the trees, downwind along the houses, got to the end of the row of houses to go to base leg and kicked the TV antenna off the top of someone's house and had to do a 180 into wind as the sports center was higher than the houses. If I had only turned 90 I'd have landed on its roof. There was barely three feet, horizontally, between my right wingtip and the guttering on the roof of the sports center as I came into wind.

It was obvious that I was still too high to land before I ran into the trees at the upwind end of the LZ so I decided to continue to box inside the houses and trees and take a downwind landing.

The box was a sort of extended turn. I was about halfway through it when it became apparent that I was going to run into a woman and her dog who were standing gawping at me. I yelled, in my best Anglo Saxon, "GET OUT OF THE F*&%ING WAY!" She stood there, looking perplexed.

I pushed out to clear her head and the inevitable turning-flaring-stalling-falling-ouch thing happened. I almost got away with it, but that the glider landed first and I kissed the back of one of my uprights pretty hard when I landed—on my feet—behind it.

"Are you alright," asked the (surprisingly pretty) woman with the dog.

"Mmm, yeth I'll be fine." I had cut something in my mouth, which seemed to be bleeding pretty badly.

She wandered off to the shops and I unclipped and looked the glider over. It was fine; it takes more than my face to bend an Airwave upright fore and aft. I laid the glider down and got out of the harness. I was shocked at how much blood there was. I couldn't really feel anything wrong but there was LOTS of blood. There were two old, obviously retired, chaps leaning over the fence at the back of the sports center so I decided to ask them if I was ok or whether I had done some serious damage to my face.

As I got to close to the fence, one of the old boys took one look at my face, went really pale and keeled over! The old bugger had fainted.

I gave his buddy a hand to help the fainter into his car and we had a fairly quick drive to the local doctor. Then he took me to the local dentist. She was really cute, tight white dress, all heaving chest, long hair and sympathy (or maybe I was in a little shock). She said I was fine and that would be 25 pounds please. Bugger, what was it that *paraplunger* said?

"No no, it's fine, we get hang gliders landing there all the time"

Got a bus back to the LZ in time to see a pilot I knew coming in to land. By the time he could see me waving at him to land someplace else, he was committed. Beardy One Canobi (Colin Harrison) then proceeded to spin in and take out both downtubes. He said that once he was about 100 over it was pretty clear that he would never get in there sensibly, so he spun it in to avoid hitting the houses, road, or sports center.

We sat in the LZ muttering dark things about *Mr. Paraplunging Instructor* and the pain we could inflict on him with the remains of Colin's downtubes. We debated whether we would do much damage to him beating him about the head, or whether we could fit one of the downtubes up his arse sideways, you know the kind of thing.

Then a few *paraplungers* came in to the LZ, so we asked them about the LZ. "Have you ever seen hanggliders come in here?" we asked.

"Oh yeah, we see hang gliders come in here lots," said the gaudily dressed *paraplungers*.

"How do they get on with their landings?" I asked.

"Oh, they all crash! We like to get down here first to see them."

Second Solo, Premier Flight

Terry Ryan

There I was, parked, at 2000 feet. The air was smooth but strong, enough to exactly oppose my forward motion. My Falcon flew itself in trim while I spread my arms and reveled in the wind. The long forgotten expression, "Look't me, mom," passed through my consciousness. I was over the end of my destination runway and not moving a bit over the ground. It gave me a moment to ponder a lifetime.

The outside world, too, was my personal vista. My heading was west by southwest; off to my right was Groveland, Fla. and highway 33 ran almost parallel to my bar. The late afternoon sun stretched the trees in the orange groves and highlighted the Westside beacons. My instructors, now 1900 feet below, whose collective will alone could have kept me from harm, watched, and waited, and rated. Why are they standing where I will need to land? The small lake just ahead with its resident alligator was my western turning point. A snapshot saved in the soul.

This, I reminded myself, is why I took up hang gliding. And the hours of study and practice have been well worth it. This flight started about 7 minutes earlier on the ground, in my harness, hooked in to the glider, staring along the tow rope towards the ultra-light tow plane they call the Dragon-fly. They're all waiting for me. I'll have to get used to this pilot-in-command thing. I run down the checklist in my head. It strikes me that this is like water skiing—but with a third dimension. I mutter something to indicate my readiness and my wingman interprets it correctly. He gives that full rotary arm motion that signals the tug pilot to *hit it.*

The ground roll is short; I'm flying within 4 seconds but must keep low and give the plane a chance to take off, also careful to stay above the prop wash and the wing-tip vortices. The powerful little tug is quick to rise. Steady as she goes; keep the plane on the horizon, and don't let the glider get off to either side. Climb rate is about 500 feet per minute. At 2500 feet the tug pilot waves me off and, as my fingers squeeze the bicycle-brake-type lever, I feel the clunk and hear the whiz as the towline releases and drops away. Pull in to gain air speed and peel off to the right. Poetry in motion as the tug peels off to the left. A steep dive, and she's gone. Yikes! I'm on my own.

A flood of do's and don'ts: relax and shake your arms, pull in your bridle, get your bearings and locate the LZ, check your ground track and figure the winds set your heading and relax. It is quiet. It is peaceful. It is a time to be in awe of the world beneath you. It is an emotional time. Unfamiliar feelings flood in from forgotten places. Let loose. Any tears of joy will dry long before you land. Your view is unencumbered for you are prone, facing down, with your "support" all above you. You marvel at your good fortune. You pity the earth-bound.

As a novice you head straight to the LZ to practice multiple figure eights on landing approach. But the wind at this level is 70 degrees across the runway and is strong and you find yourself "parked" on the up-wind leg.

I check my ground track again. Uh-oh! I'm loosing ground—actually flying backwards. This is what they warned me about; don't get too far down wind. I pull in the bar for more speed, but no headway. For an instant, panic. I haul in the bar; now gaining ground but loosing altitude. But it's OK because, at 1500 feet I reach gentler winds and go in to my figure 8's. Jim taught me how to enter my turns with confidence, to push out and carve the turn, and to exit the turn right on track. You know when you've done it right by the feeling you get in your body and your soul. This experience is not possible on the training hill.

The sound of the wind in the wires is your speedometer. Your other senses tell you location, attitude and direction. Subtle body movements control everything. Hang gliding is a sport, a discipline, a passion, a thing spiritual. In learning to fly, I have also learned to read the clouds, the birds, and even the grass. I notice things that are invisible to average folk. Hang gliding is amazing and fulfilling. I applaud those who have gone before me.

Michael Robertson got me started in all this years ago and I am eternally grateful. More recently, Campbell convinced me to fly at Quest by his unbounded enthusiasm for the sport. Jim took me under his wing (no pun) and taught me how to *follow* the plane, showed me my first *thermalling*, and how to pick my *spot* on landing and watch the angles. Russell helped me perfect my oscillation recovery, landing set-ups, and, most important, how to relax. Paris taught me how to carve those turns and gave me my final passing grade. And Leslie gave me advice, confidence, and lots of photographs.

Alas, it is time to land. Should I make that one last turn? No! Better to go long—there's lots of runway. Too short, and I'm in the watermelon patch. Check your *spot*. Straighten out. Pull in for speed. The windsong is much louder now. Hold it. Minor corrections—gentle—nothing hard or hasty at this point. Level off or *round out* just above the road. Skim in over the grass at about 4 feet while you bleed off speed. Push out, gently, and flare—NOW! Perfect landing. Your sub-conscious registers a few cheers. But you are lost in your own thoughts; already re-living the flight.

I am struggling out of the harness when someone comes up and hands me a Coors Light, the drink of choice at Quest Air. Friendly people, a common passion, and cold beer—what more can you ask for? It's been a great flight and a great day. As we all head to the hangar, we know the talk that night will be of flying. And later that night, the dreams too, will be of flying.

Flying In Clouds

Steve Lantz

There have been many articles as of late in both Hang Gliding and Paragliding magazines about flying in clouds. There is one thing that these articles fail to mention, that *no human can fly in clouds without the aid of instruments.* Sometime around 1980 I launched from the Gold Hill launch at Telluride. It was a beautiful morning with cumulus clouds forming on the western horizon and light breezes coming up the most beautiful hang glider launch in the world. At 12,000 feet, launching at telluride is always a challenge, but the unbelievable beauty and excitement at being there usually makes up for the lack of air density at altitude.

After two hours I flew back over launch at 14,000 feet and drifted southeast of Telluride toward Silverton. Earlier I had noticed a thunderstorm developing to the west but in my enthusiasm for the moment had failed to keep track of it. The sky had gone from crystal clear to about 80% cloud cover, many of the cells sporting black bottoms. There were gliders everywhere and we were all having a great time at cloud base.

A lightning bolt struck a peak three miles in front of me just as I realized the cumulus I had seen earlier was now directly above me. My vario pegged out at over 2,000 fpm up and in a flash I was in the cloud. I was flying the latest, greatest rigid wing available at the time, a Manta Fledge. I deployed both rudders and stuffed the bar to my knees, but my vario remained pegged at 2,000 plus, and the turbulence increased until my hands were being torn from the control bar and I was slammed against the keel. My hands were white with ice and frost as were my down tubes and the leading edge of my wing.

I was not flying with oxygen in those days, in fact most of us were not. The fantastic cannular system developed by Patrick at Mountain Aire was not in common use as of yet and the old systems were heavy and cumbersome. Not a good excuse for not using oxygen, but the fact is I had none. The last thing I remember is reading 19,900 feet on my brand new Ball flight deck.

I came to with my glider in a forward tumble and left spin. The right wing was broken at the last compression strut bay and the red and black glider was completely white with ice and frost. Actually, I could still see streaks of red, but then I realized that it was my blood.

Suddenly I fell out the bottom of the cloud and everything was crystal clear. I was in a steep, nose-down, violent spin with a broken wing; and I was below the top of some of the peaks in the area. I grabbed my hand-deployed parachute and threw it as hard as I could. Nothing happened. I watched the top of a peak go through my horizon. Then I saw my parachute, hooked to the rudder on my broken wing. It ripped loose and opened with a tremendous opening shock. I looked at it for only an instant and saw a giant rip in one of the gores. A split second later I impacted the ground, still in my bulletman harness. I landed on a very steep shale slope and slid for several hundred feet. The harness and the steep slope saved my body and legs.

I was shaking violently from the cold and shock, completely covered with blood, frost and ice. My face was severely injured; my front teeth were missing and there were deep cuts on my chin and cheeks from being slammed around in the glider while I was unconscious.

I lay there, in and out of consciousness for a while, and then made another decision that could have cost me my life. I decided to walk back to Telluride. I had begun sweating profusely because of the heavy clothing I was wearing for high-altitude flying. Still lying there, I took everything off except my jeans and T-shirt, left the clothes in a pile, and got up and started the steep descent down the mountain. I was still bleeding profusely and was acutely aware that my front teeth (twelve in all) were either missing or sheared off at the gums. I had gone only a few hundred yards down the mountain when I started shaking uncontrollably and became unbelievably cold. I crawled on my hands and knees back up to the crash site redressed in my flying gear, and once again started back towards Bear Creek Canyon and Telluride.

About an hour later a helicopter passed overhead, going directly toward the crash scene. Another hang glider pilot had seen the parachute and glider hit the mountain, and had flown back to Telluride and launched the chopper. Had I stayed with my glider I would have been rescued quickly found and rescued.

.Several times I sat down and passed out, but was able to recover enough to get up and proceed down the canyon. Two hours after the crash a search crew of fellow pilots found me and radioed the chopper to pick me up. This was the first time I had ever landed in the town park and not enjoyed it. A quick shot of morphine and the rest was easy. My wife and my good friends Walt and Judy Nielson drove me to Grand Junction where a plastic surgeon used over 200 stitches to put my face back together. Over the next two months I endured twelve root canals in my sheared-off teeth.

I have had many hang gliding pilots tell me what they would have done in this situation and that for them it is no problem to fly in clouds. Some tell me they do it all the time. Flying in clouds is not only illegal, but it is virtually impossible for any human to fly in clouds without the aid of instruments. Do it and you will eventually end up injured or killed. Airplane pilots spend thousands of dollars to equip their aircraft with the needed instruments to fly in clouds yet some still become disoriented and lose control by attempting to second guess their instruments.

Post Script: I wrote this story as a warning to other pilots not to be as stupid as I was in playing near the clouds. As an ex-navy pilot and lifelong airline pilot it is very difficult for me to admit my lack of risk management and shear stupidity in this instance.

"CLOUD HOPPIN'"
Doink!
Boink!
Poink!
Goink!
©skyout
Jules Makk 2001

Old Dogs
New Tricks

Still Havin' Fun, After All These Years!

Doug Johnson

Having flown hang gliders for 21 years, on a fairly regular basis, one would tend to think that he had seen it all. Done it all. Heard it all. Well, most of it anyway. The flying. The friendships. The war stories! You still show up at the flying sites because every flight is just different enough to be unique. Some flights are more memorable, others very similar to dozens of others. But, a flight that I had last summer was quite memorable. The flight I'm talking about came from out of nowhere. Totally unexpected! I'll never forget it. At least I hope I don't. I usually fly my personal glider with a camera, but, wouldn't you know it, that day I didn't pick up film. Bad preflight? Since I don't have the pictures to do my talking for me, you are forced to read this instead. I'll use the pictures etched in my mind to put the details of a really fun flight on paper. This should always be done immediately after the flight for better clarity and detail. More emotion and feeling would come out. Sure, I log all of my flights, but we can always keep a more detailed account. I was told to get this flight on paper right after it happened. I should have listened! Letting nine months pass before getting this down won't make it any easier!

I am a Tandem Instructor with the *Superior Dragonflyers*; I teach via aerotowing using a Dragonfly out of the Richard I. Bong Airport in Superior, WI. The forecast called for light winds and a wide temperature range between the forecast low and high. This meant the dew point was low enough to allow the lower overnight temperature. Dry air! It was to be a great day for soaring. I told myself that to get to the airport early. I would need extra time to set up my own glider. If the tandem lessons started to get too bumpy I wanted to have my glider ready. We hauled the Dragonfly and tandem hang glider out of the hangar for the scheduled morning lessons. I also took my Moyes SX6 out onto the field and set it up. I tied it down and went to work giving tandem lessons. Sure enough, by 9:30, the thermals were starting to affect my students' learning curve. We parked the tandem glider and I started to ready myself for a little fun of my own.

I left the launch dolly at 10:30 behind the Dragonfly piloted by Jerry "Engine" Anderson. As we were climbing away from the field, I was already flying through some pretty good lift. And some pretty good sink! I stayed on tow until I found what seemed like a really good thermal. Altimeter check. 1700' AGL. High enough for me! Release. Turn. Ah, there it is! Or is it? Two or three good 360's and it was gone. Dang. OK. Switch to *search mode*. I found another little bubble starting to come up from below. Altitude check. 400' AGL. Possible low save coming here. Done it before. I slowly work the thermal from the west side of the airport to the east side and circle over other gliders setting up below. The students at the picnic table are all eyes as I get smaller and smaller in the rising air. I top out at cloud base, 4200' AGL. The drift is just too much out of the southwest to be usable for XC. I have been drifting directly toward Lake Superior; I decide that I will just hang out and just see how many hours I can clock.

Here's where the flight became so memorable, the part that will keep me flying for as long as I can. Normally, when you reach cloud base, you have accomplished your mission as a soaring pilot, which is to get as high as you can in the thermal. And normally, when you get to cloud base, you leave the area of the cloud to avoid being sucked up into it. As you leave the area under the cloud, you are leaving lift and flying into sink. Usually, there is an area near the edge of the cloud where there is a vertical wind shear occurring. As the lighter, heated air under the cloud rises it is replaced by cooler, heavier air from above the cloud. One must be aware of this and add extra speed to compensate for the turbulence. The less time spent in this area the better. Sometimes pilot experiences a sensation referred to as *going over the falls*. Not fun when you are looking at the horizon that was just behind you! So, there I was, starting to *white out* at cloud base. Altitude: 4200'. I was up in the dome, the belly of the cloud. Wispy veils of cloud were hanging down all around me. I turned my glider toward the airport to the west. I pulled on some extra speed to go through the veil at the edge of the cloud. I went from dark to light, gray to blue, up to down, up to down...

Up to down? Hey, there wasn't any turbulence at the veil! I'm out in the blue sky, no longer under the cloud, and I'm still going up! Going up at 500' per minute; and it's really smooth! At this point I had a vision of all of the SKYDOGS, standing on launch at a ridge soaring site somewhere, screaming, "TURN." What's wrong with this picture?

I was still leery of the turbulence, being so close to the cloud, so I didn't slow down. I did, however, start to bank the glider into a shallow turn. As I came around it was hard to gauge how close the cloud really was and I flew back into the veil. Still, there was no turbulence. I elongated my 360 so I could fly out away from the cloud. The lift was really smooth. It was the smoothest air I had been in all day. After several 360's, I noticed my shadow on the side of the cloud, that is, a shadow with a 360-degree triple rainbow surrounding it. I'd only heard about this from a few other pilots, but I'd never seen one. New ground. Still transfixed by my *Glory*, I climbed about 1000' up the windward side of the cloud. On the radio I learned that the sight hypnotized everyone on the ground. A jealous (or maybe sarcastic), "Yeah, we see ya," was the response. Climbing up the outside of a cloud isn't supposed to happen. I caught up with the top of the developing cloud and watched the top billow beside me as I climbed to 6000'. My hands were freezing and I had drifted out to the shore of *Gitchigumie*.

I looked northwest toward Duluth. Grandma's Marathon was in progress. At the finish on the northwest end of Park Point (an 8 mile long sand bar at the western end of Lake Superior) was a crowd of 30,000 people, big tents, food, and beer. I was 5 miles away. Could I, should I, fly over there? Nah, this flying day was too good end after only one thermal. Sure, I could make 5 miles, cross wind, into a big blue hole. But it would be the end of my flying for the day. No way. I pulled my fingers out of my gloves and hooked my hands over the control bar. I turned and headed back toward the airport. I was still going up.

The lift was still very smooth. I have launched above the clouds and flown down through them, but I had never started below the clouds and flown higher. Maybe I was still in bed and dreaming. Was I having an out of body experience? After all, it was a really good forecast! The crisp contrast of the sun shining on the tops of the bright white cumulus clouds with the dark greens and blues in the shadows below was breathtaking. I had about 3 miles to go to get back to the airport. There was about 50% cloud coverage and most of the cumuli were 400-500' thick. One out of every ten were like the one I had just left; tall towers of cloud. As I flew toward the airport I had to slalom through these towers like a skier. I finally quit climbing about half way back at 6400'. I was frozen. Ah, low dew points!

When I got back to the airport, I was at 5000' AGL, still 1200' above cloud base! I tried to milk every foot of altitude that I had to put off dropping below cloud base for as long as I could. Normal physics and micrometeorology took over and soon I was back down where I have historically been able to fly a hang glider. I played around for another hour, staying above 4000'.

I was a little sad that my time above the clouds was so short lived, but my hands were telling me that they were glad it was over. I saw Shelley, my wife, pull onto the field. This always means there is the possibility of something to eat. My frozen hands were telling me, "Find Shelley". I was cold and a little hungry, so I pointed for the ground. 1:40 hr total airtime for the flight. I ate lunch, warmed up and launched again at 2:00 pm for another 1:20 hr. 3 hours total airtime for the day! Plus several tandems in the morning and a couple more that evening.

Now, I must admit, I have flown higher than I did on this flight. I've been to 17,999'. And this wasn't my longest flight, time wise; my PR for duration is 6:45 hr. And it certainly was not about distance, either; my longest XC is 152 miles. But, the really nice thing about this flight was that I was able to get out of my own bed, go to the airport and fly. I was able to share my experience and excitement with my students. It was a good lesson for them, "Look what you'll be able to do some day." My wife and some flying friends were there. I was pretty excited when I came down from this flight. I have worn out several cars driving all over the country and I have lots of great memories. My logbook is getting fatter still and my hair is getting grayer.

Maybe I'm just getting old, but I really had a good time. I'll take it! No problem. I am still able to take advantage of the conditions that are here for me every once in a while. I've been watching the sky here in Duluth since I was 5 years old. When I pointed out cloud streets to my mother and described them as "parades of circus animals", she thought I was a little goofy. I was lucky enough to grow up here, on the north shore of Lake Superior, and be exposed to the cross-section view of cumulus development on the south shore. I'm sure the coolest thing about this flight is that it happened right here, close to my roots. Close to where I first thought about flying. Now that we have a Dragonfly in the neighborhood, we can have some fun here at home between tandem lessons. While we may not always have the best conditions here, it does turn on once in a while. So, we fly and have fun after all these years!

The Dune and The Dragonfly

Mark Bolt

To make this short and sweet, I only know how to fly a hang glider, and after 21 years just recently learned how to fly a dragonfly at Cloud 9 Field, Michigan. I started training at a gravel pit in April of 1979, with a half hour ground school and one demo flight off the training hill. I fell in love with the experience of flying hang gliders. The rest of my training was self-taught.

My first soaring flight was off Greenpoint in Frankfort, Michigan, a 375 foot dune. By fall of 1979 I had many hours dune time. I then traveled, to Lookout Mt. Tennessee for my mountain flight experience. In June of 1980 I spent a month in Owens Valley, California and learned to thermal and it was there that I entered my first XC competition. The only reason I entered the competition was because they took pilots up the mountain and picked you up at the end of your flight. I did the Owens Valley competition again in 1981 but did not compete again until 1995. Between 1981 and 1995 I flew mostly in Michigan, New York Finger Lake Mountains and Tennessee

From 1995 to now I have been mostly flying competition, which has greatly increased my flying skill, by flying with good pilots and pushing my comfort zone. I have found that competitions have three distinct benefits for a new pilot. The first is developing the skills to stay with other more experienced pilots and knowing that your glider is good enough to keep up with them. The second is learning to do things on your own. The third is to learn to keep up with the main gaggles of leading pilots in any competition.

I just love airtime and flying hang gliders and it is hard for me to race out of the sky, but I have a lot of fun. In my last two competitions I had 12 days of flying back to back and logged 46 hours airtime and 600 miles XC, I like it!

Memorable Flights of a SkyDog

Bob (SkyDog) Grant

I was first introduced to sport flying while an avid water ski enthusiast. I belonged to *The London Ski Serpents* water ski club. We had two flat kites, which were towed by a 120 ft. rope, which always stayed attached to the towboat. Normally the highest we would fly would be about 60 ft. off the water swerving back and forth behind the boat and doing all kinds of neat tricks like hanging from our knees and turning backwards. In the fall of 1971, Bill Moyes was doing a tour of the United States and Canada, putting on towing exhibitions at many of the fairgrounds along the way.

Well, Bill Moyes did a show at our fall fair, The Western Fair, right here in London, Ontario. That was the start of it all for me. A water ski friend of mine, Tom McClatchie, soon purchased one of Bill's gliders. I would watch him fly up and down Wildwood Lake, just 30 miles from our home. I knew that I just had to fly like Tom and Bill.

Tom had promised to let me try it soon, but being rather impatient and with a little (maybe more than just a little) encouragement from my friends I was going to try flying. While Tom was on a picnic with his girlfriend down the lake somewhere, we hooked that 13-foot-leading edge Moyes glider to the boat and away I did fly. I passed Tom minutes later. He must have had a fit thinking that I would kill myself, not having taken any lessons. As it turned out, I had a great first flight, releasing from the 500 ft towrope and landing perfectly on skis in front of the cottage. Well, I was hooked on the sport and was immediately off to purchase my first delta wing from the now famous Michael Robertson who lived near Toronto, Canada.

My mentors were Bill Moyes, Bill Bennett and Bob Wills along with hundreds of others. I looked up to many of the big names in hang gliding and longed to fly with those wonderful, exciting and innovative people. In 1975 and 1976 I lived out my dreams and along with my flying buddies, Chris Smith – (Cloudbase Harnesses) Sandy McDougal and Gary Kneves of London, we drove the 45 hours to the Escape Country World Open Hang Gliding Competitions near San Diego, California. I entered those competitions but did not place very well, but I sure did meet many of the top pilots of that era. I recall getting a ride up to the 1500 ft. launch at Escape Country with none other than Bob Wills (founder of Wills Wing Gliders) and I think that was probably one of the most memorable events to have happened to me at those competitions. Bob was a very soft-spoken, enthusiastic pilot and sharing stories with him was exquisite. They stay with me today.

My most memorable flights are many, some so beautiful and others so scary that I don't even want think about them. For some reason this one flight still flashes through my mind occasionally. It wasn't the greatest flight for length or distance but to me it left me with a somewhat indescribable feeling. As it turned out I was alone at what I call my home site, Hammondsport Takeoff, near Rochester, New York. I had driven there on a Friday but no one else showed up so I knocked on the landowner's door and asked if he would help me launch. Dick Paroulski, the landowner, was only too willing; so I was off. It was a gorgeous day with nice cummies popping up late in the afternoon. At Hammondsport, we often saw hawks and turkey buzzards, but on this incredible day I had a Red Tail pop out of the trees and slowly catch up to me at about 1500 ft. As I was slowly turning in the 400 fpm smooth lift, the Red Tail was coming up and gaining on me. I became fearful that the Red Tail might bump into me, as I am sure he did not see me. When he was about 20 feet below and in front of me I let out a giant scream that made the little devil flip over and dive away from me. Boy, that was close, and so spectacular to be so close to a beautiful bird, sharing the same air. I continued on to fly by myself and made a cross-country attempt, which took me 20 miles to Corning, New York. I landed on a riverbank right in town and received a ride from the first person that I encountered. Most people are so nice, especially when they are excited about seeing a hang glider and pilot land next to their home. I think what made this flight so memorable is just the fact that I was all alone and fending for myself among the clouds and ultimately making the correct choices to get me safely on the ground after a two hour flight. There is something about being alone up there when no other pilots are in the air and no one is on the ground waiting for you that made me feel good. I just don't know why.

Another mystical flight took place at Wallaby Ranch in Florida just last year on another really nice thermally day. I was climbing up to 4000 feet above the Ranch and found myself whiting out and thought... OK that's cool, but I had better get out of here. I headed toward the brighter side of the cloud. As I was leaving the cloud, I turned and looked back at the cloud and much to my surprise, there it was, a very large shadow of my glider pasted on the side of the cloud. It seemed that this well-defined shadow was about 300 feet wide and wow! What an awesome sight. All through my 29 years and seven hundred hours of airtime, this was the first time I had ever seen this happen. After landing and talking with other pilots and relaying my sighting, they told me that this occasionally happens and is a picture to behold, if only I had taken my camera on that flight.

I experienced several wonderful flights at the Canadian Nationals (around 1980) at Mount St. Pierre, Quebec. This is a very picturesque site with the giant St Laurence River out front and mountains inland for miles. One of many sweet flights was experienced there when the air was so smooth that we could float anywhere in a wonder-type wind. These are the times when I like to do my *wingees*, which are usually less than 90 degrees but feel like 150 to me. That sure is fun. If any pilot reading this interview gets a chance to visit and fly Mount St. Pierre, it would be well worth the effort, and an experience you will never forget.

My scariest flight, ever, was one summer's evening. I headed down to the river, downtown London, to do a little towing after work. After getting the boat in the water and ready to tow, I found out that an old friend, Nelson Stephens, would be driving the boat that evening instead of our regular driver. Nelson had towed me previously on my 13 ft. Moyes, but not on my new high performance Delta Wing glider. He didn't realize that much less speed was necessary to tow the new Delta Wing. After a pop-launch off the beach I found myself going up and up and up and screaming. My "slow down" signal went unheeded, so I tried to release, which might have caused a loop, or something worse. But at that point it seemed the lesser of two evils. When I tried to release, the mechanism failed. I was fastened to my glider—a screaming rocket! Locking out, I was heading towards the green grass next to the pollution plant. I was crying in my mind and thinking about my three kids just when all of a sudden, WHANG, Ken McBurrney released the 700-foot rope from the boat and I was doing a great up-and-over wingover at 50 feet above the water. Somehow I pulled off a perfect water landing. I had nightmares for a long time after, reliving those few moments. What makes us keep flying after such a close call? It must be the love of flight.

The flying is great, but it is also the getting together with other pilots before and after flying that makes this sport so great. Sharing stories from so many different pilots and hearing their excitement always fills *me* with excitement. Seeing a new pilot show his overpowering enthusiasm after a simple do-good flight is magic to me. I will always cherish the many friends that I have made throughout me hang gliding career.

You might ask who is the most memorable pilot I have flown with, but to pick one would not suffice, as there have been so many. The one person who comes to mind is Chris Price, from the old days with Bob & Chris Wills. During 1975 I was reading an article in Hang Gliding Magazine authored by Chris Price. It was about a flying trip in the mountains somewhere out west and the content of that article made me want to go there so much that it was overwhelming. Chris's writing made the trip so exciting and magical. Then I recall meeting Pete Brock (Ultralite Products) and his family at Escape Country where his nine year old, Hall Brock, was flying a small standard. I filmed the youngster as he landed flat-dab on the target from 500 feet up! Hall was a beautiful young pilot and I will always remember his happy face from my movies. I used to run into Larry Tudor, one of my favorite pilots, at many meets. It was always so nice to talk with him; and what a great pilot he continues to be. The list goes on and on; there are so many wonderful Hang Glider pilots to remember.

100 Miles of Exxtacy

Mark Poustinchian

Not long ago I bought an Exxtacy. The local pilots' expectations were high, and the pressure was on to do some big miles very soon. My longest flight of the year had been a 48-miler, which I made in February on my Laminar ST. After that we had the worst flying conditions in March, April and May that I can remember.

On the day of the 104-mile flight, after setting up the Exxtacy, I walked up to launch and waited for signs of thermals. I could not spot any birds or any indication that it was going to be a good day. Finally, I decided to give it a try and launched at about 1:30 PM. The air turned out to be a little punchy, but fortunately there was enough wind to help maintain, and I worked small thermals to get over the mountain. It took a while, but I finally spotted a bird climbing in front of the mountain and was able to get there very quickly to find 200-400 fpm lift.

I had my GPS mounted on my glider and a cell phone in my harness. I told Samantha that if it turned out to be a good day I would fly as far as I could. I really didn't think I would break my own state record of 95 miles, which I have held since March of 1995, especially considering the conditions and how difficult it was to hang on to the thermals.

After an hour I was 20 miles away, south of the Arkansas River, and had made one low save so far. The workable thermals were very broken, but good enough to maintain or slowly climb. I started to cross the river riding a thermal that was rising off the big, dark, dry fields just south of the river. My best altitude up to this point was around 4,700' AGL, and it was not easy to stay over 4 000'. I had to work bubbles and trash thermals often between 2,000' and 4,000' AGL while drifting with the wind. I tried to be patient to preserve the precious altitude that I had to work so hard to attain.

After crossing the Arkansas River and Interstate 40 I got very low again. Only a few hundred feet over a field, my harness already unzipped, I found another trash thermal. I gladly jumped on it and worked the trash air to 5,020' AGL. I was on my way once more. This would be my highest altitude of the day. I got below 4,000' very shortly after that, but by this time I knew that I might have a shot at the longest Arkansas flight of the year; 61 miles would do it, and it looked like a real possibility. I turned the GPS on to get a reading; the low-battery signal was flashing. I turned it off to save the battery for a reading on my landing position.

I was several hours into the flight when I noticed that the drift was taking me toward the Boston Mountains, a major barrier to long X-C flights. I had crossed these mountains only once before, a few years ago. That day I had been getting to 5,500' AGL over the flats with ease; clouds were plentiful and I had a 10-15 mph tailwind. I had stayed with a big cloud for a long time, avoiding looking down at the peaks. The fields and the valley on the other side were obscured by several peaks with a top elevation of 2,600' above the valley. The high peaks and rolling, tree-covered mountains continue for a good 10 miles without any place to land. I knew there was a nice valley on the other side that I could not see, even from above 5,000'. It was a very memorable flight that I will never forget. On that day I spotted another fresh cloud from a couple miles away; I was able to glide to and stay under it until I was finally able to see the valley on the other side. But on this flight, with the prevailing conditions and blue sky, there was no way I would even try to cross. Deep inside I am still a conservative pilot.

In order to avoid the Boston Mountains I headed west between the thermals and tried to go around them. I reported to Samantha that I was still up and on my way, and she gave me some *go for it* encouragement. I soon flew over another Arkansas hang gliding site with a 300' AGL northwest launch called "The Secret Site." A hang glider pilot, Charlie Gillespie owns it, and he flies it on northwest days. Surprisingly, the record from this 300' hill is 62 miles, which was set a few years ago by John Flatte. That's not bad for this part of the country.

At this point I was determined to stay up for as long as the sun and thermals would allow. I reflected on something Larry Tudor had told me: "It's not over until your feet are on the ground." What a great way to put it! I ignored the rolling hills and trees below, including a few decent landing areas. As I flew on, the fields were smaller and harder to come by. In the past I had always tried to land next to a major blacktop road to make retrieval easier. I determined not to worry about that; I had my cell phone and my GPS.

I can't remember how many thermals I worked; there were many and they were not very strong. As the hours, miles, and rolling peaks and valleys passed, the thermals got a little smoother. The Exxtacy offered unbelievable glide between them. It was getting close to 5:00 PM but I was still able to climb in much better thermals. Unfortunately, my peak altitude was diminishing with each climb, and the thermals started to fall apart below 4,000'. The ground was also rising below me and the altimeter was showing more than I really had.

Not long thereafter I got low over a big field I had picked out from a distance. There appeared to be a house next to it, but up close it turned out to be nothing more than a storage shack. There was no sign of anyone nearby. No roads either. How was I going to carry my heavy glider out of there? Would I have any usable signal on my cell phone? I was getting worried. All I could see around me were tree-covered hills. I needed some major altitude to get my butt out of there.

This was to be my lucky day; a small hawk appeared out of nowhere and saved me. My little friend turned and turned and was climbing toward me. We shared a 200-300 fpm thermal, drifting with it over the hills on the north side. I was able to see the next valley again, but stayed with zero sink as long as I could. My feathered friend turned west and disappeared on the horizon while I was still drifting with some small bubbles. "Thanks buddy, I'll never forget you," I whispered. What a great feeling; it doesn't get any better than this. It seemed like God was watching over me and saved me every time I needed help.

That was my last thermal, which topped out at about 3,500', and I was flying over roads and cars and nice fields again. I kept on drifting to the northwest and picked the last field at the end of the valley as my landing zone. As I got closer I saw cars on a blacktop road next to the field, and a lake nearby on the west side. The ground was rising, but very slowly. I ended the flight with a nice, easy landing at 6:07 PM.

The GPS was in search mode. With all the turns and zero sink I had worked for so long, I figured it might be close to 100 miles, but I feared that I had once again come very close without passing the magical barrier. Finally I got a fix and, oh my God, I couldn't believe it. 104 miles! I screamed with joy as tears filled my eyes.

The signal on the cell phone was good, and I called Samantha to let her know that I had made the first 100-mile flight in Arkansas. She was still going west on Interstate 40, hoping to make contact with me, but I had been flying northwest, further and further away from the Interstate. She was about 60 miles away, so I had plenty of time to pack up and get to know landowners Leslie and Elizabeth Krause. They were very helpful and provided directions for Samantha, and told me that I was welcome to drop in any time. I had landed in northeast Oklahoma, next to Highway 59, about 11 miles north of Highway 412 on the east side of Lake Eucha.

I was very satisfied with 104 miles on a marginal day on my new Exxtacy. Long flights are possible in Arkansas, and we have much better days. I told Samantha that she could have all the tandem flights she wanted for the rest of the summer. Without her help it would be very difficult to make these enjoyable and record-breaking flights.

I hope to get a chance to meet some of you in Arkansas. Every year we sponsor the "End Of Summer Mountain Nebo Fly-In" at the end of August.

The Rich Tapestry Of Flight

John Reynoldson

It's a wet and windy autumn Sunday afternoon. I am supposed to be a hundred miles from here, at a microlight convention. But it's a long way to go if there's to be no flying, and we've had thunderstorms raging at the walls for days. If there are hardy souls at Wangaratta this weekend, I can only assume that their wings remain furled, and by now they are contemplating leaving the hangar on the long trek back to town.

If anyone ever asks you to write about your "greatest, or most memorable flight", turn and walk way, or better yet, run. Failing that, try to ignore the consequences and reach for the nearest blunt or sharp object. That's what I wish I'd done, because I don't have a "greatest" flight. I racked my brain, (always a chancy proposition at best), and all I can offer are some vignettes of flights that come close to qualifying. I call it, *the rich tapestry of flight...*

Oddly enough I don't remember my first actual flight in a hang glider, though you'd think it would stick in one's mind. I remember the day, trudging up and running down a low rise at the beach, avoiding mutton-bird burrows and trying to get airborne, but I don't actually remember the airtime! But then, it was the 70's and that, I think, is excuse enough.

It's hard to forget my inadvertent first soaring flight, when I lifted the nose just a fraction too high while adjusting my harness on a windy ridge. I suddenly found myself high above it.

My one and only parachute deployment (touch wood) occurred when my new glider and I entered a thermal containing leaves and twigs, only to find ourselves upside down, with one of us broken. Has to be a keeper. I remember even more vividly the half hour up a gum tree when the wreckage reunited with the origin of the twigs and leaves.

A very recent treasured memory is my first hundred-mile flight, achieved at a cross-country clinic with significantly more ease than expected. Only 25 years after taking up the sport! My previous best had been 90 miles, achieved 13 years previously. My very pregnant ground crew was there for the retrieval (the consequences of which were to limit my XC operations for over a decade, but I love them deeply). This pickup was also notable for having to scare away a (very) poisonous snake from the pack-up area with my longest batten.

This memory wasn't one flight, but many. I spent two weeks at Byron Bay one summer, and the cliffs were on every single day. I had never thought until then that I would actually decide not to fly on a perfect day, but it eventually happened. Too many wingovers, and too much sun.

I tried to thermal a brush-clearing fire at Mt. Blackheath in very stable conditions, then left far too low. I crossed the tree line in the landing area, downwind, with no height to turn. Every single batten in my EF5 rigid wing took on a reverse camber. I have the photos to prove it.

That first high flight from Mount Buffalo, in still air, is a magical moment that comes only once for each pilot. You almost immediately have 3000 ft of altitude below you, and the world seems to stand still. It ranks alongside the first sight of your "glory" on the side of a cloud as you climb past cloudbase.

Cruising away from Boundary Peak toward Janies Ranch in the Owens Valley under a major wave rotor cloud, watching my wing tips dancing the Fandango in the choppy air. This after having gone hypoxic in the same flight by forgetting to turn on the oxygen, resulting in an insane sight-seeing trip to within 200ft of the very peak of White Mountain in the middle of a contest task during the 1980 XC Open competition.

Getting "stuck" on a small coastal cliff at Cheviot Beach (where Australian Prime Minister Holt drowned years ago) for about an hour when the wind dropped out, without enough height to make it around the points back to the legal soaring area 2 kilometres away. Frantically trying to decide whether to stick it out or land and explain what I was doing on a restricted Army base. I've never been so sick of 100m of cliff before or since, but the prospect of standing on unexploded ordinance on the beach had very little appeal. (The wind did pick up, and I did make it back.)

Pulling off a superb spot landing in the only cleared area in a very big forest. Then finding on final approach that the edges of the clearing are lined with beehives. Bees bouncing off one's helmet make a very interesting sound indeed.

Sheer terror when I modified my own homebuilt hang glider with a double surface, only to find that it had become divergent. To this day, I have no idea how it pulled out of the dive. I can only assume that Higher Powers have not yet exhausted the fun to be had by jerking my chain.

The serenity of cruising around for an hour and a half at 13,000 ft when I was supposed to be doing 10 tows that day to gain my towing endorsement. (And I did them too, but we were packing up in the dark!)

The first flight in my new Lynx B, finding out the hard way that the glider, which had been used in a static display by the manufacturer at a trade show, had had the deflexors wound out real tight so the sail would look clean on display - and they hadn't been returned to flight configuration. Can you spell supersonic? Can you spell ANGRY?

Landing up to my waist in a small farm pond. Don't ask, or I might yet find that blunt object!

Lucky 13

Francois Dussault

It was a special and memorable day because it was the 13ᵗʰ of September 2000, and my 13th season of hang gliding. Unfortunately this summer had not been very good for hang gliding, few thermally days because of cloud cover by noon, and few wonder wind evenings.

The morning of this memorable day was absolutely nice, and I went to my job with my heart at 60 mph. At 10:00 o'clock in the morning, I told my boss that I had to fly... I absolutely must go flying today! My boss understands my passion for the sport and she is always happy and supportive of me when I ask her to take leave time to go hang gliding. I suppose maybe its because she's happy for me.

Some of my hang gliding buddies joined me at Grand Morne around 1 o'clock. Grand Morne is our club site, only about 15 minutes from our home in Thetford Mines, Quebec. That means it's easy to go flying every day that the weather is good; we often go after work at the end of the afternoon. Everyone met at the landing area where our club Jeep is kept and we loaded t the gliders onto the jeep and kept on driving until we reached the launch. What a surprise! 12 to 15 mph west wind. It was perfect conditions for a perfect day.

The flying season was ending for us in Thetford Mines. We expected to launch and soar at1000 feet over the ramp at most, but not more. In September the chances of a sky-out day are not frequent, especially after a long and bad summer for hang gliding. After setting up the gliders, the wind increased from the NW, too strong for a safe launch. The wind is frequently strong at the Grand Morne. The clouds are nice and look great for thermal activity, but we can't launch.

At the end of the afternoon, around 4 o'clock, I prepared for a late afternoon post-thermal wonder-wind flight. After a good launch in the NW wind, my vario told me that thermals were still active. It was pretty amazing for thermals to be so strong especially because the air was almost smooth. I quickly climbed to 4000' feet, very close to cloudbase. I circled and tried to find some calm air under the cloud but the turbulence was so strong. I decided to go in front of the cloud and try to fulfill a very old dream of mine, to soar the cloud from the wind side and go over the cloud. I was very disappointed because the turbulence in front of the cloud was even stronger than under it. Finally, I made the decision to go XC, because I was still at 4000 feet and slowly leaving the mountain. I was totally amazed; behind the cloud, I began to climb again, even without turning 360-degree circles.

What the hell? I was climbing behind the cloud in smooth air. I continued to climb until I was even with cloudbase, and soon I was looking down on the cloud. What has happened here? It's a better flight than in my dreams of cloud soaring! The view was so nice and so beautiful. I was at 5000 feet, but I didn't understand what was happening. But it really didn't matter because this flight was so exiting and even after many years of flying experience, it's always possible to be surprised in this wonderful sport.

My altitude was still good, so I decided to keep on flying SE with the strong tail wind. I estimated about 20 miles of XC before I could land. It was not an easy glide, and I decided to tighten the VG on my Sensor. The air immediately became weird and I lost a lot of altitude. Very quickly I descended to 2500' feet and realized that a 20 miles XC flight would be impossible without another thermal. At 5:00 pm there was probably little chance of this happening, so I finally landed in strong NW wind, every bit as strong as at launch.

I was very exited about my flight even though I did not fully understand what had happened. In the LZ I did not tell my flying buddies what had happened in the air; I was still trying to figure it out in my own head. That night I told my brother, a sailplane pilot, about my amazing flight. He suggested I contact his friend, another sailplane pilot and meteorologist, to ask him about the unique condition. I learned that the wind was NW close to the ground and SE at altitude which permitted convergence at about 4000 to 5000 feet. That is the reason I climbed out behind the cloud instead of in front of it. That was also why my attempt at going XC was in the wrong direction when I was high; what I thought was a tail wind, was really the wind front! That's why the condition seemed so weird at 5,000 feet and did not change until I dropped down to 2500 feet, back into NW wind.

This was a special day for me, a lucky 13-day and a flight I will never forget. It is so nice to be able to participate in such a great sport with so many good flying buddies to share the experiences.

SOME JUST GET LUCKY!....

The *Go To Jail* Field

Lori Allen

When I decide to do something simple, like an unscheduled landing out, I don't mess around. It was a beautiful weekend at Lookout Mountain Flight Park (LMFP) in Rising Fawn, Georgia. It was northwest and soarable, and I couldn't wait to drive the 10 minutes up to launch and get set up. Living in the LZ of one of the world's premiere flight parks sure does have its advantages! I was living here and loving it!

Since I tend to be easily distracted at launch, running into friends and answering questions of the various wuffos who come up and gawk at the "hand gliders", it took me awhile to finally set up my Wills Wing Supersport and it was late in the afternoon before I finally launched. I had no problems getting up in the smooth ridge-soarable air. Immediately gaining 2,000 feet, making the trek to the "Point" (Point Park overlooking Chattanooga, Tennessee) was a given, so I turned north and was on my way. There were only a few pilots in the air, but I wasn't worried—I had made the 21-mile round trip several times.

I meandered down the ridge maintaining a steady 4,000 MSL, gazing down at the lakes, trees, and homes dotting the bluff. I made the crossing at Steadman's Gap and passed over the distinctive Covenant College, and breathtaking Sunset Rock. Reaching the Point was a piece of cake. As I circled above the monument of Point Park and gazed at the scenic Tennessee River bordering downtown Chattanooga, I looked at my watch and realized it was getting late. I turned back towards LMFP. Although there were few landable areas and a definite "no-land zone" below Covenant College, I wasn't concerned about making the return trip. Although I had no XC flights under my belt as of yet, I figured that if it was so easy to get to the Point, it should be no problem getting back.

Well, so much for resting on my laurels. Over Sunset Rock the lift suddenly shut down. I thought to myself, "Well this is probably a sink pocket. Just keep heading back and you'll hit more lift; this is just the right time for a really nice glass-off." Wrong again. I was sinking lower and lower; and as I got below ridge level, the trees kept getting closer and closer. I ventured further and further into the valley and there was nothing underneath me but more trees. (Crap!)

Off in the distance I saw some fields and knew that I had the first one made. But the thought of landing there caused me much concern: it was the dreaded "no-land zone" below Covenant College. Over the years a number of pilots have had the misfortune of being carted off to jail by the Dade County Sheriff's Department because of a rather hostile landowner. Unfortunately, I didn't have much choice. I circled above the field to determine the best landing direction. I thought I saw a road adjacent to the field for easy access.

As I turned on final I realized I had to deal with some pretty tall grass and be prepared to flare early. I flared and kept going down, down, down! I ended up on my butt staring up at grass that was as tall as me. (Wonderful!) I dragged the glider through the thick grass to some nearby hay bales, which gave me a place to throw my equipment while I proceeded to break down. I was breathing a sigh of relief because nobody appeared to give me a hard time. (Yes!) I was about eight miles from home as the glider flies, and I didn't have a radio or phone.

I'd never before carried my glider for more than 20 feet by myself. I struggled to get my harness, then my glider up to the road—which turned out to be a little used farm road. To get the glider over the barbed wire fence, I propped my harness on the barbed wire, then slid my glider over to keep from tearing the bag and sail of my glider. Luckily, the only damage to my harness was a small rip in the bag.

Which way do I go? Right or left? I chose right; I didn't get very far before I came upon a rather intimidating creek and decided I didn't want to deal with that. I retraced my steps and traveled the other direction. After climbing a hill, I eventually found a house (yes!) and knocked on the door. Nobody answered the door, but as I was about to leave, an elderly lady hailed me from the upstairs window.

I told her that I had landed in a nearby field. She indicated that they owned several of the fields in the area and that there were clear *no trespassing* signs everywhere. At that point a rather mean looking man (who thankfully didn't move around too well) ambled out the door, sat down on a nearby stump and just stared at me and he looked pretty doggone ticked off. I started groveling big time. I explained that I had to make an emergency landing although I was aware that there was to be no landings on any of his property. I further reasoned that landing in his field instead of the trees would help preserve his property; the rescue squad wouldn't have to tear up his field to get to me. He seemed to accept that, but he also informed me that he has had every pilot who ever landed there jailed for trespassing. As long as I left immediately, he said, he wouldn't press charges. I was thanking my lucky stars that I was female, which is probably what saved my hide.

My gratitude for my gender faded quickly as a big truck drove down from another house up the hill. An even bigger, meaner, positively evil-looking man (who was younger and more mobile) got out and started staring at me without saying a word. . This had to be the son. I thought to myself, "Oh God, what have I gotten myself into?" But the elderly lady telephoned my friends and arranged for my rescue and gave me directions (yes, I'd have to cross the creek) to get off their property.

I kept glancing behind me as I returned to my equipment in the field, praying that the "evil one" wasn't following me. He was way too scary for my comfort.

Luckily, I made it back without incident and began to move my equipment. There was no way to cross the creek without getting wet. I grabbed my harness, propped it on top of my head and crossed the creek with only a few mishaps. Getting my glider across wasn't as easy; I kept sinking up to my knees in the mud and managed to lose a shoe. I did manage to get it across and collapsed in the grass for a few minutes to catch my breath. I decided that retrieving the shoe wasn't worth the effort.

I continued down the road with my harness. About a half a mile into the hike and feeling pretty tired, I heard the familiar diesel sound of the dreaded big truck. The "evil one" followed me all the way to the gate where my good friends, Kenn and Doris Pollari, were to meet me. He didn't say a word—just followed me and stared. The movie, "Deliverance" came to my mind, and I simply prayed and walked and ignored how much my left foot was hurting. And I still had to go back and get my glider! Thankfully, I had hidden it after crossing the creek.

Kenn and Doris weren't there! I climbed over the gate. The "evil one" turned around, not an easy stunt on that road, and headed back in the other direction. I breathed a sigh of relief—but in the back of my mind I was wondering how the hell he got that truck across the creek! There must have been yet another road.

It was getting darker and darker, and long past sunset when I saw the familiar headlights of the Pollaris' Subaru Outback and waved them down. I explained my situation to Kenn and he offered to hike back with me to retrieve my glider. Doris, bless her heart, happened to have an old pair of shoes and sacrificed the left shoe that she insisted she was going to throw away—it was a little loose, but better than nothing. My glider and I were soon reunited, without any further confrontation with the "evil one."

We loaded everything up to head home. I was pretty doggone muddy and I didn't smell too good either. Peee--yew! Yes, you guessed it—I smelled like feces (hey, I don't want to be totally predictable here!). However, they were good sports, and urged me to climb on in. For some crazy reason, they thought that being the first to hear about my misadventure was worth it. Between the gagging from the smell and the laughter from the story, it was a memorable ride home, although not nearly as memorable as the experience; one I don't care to repeat, thank you very much!

My first coherent thought after my little adventure was, "Doggone! If I can survive an experience like that, going cross country should be a piece of cake!" It wasn't long after my adventure in "no-lands" land that I got my ham license and a 2-meter radio. My first true blue XC experience was a 22-miler, open distance, south from Henson's Gap, Tennessee.

But that's another story.

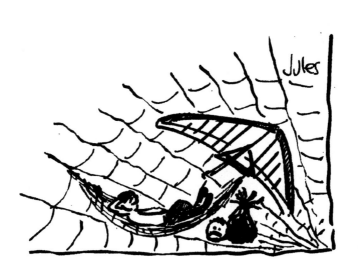

Simple Steps to Getting Up at Mystic

Gilbert (Chainsaw) Griffith

Mystic is the local hang and paragliding site owned by the North East Victorian Hang Gliding Club, Australia. The height is 2615'ASL or about 1800' above the valley floor

Dumb idea eh? Who needs advice on how to get up at a novice rated site? Anyone thinking that hang glider pilots need instruction at such an easy site as Mystic must be stupid. But just this morning paragliding pilot extraordinaire Brian Webb, current president of the Hang Gliding Federation of Australia, suggested this article after watching early afternoon antics and scratchings while recuperating from a morning's flying.

As a weekend pilot I have to take every opportunity I can. So first of all this means putting my radio on charge, getting a good night's sleep, not too much to drink, and getting up in the morning.

If it looks flyable, I listen to the weather box and note the trend. I look for slowly increasing wind speeds without too much gust factor (50-75% is my personal limit).

At about 10am I'm hanging out waiting to finish work if it's a Saturday, the car is fuelled and checked, and I'm itching to go.

The first part of getting it up on Mystic is being there, so by 12.30pm or maybe a little earlier on Sundays, I'm on my way with a vegemite sandwich for lunch. No sitting around discussing the weather or trying to sober up, just get there and set up.

Setting up gives time to notice the cycles, watch the paragliders and notice where they find the lift and how high they're getting.

At Mystic, 12:30 to 1:30 seems to be the best time of day to launch. I wait for the start of a cycle by watching the pine trees 100 metres down the hill; if they are not moving I don't go. Same goes for the trees on the spine to the left of launch (the resident thermal is named Marcus), if they're moving you can be pretty sure of lift over that spine so you do a left turn immediately after take off. I don't zip up until established in good lift, which aids concentration in the early part of the flight. The only time I'll take off in still air is if I can see someone hooking into good lift within my gliding range. If you can see the lift, go for it. But you want the start of a cycle, not the end, so don't wait too long. If you fail to hook up with Marcus there is another resident thermal on the right hand ridge in front of launch called Emily. Sometimes there is good lift in the bowl and you'll find it as you cross. More often there is sink. Emily often cycles at around 10-20 minutes so in a dead part of the cycle you may bomb out, or have to work zero sink very carefully while waiting for the next bubble.

The first 500' gain is the most difficult at Mystic. Thermals tend to be narrow and sometimes just little bubbles so you have to work them gently if they're light, and very aggressively if they're strong. Once above launch they can change direction, particularly if there's a southerly wind, so you need to explore a bit while climbing to follow the core as it moves around. Keep an eye on all the other pilots, so you have a map in your head of where they all are (safety), and so you can see when someone finds a better core. The best core of the day only happens once or twice each day. This is when thermals from the three valleys combine and form a strong thermal that can take you to 8000' ASL in minutes. Even breaking through any inversion is possible if you catch this one.

For the crossing to Clear Spot, most hang gliders need 4500' ASL or more. If there's a lot of sink, I push on and always find lift about ¾ of the way across. Trust me. There is an option of heading to the right and picking up lift on the ridge lower down, with the last resort of bombing out in Bakers Gully. You have to know when to bail out early, as sometimes the sink in Bakers Gully valley is strong enough to put paragliders down in the trees before they get to the paddocks. I've been caught very low in here a few times and only got out unscathed thanks to my Atos and a small bubble of lift.

Back at Mystic, if the thermal half way down the ridge to the right of launch (Emily) is not working it often pays to glide along the left-hand ridge where thermals are often triggered and may be off to either side of the ridge line. The far end doesn't often work so you can cross towards the LZ early in the hope of picking up a thermal from the base of the Mystic bowl. On my first ever paraglider flight I found lift at 100' above the LZ which took me back to launch height.

Never give up.

You can visit the North East Victorian Hang Gliding Club web page at http://www.home.aone.net.au/gilbert/nevhc.htm

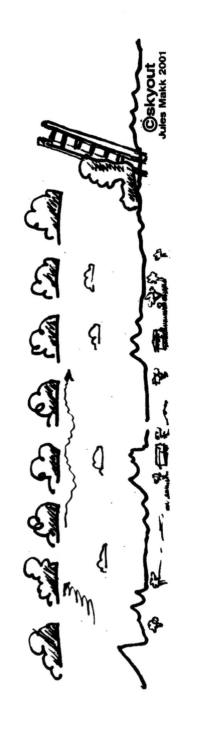

The
Sky Dog
Howls

Follow Me, Said Her Tail Feathers

Michael Robertson

During my 33 years of hang gliding I have been asked countless times by students and others, "What was your most memorable flight?" My usual one line answer is, "The last one." But as I ponder the question for the purpose of this book allow me to fondly remember a few flights that really stand out.

There was the seven-hour. XC into the interior of the Gaspe Penninsula from Mount St Pierre in '82 on a Moyes Mega. It took only a couple of hours to meander back into no-man's-land and the rest of the time to get back out! Some ravens helped me in a big way. I'll choose a couple of other flights in which birds played a role to write about here.

There have also been many tandems that were life-altering experiences for my passengers. I have to mention one in the latter category because the ability to share flight with non-pilots is a special gift for which I thank the sport.

A woman with advanced Cerebral Palsy came to our hydrostatic winch tow park with a friend. She was in a wheelchair and hooked up to an oxygen tank. After considerable preparation, we got her and her O^2 into the Falcon 225 and took off. She was very silent and I wondered if everything was OK. Then she turned to me and her beaming smile framed by small hoses transformed my doubts. We caught a thermal and played in the sky for only15 minutes or so and landed smoothly. A few months later a *Mobility Magazine* arrived with an article written by this woman. She sweetly described how the experience had transported her to another dimension, free of pain and illness, how she had felt like a dream-bird and was so appreciative of our efforts to take her up and away. In the post-script the editor explained that the author had passed away peacefully a few weeks after writing the article!

It was 1978 or thereabouts. I was teaching an instructors' course in Vancouver BC. We headed for the home of the Bigfoot, to Aggassi, for our free flying (a mandatory part of any IP, eh). As we drove past restaurants offering Sasquatch burgers the mountain loomed. West facing, all the air from the Pacific funneled by the Fraser Valley onto its waiting slopes.

We drove only half way up and marveled at the beauty. The confluence of 2 major rivers formed a large delta out front, which augmented the vista. It would be hard to imagine a more perfect location. I set up my beloved Condor, from the original UP, a glider we would now sit on the side of the road as a sign to rot. This was the model that Ken DeRusey, he of the dry wit and wily wisdom, used as a teaching glider into the 90's on his *world's best training hill*, the Mesa, in Santa Barbara.

I launched into a seemingly light breeze and made a pass down the ridge mesmerized by the splendor of the valleys and their rivers' run. As I turned back toward launch it had disappeared! I looked around thinking, "Where is it? Shoot, maybe I'm sinking out! I wonder if I'll even make the LZ?" Then I finally spotted the other gliders about to take off and realized that in one pass I was already 500' above them and climbing in glass smooth ridge lift! I had no vario.

I waited for the rest of the flock to join me about 1000' above the top. Occasionally gentle marshmallow thermals added to the ease of staying up and the mountaintop gradually ceased to be prominent. The breath-taking panorama provided a 360-degree plethora of peaks. Now the object of this exercise, for me, was to watch the thermalling skills of the dozen aspiring instructors below and observe their air-sharing etiquette. My eyes were glued to the scene below. A casual glance to the side suddenly stopped my gaze cold. There, parked a few feet off my wing tip, was a big bald eagle. She was looking at me and I got the distinct impression there was a smile in her eyes and on her beak!

Once we made eye contact she headed out toward the middle of the valley. "Follow Me," said her tail feathers. I did. My penetration was anything but eagle-like, but she courteously waited for her clumsy distant cousin. We arrived at the confluence of the two rivers over the delta with my extra altitude traded away. Just as I was contemplating whether to stay out here with *Her Eagleness*, bail back to the ridge, or head for the LZ, she pierced the air with a gleeful screech and we began to rocket up in her house-mother thermal. I recall wondering how high heaven might be as we circled together, specking out 'til the horizon was a curve and what had been my world became a postage stamp. It was as if I was looking the wrong way through a powerful telescope. I didn't have an altimeter but I probably should have had oxygen.

As we topped out over the mountain she took another look at me and headed over the back. To my everlasting regret, responsibility got the best of me and I decided to hang with my class of dots below and let her go.

Many years later a fine Canadian wildlife painter, Frank de Matteis, traded me an original oil painting depicting the flight for his beginner course. The background in the painting is flat but the Bald Eagle is gorgeous. Hanging on my office, wall it serves as a constant reminder of one of my life's ultimate flights.

Venezuela's La Victoria site provided another memorable flight. My longest XC of only about 100km featured an amazing bird-save. I had launched from the radio tower that provides the road for the site on my WW 167 Sport and as usual climbed to 14,000 feet. My flying buddy of the day bailed at the 35 km mark more because a cute South American lady had landed there than because the lift was gone.

I was feeling literally on top of the world, thinking my altitude would last forever and that it could be replenished easily and at will. I blundered into a box canyon and realized way too late there was no way out the other end. Suddenly I was in trouble. There were no roads cutting into the dense jungle beneath me and the sides of the ever over-shadowing ridges were steep and impassable. My mind scrambled thru the options: head back the way I came, doomed to land in the trees but shortening the walk out; try a fly-on-the-wall landing on a gentler slope and hope another pilot spotted me; head further into the abyss and pray for a miracle.

Then I saw two turkey vultures circling over a wisp of smoke way in the corner of the dead end valley. It was all or nothing, my only hope. I arrived in the fire-fuelled monkey-fart at about 500 feet AGL and started circling with my saviors. The first 200 feet took 10 turns. The next took only two. And then we were out of there! I have several photos with both vultures in them. One I took at 13,000 with the altimeter partly in frame and the Venezuelan countryside stretching lazily away. Another showed a view of the mountains in the background and a third showing a large lake like the one near which I found a perfect LZ. Perfect because it had a large shade tree, dust blowing to show wind direction and major roads on two sides to get a ride back to the hotel.

But the saga wasn't finished yet. My good luck stretched to provide a flat bed truck whose driver happily agreed to take me back (2 hours out of his way) to La Victoria. Then he proceeded to stop at virtually every bar along the way to regale the patrons with stories of his "Icaro" and solicit quenching of my formidable thirst. Yes Virginia it doesn't get much better than this. I think I remember rolling into the hotel at 2AM with a smile as big as the Venezuelan sky and a driver as drunk as a proverbial skunk.

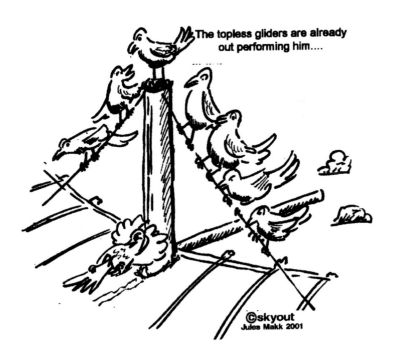

Dan the Man

Scott Jewell

As the sun wearily made its way above the early morning horizon, our hero was there to greet it. There are few pilots as committed as Dan Walter. With the exception of one well-baked individual, there certainly isn't an earlier riser. Dan is always prepared for that elusive East Coast morning lift-off. It was Dan's diligence to fly higher and go further that stimulates me to tell his tale. For reasons that will soon become apparent, you'll understand why Dan is unable to spin this yarn himself.

The wind was blowing into Dan and Robin's hill at a brisk 10-20 mph at about 9:30AM. The date was May 6. Dan had been set up for hours, waiting and watching as the day began to build. The weatherman was calling for increasing wind velocity and also for a spring snowstorm to move in later in the day. The forecast alone was enough to deter all other pilots from even playing Paul Voight's "Whack Tape", let alone going out to fly. Dan, on the other hand, bundled up and headed out to his favorite site.

While the rest of us were rising from our beds, excavating the sand from our eyes, removing the cotton from our mouths and swearing we'd never drink beer again, Dan took four strides towards the precipice of his own hill and transformed into a graceful hybrid of bird and man. Even with the high winds, lift was sparse. Dan worked the ridge like an Amish man honing his favorite plane. At a mere 500 feet, Dan hopped over the back to the airport with intentions of landing. He was surprised to find a small bubble of lift. That was the last time Dan thought about landing for the next four hours.

Anyone who has gone cross-country from Dan and Robin's hill knows that the main stumbling block is having enough altitude to clear the forest beyond Towanda. When Dan arrived at Towanda, he had 5,000 feet. Crossing the vast green sea below was not an issue, or so he thought. Halfway over the forest, Dan encountered moderate but consistent sink. Knowing he was committed at this point, he knew that if he didn't think quickly, he was headed for the trees.

At a time when most of us would have been looking for a friendly willow tree, Dan's level head came up with a clever solution to his predicament. Prior to launching, he'd dressed in multiple layers of heavy clothing. At 3,200 feet,

Dan began to skillfully peel off a layer of his Arctic attire and drop it to the ground. The moment that article of clothing left his finger tips, his rate of descent slowed from 500fpm to 400fpm. With 10 miles of future charcoal between himself and the next workable ridge or LZ, Dan concluded; "If a little is good, more is better."

By the time Dan had reached Tunckanock, he'd gotten back up to 4,000 feet and had hooked a whopper. Although he was dressed in nothing more than his CG harness, bar mitts, and a smile, he stayed warm. Dan must have genes in his ancestry that run directly back to Australopithecus, because the man has hair the likes of which even Rasputin has not seen. After shedding his skin, Dan thought of one more way to lighten his wing loading, but he saved that until he flew over Scranton. That evening the National Weather Service reported a strange acid rain with a yellow color that fell upon an isolated area near the Scranton Airport.

After reaching the town of Wilksbarre, Dan was finally stopped, not by sink or exposure, but by the Pocono Mountains. With 3,000 feet of altitude, Dan made the decision to land at the Wyoming Mall. Dan's approach was flawless, but when he went to unzip his harness, the zipper momentarily caught in his manhood. The instant sensation of pain caused him to deviate slightly from his course and dragged his lower body through a rather large burdocks bush. Somehow, Dan managed to pull off a no-step landing despite the circumstances.

Dan managed to walk his glider to the edge of the parking lot, unhook and begin the tedious job of removing the one hundred or so Velcro balls that were now affixed to his lower torso. He was so wrapped up in his preening that he failed to notice a young lady who had come over to see if he was all right. Judging from her reaction as Dan stepped out from behind his glider, she must not have ever seen a hang glider before. The woman's screams of exuberance were heard all the way to the mall security office, where they sent out a small congregation to welcome him. The people of Wilksbarre were so friendly, that they gave Dan his own personal room for him to wait in until his ride arrived. The room was furnished with his own personal bed, toilet, and a soap-on-a-rope in case he wished to use the shower. Why, they were even kind enough to shave off the remaining burdocks and place a small Band-Aid on his zipper wound.

Once again, Dan has shown us the difference between a good pilot, and a great pilot. My hat's off to you Dan, (but that's as far as I'll go).

The Touch

Mark Grubbs

Hang-gliding is full of perspectives and experiences that groundhogs would never dream of. For me, some of the most rewarding ones have occurred while sharing the air with birds of prey. Throughout my flying career I've had the usual experiences with the big birds, and the thing that I find most fascinating about them is that hawks or eagles seem to regard me as one of them. They seem to recognize that I'm just as motivated to stay in a thermal and climb as they are, and are willing to share the lift. It's like going on a wild animal safari; jumping out of the jeep and hunting prey with the lions. I'm in their arena, not just looking at them from the other side of a fence at the zoo.

I've seen red-tails look right at my face from just beyond my outside tip as we circle together in a thermal, and they seem to regard me, not the wing, as the "pilot-in-command". Maybe they realize that a few of those two-legged, wingless things on the ground have learned to imitate them.

During a late afternoon soaring flight at Mission Ridge, I watched a group of young red-tails in a launching and landing clinic. They lined up single file on the edge of a soarable knoll. One by one, they would stand still, stretch their wings out to full span, and take three or four steps down the hill on their talons and launch, just like hang gliders. They would make several soaring passes in the light ridge lift, then execute a downwind, base and final approach and flare just at the rear of the line, presumably to do the whole thing over again. The hawks were imitating hang gliders!

A few years ago, in the late fall, I was soaring at Ft. Funston on a smooth, buoyant, straight westerly day. Just over the golf course I noticed one of the locals, a red-tailed hawk, parked over the trees at my altitude, probably looking for lunch. I believe biologists refer to this maneuver as *kiting*. I approached the hawk from the north and as I got closer I noted that she was looking sideways at me, but showed no intention of moving. I guessed that she had been around enough hang gliders in her career that she wasn't bothered with my presence. I got close enough so that as I did a gentle 180 away from her, my outside tip came to within a few feet of her. My intent was to convince the hawk to forget about lunch for a few minutes and to come and play with me. I looked back after rolling out of the turn and, as I had hoped, there was my red-tailed buddy, following me. I cruised north to the end of the bowl in front of the golf course and began a slow roll back to the south. Keeping formation, the hawk began to turn just as I did, so that when we'd both rolled out, I was following her. As we came upon the south end of the bowl, she began to roll back to the north, which I mimicked, so that she was again following me.

We repeated this routine several times, creating, as far as I knew, the world's first impromptu avian/ human aerial ballet. I was amazed at the connection I had made with this untamed animal. She had chosen to acknowledge my existence instead of doing the usual evasive maneuvers that hawks often do when a hang glider comes along. She was regarding me as just another big bird.

After several minutes of this, my new flying buddy remembered that she was hungry, broke our formation, and headed back to her original kiting spot. Since I wasn't ready to stop playing yet, I climbed just a bit higher, turned downwind, rolled out and lined up on her six-o-clock and passed about three feet over her head. During this close pass, she never altered her position, and her head movements alternated between scanning the ground just below her, and attempting to look up and behind as I approached from her six-o-clock high. I noted that it was difficult for her to twist her neck enough to see above or behind her.

I know that biologists try not to anthropomorphize animal behavior; that is to say; to not interpret an animal's behavior or motivation as anything resembling our own. However, I'm sure that my red-tailed friend must have found my close passes to be a good compromise of her need to search for lunch and a desire to clown around with me. I made several of these passes, with my basetube passing as close as three feet over her back, and she never flinched.

The temptation was too much. I knew that my friend would soon spot a tasty, warm, writhing mammal in the trees and dive for lunch, or another hang glider would come along and break up our party. I had an opportunity to do what non-pilots can't even dream about.

I had to do it.

On my final pass, I started my run just a little bit lower. The wind was straight west at about 20 mph. Our sink rates were almost exactly the same in the buoyant ridge-lift. I pulled in just a bit, increasing my closure rate to a still dream-like two mph.

Time stretched and warmed. It began to pass at a dreamlike pace, the way it does when I'm in smooth, soarable and silent air.

The hawk's attentions were no longer half-focused on the ground. She tried to look up and over her back, at me. Wings and feathers twisting in smooth corrections of airspeed, to match mine. My closure rate was almost imperceptible. Her wings were now directly under me, one foot below my basetube.

I reached down with my bare right hand and lightly touched her on the back.

A sudden realization must have come over the hawk, like when a puppy and a kitten play with each other, and then their instincts tell them that it's not the way they're supposed to behave.

As I passed in front of her, she rolled to the right, almost ninety degrees, stalled, and perfunctorily extended her talons. It wasn't a panicked or frightened gesture, but more like the hawk body-language equivalent of, "It's been fun, but if my mate catches me fooling around with you, you're in big trouble. So, leave now, or my instincts will force me to tear through your Oakley Factory Pilot Eyeshades and scratch your eyes out!"

So I left.

I headed north, back to the world of humans, and thought about what I'd done. For sure, it was a beautiful thing; and maybe I should have kept my hands to myself. But maybe I was doing just what the writer of "High Flight" had suggested, "Slip the surly bonds of earth, reach out a hand, and touch the face (back?) of God."

In Search of the Magic Moment

Jules Makk

Since taking up hang gliding in 1983, there have been a few really exceptional days in my experience, the magical moments that glow incandescently in my memory as pure joy.

One was a spectacular flight in an orange-pink emblazoned sunset on the coast that saw a simultaneous moonrise from the other side. To soar in the steady air currents by moonlight and to see the lights of houses and street lights blinking on in the distance marking the edge of the land and sea.

Then there was a winter convergence flight over a mountain in smooth, gentle lift, to play among the wisps of cloud vapor, climbing up the sunny side and diving through translucent veils of puffy white to burst out the other side. No other encounter has given me a truer perspective of my flight and motion in three dimensions through the air.

There was the 40 km. glide over the flatlands in warm buoyant air from 9,000ft, and the last thermal, to watch the lengthening shadows on the ground and cross the countryside in undisturbed peace and serenity.

They don't happen overnight, but they do happen. After having my share of accidents, bumps and cuts and scares, I have become conservative. I pick fewer days to fly, with a broader margin for error, still looking for that exceptional day.

A few years ago I was flying at Myponga ridge, south of Adelaide, a popular flying spot in the winter north-westerlies. A bank of sea surface level fog approached the ridge in the 15-17 knot breeze and crawled like a lazy cottonwool caterpillar up the face and dragged itself over the launch. It drifted up the shallow slope to the low hills at the back, and then dissipated like a steamy ghost. It was amazing to me how slowly it moved. My perception of the air movement and my speed through the air as I imagined it, seemed to be far more than was apparent by the tardy progress of this low slow cloud. Normally we can't see the air we soar through. The overall sensation was of being suspended in time. I quite easily maintained 500ft over launch and I had a camera handy.

Of course, the magic moments probably happen more often than we have time or opportunities to fly, but they do happen. With over a thousand hours of flying and many thousands of road kilometres behind me, I watch the sky expectantly, projecting my thoughts and fantasies towards the question, what's it going to be like, up there today?

Soaring From *The Foothills*

Karen Holbrook

Wednesday March 28, 2001

Where were you today? You guys missed it, a great soaring day at the Flight Park.

Brad and I were at the flight park alone. We debated the flight conditions briefly, but it was a go! Brad and I discussed flying Moore Mountain, but I talked him out of that for reasons I will not divulge. Mike Wooten called to check out flying conditions. The report was good; Wooten was on his way.

While waiting for him to arrive at the airfield, Brad and I set up our gliders. Henry Muller arrived to do some modifications to his trike, and we spoke to him briefly. When Wooten arrived he began setting up his Millennium.

I was ready for flight; Brad towed me up. Thermals were happening! I released at 2200' AGL in a great thermal.

I drifted with the thermal until I was 5,043' AGL. There were a couple of times that I thought I had lost the thermal. As I was gaining altitude, I thought that if I got to 4000'AGL I was good. But when I hit 4000 the vario was pegged! I thought if I reached 4200'AGL, I was out of here! Winds SW and good! I reached 4200' AGL and was still climbing. Yup, I was gone! 5043' AGL, Moore Mountain was far away and in a haze. If anyone on the ground could have heard me, they would have committed me to an insane asylum. "YeHaw!"

As I drifted with the thermal, the flight park began to cover with a haze, and Moore Mountain began to clear.

I was committed to something by then. As I looked over the beautiful countryside, I was picking fields for possible landing sites, should I need one, and I was making sure there were no horny bulls in the pastures.

As I got close to the Brushy Mountain Range, I was down to 2300' AGL. I saw some folks at the Apple House on Highway 16 watching me, and some of the traffic on the highway slowing down to see what fool was up in the air on a human-size kite. I Love it! Then I found a mountain, Ten Acre Rock, setting all by itself and I figured I could catch a thermal from it. My guess was right; I gained altitude to 3993' AGL. Sure do love my Saturn, and it's VG.

Since I was from the 'far side' of North Wilkesboro, I considered flying further. I again started to locate possible landing fields. Should I go across the mountain range? I had gained altitude to above 4000' AGL; the Green-eyed Monster almost had me. I spotted several possible LZs, but I changed my mind and turned back toward Moore Mountain. Better safe than sorry. Occasionally, I thought of several hang glider pilot friends of mine. Sure wish they were here to...

Nope, this is my flight!

As I crossed Moore Mountain I noticed a vehicle parked on top. What were they doing? Then I spotted a white truck on the dirt road. Was it Wooten's truck? Had Brad, Mike, and Smitty figured out where I was?

No, it was Chris and Tammy. I noticed the PG equipment in the bed of the truck. Oh, well, guess no one cares; I sure didn't.

I followed a couple of Red Tail Hawks, in toward the ridge. Several Black Vultures flew with me. I ridge soared for forty-five minutes, gained and maintained altitude of 2200' AGL.

I was getting a little tired, and it was getting late. I figured I would have to search for a phone to use, since my cell phone has no signal on or around Moore Mountain. Little did I know. The guys must have been a little concerned as to my whereabouts. I found out that Smitty, bless his heart, is a worrywart. After two hours, he continuously reminded Brad and Mike that they should look for me. And was I OK? Hell yes! I was fine as frog hair.

As I made my landing in the LZ, I heard an aircraft motor; it was Brad in his Dragonfly. He did a fly by over the LZ, and I knew that meant someone would be by shortly to pick me up. As I sat on the BUZZARD bench, I was re-living the flight. Again, what if someone heard me? Oh yeah, an insane asylum for sure. By the way, nice bench. I realized only then that I had a blister on my finger from the VG!

A little while later, I saw Brad's truck approaching the LZ, and Smitty riding shotgun. As we were loading up the equipment, Chris was making a tandem PG flight into the LZ. Of course we couldn't leave without hello and conversation. I found out that a search party had been underway; Brad in his Dragonfly, Mike on his Foxbat trike, and Mark Schindler in his Avid Flyer to all surrounding areas.

Thanks guys. I do love you all. Thank you for all your guidance, encouragement, suggestions, and assistance. Without you, I'd still be on the ground. To all the hang glider pilots, I enjoyed the flight tremendously, and sort of hate that you didn't get the flight of the day. Not!

Look out guys, this girl is on her way. And there is no turning back now. Guess I'll have to carry money with me for XC pick-ups.

I'm still high!

Homecoming Game

Ralph Hyde

Editors' note: The following was excerpted from 'Twenty Years Ago... A Hang Gliding Journal About the Early Days of Sonoma Wings, Volume 32 Published on the Internet at: http://www.crosswinds.net/~skyfun

Saturday, October 22, 1983 - 7:53 AM

Up getting ready to head for Elk Mountain for our fall cross-country weekend. Looks like a nice sunny day for it. Slept fairly well last night after going to bed around ten. Awoke early this morning.

Sunday, October 23, 1983 - 4:25 PM

Got home from a good weekend at Elk. To my surprise and delight, I was the winner of our Sonoma Wings cross-country contest, flying all the way to the High School at Upper Lake. But first, let me review.

Got off Saturday morning by myself at 8:40 AM, cruised on up to Elk. Saw Stretch and Anne getting gas near Upper Lake, stopped and said hi. Found Roy in Upper Lake with the hot tub, waiting for Stretch and Anne. We went to the restaurant for coffee, and Rich Sauer joined us there.

Then, on to the campground at Elk. Ivan, Jon, and Hank soon arrived. Bones, Sharol, and Don Piercy had already gone up the mountain, as well as Gordon, Susan Grey and others, whom we saw on top. Susan had her new Duck. We greeted people and got set up.

Sharol launched first about 12:45 on her Comet, but it was a bit too early, and she was gradually flushed down the mountain. It was evidently a fairly marginal day, so we didn't have high hopes for going far.

Stretch lined up next, and I lined up behind him, as I expected the launch would get crowded quickly when anyone was able to stay up.

Stretch launched at about 1 PM, and was able to get up in a thermal beyond the point.

I launched next on my Comet and flew down to the point where I scratched for awhile, getting some light thermals but not getting up much.

Roy and Anne launched next. Roy got up, but not Anne, who eventually got flushed out, but worked low in the canyon for a long time.

I eventually got a good enough thermal near the point to get up and back behind the ridge, and soon was up to 5100' or so with Stretch and Roy, and soon others. Roy, then Stretch, headed out towards Pitney Ridge.

I worked the lift longer, with Bones, Gordon, Tom Denny and others, and finally left with 6400', heading for Pitney, holding my altitude pretty well.

I soon saw that Roy and Stretch had landed in the creek bed west of Pitney, and I talked by radio with Stretch. Another glider was ahead of me, and Tom Denny made it past Pitney, but down to the creek bed beyond.

I made it through sink to the peak of Pitney where I expected and found good lift, so stayed there quite awhile, thermalling up to 5100' or so before heading on diagonally to the south towards Upper Lake, looking for fields along the road that I could land in if necessary. The valley is planted mostly in walnut and pear orchards, so decent landing areas are few and far between, especially next to the road. The creek bed is a possibility in some places.

Kept going, over a tended fire in a field at one point, where I got some light lift and circled a bit before continuing on past more landable fields. Finally I saw the High School in the distance, which I thought I might be able to make, so headed that way.

As I got closer, I saw that there were a lot of people in the stands, and that there were teams at either end of the football field.

Just as I came over the north end of the field with about two or three hundred feet of altitude, the announcer started to welcome the people to the game over loudspeakers. I shouted down, "Helloo," then waved, and many people waved up to me as I flew the length of the field. I felt pretty good, like a barnstormer, the pre-game entertainment.

I decided to land on the softball field, which was adjacent to and slightly east of the south end of the football field, with home plate and a backstop at the northeast corner. There were sprinklers active in the right field area just south of the football field.

In fact, I didn't have any other options, as there were neighborhoods to the west and south and orchards to the north and east of the High School. I was committed, whether I liked it or not. It was fairly tight, but I thought I could squeeze in.

I circled over the backstop and adjacent orchard before approaching that field. But I found I was too high to get into the field from there, as I wouldn't be able to get low enough over that high backstop to go on final.

So I had to make another turn back toward the football field, then a 180 over the sprinklers in right field, and back towards the pitcher's mound, turning right towards the left field corner, skimming the ground, then flaring hard about 20 feet short of the fence. My feet came down under me, then slipped on the wet grass, and I sat down under the flared glider for a three-point landing, feeling very good that I'd made it down safely, especially in front of all those people.

Everyone cheered when I landed, and soon a bunch of kids came over, and a few high school girls brought me some cold Seven-Up.

I felt like a celebrity. It turned out that this was the Homecoming Game. I was the accidental pre-game show, coming over at 2 o'clock, just as the game was about to start, and I basked in my glory for a while. I was reminded of Rich Pfeiffer and his Rose Bowl fly-in. He got in big trouble for that one; no one here seemed to mind.

I tried to call my friends on my CB radio, but couldn't reach anyone. I'd seen another glider circling behind me, but he didn't make it as far. It was Jim Leech, a Bay Area pilot.

Folded up my Comet with the help of a kid named James, and eventually carried it out of the back parking lot and over to the next corner to try and get a ride.

It turned out that Anne and Stretch came looking for me, but went past the High School without seeing me. I did get a guy in a pickup truck to give me a ride a few blocks to Main Street, and I waited there.

Talked to some people for a while, and the druggist, Ted, said he'd give me a ride after he closed up. After an hour wait or so, he and his wife Diane gave me a ride back to the campground. I thanked them and invited them to stay and party with us, but they had something else to do.

Anyway, I was given many congratulations, felt very good, ate it up.

Eventually I set up my tent, had salad for dinner, and got in the hot tub with Stretch, Anne, and Roy, and eventually Hank, Ernie, Jon, and Gordon. Spent a pleasant evening. Got to tell my story a few times.

Later it clouded over and began to rain lightly, so I put up my rain flap. Eventually went to bed, and it rained on and off throughout the night.

I slept occasionally, I think, got up to a foggy, damp morning around 8:30, and we (mostly Don and Sharol) cooked up some breakfast for a few of us, while others (Hank, Ivan, Gordon, and Jim Leech) went to town for breakfast.

It sprinkled some more during the morning, and soon people started giving up on the weather and leaving.

Roy, Stretch, Anne, and Gordon went up Pitney for a short flight, but most of us stood around 'til afternoon, finally packed up, said our good-byes and headed home.

Mam Tor Dual Flight

Roger Lennard

Author's note: As you may be aware, the Foot & Mouth disease in the UK means that flying is suspended. The attached report reminds me of an excellent flight and makes me look forward to many more when we can take to the air again.

It was getting closer to mid morning as we reached the landing field below Mam Tor. Steve, the instructor, pointed out common routes to it from various surrounding peaks. From this viewpoint it seemed that the trees and power lines could pose a significant hazard to anyone trying to make a final approach. Extra care needed to be taken at this time of the year because it was now lambing time and the last thing a farmer wanted was a hang glider scaring the pregnant ewes. The wind had shifted direction slightly and was light; smoke from a factory chimney marked the direction.

We checked out one possible launch site, but consideration of the wind direction ruled it out. This left only Mam Tor itself, which at a height of about 1,000 feet above where we stood looked rather impressive. The van wound its way up the steep sided gorge past hikers and holidaymakers waiting for guided tours of the speedwell cavern. At the roadside we unloaded the glider and walked the final few hundred metres to the summit. A seventeen-foot glider in its bag arouses some curiosity from hikers who, not quite sure what to say, ask if you are going hang gliding. A variety of quick remarks spring to mind but the most appropriate response was to say, "Yes, if the conditions are right." (The British have an obsession with weather conditions).

At the top there's no hurry to rig the glider. After all, the view on this late April day was worth savouring. A handful of paraglider pilots were rigged and ready, occasionally taking to the air when the wind strength, and therefore the upward deflected air, increased. They crossed from side to side along the ridge, varios bleeping as a mass of rising air carried them higher. We watched closely, visualising the uplift and sink areas.

The tandem glider, a large 'Discovery', was unfurled and asssembled. Battens were slid into their pockets and wires tensioned. All parts were carefully checked for wear and correct fitting. The lower 'A' frame was left flat so that no sudden gusts would lift the glider and throw it over the back of the ridge.

We put on the long pod harnesses, which have a hang strap at the back and a sort of remote-zipping sleeping bag pouch for your legs to fit into. Pilots obviously cannot zip their legs into these before being airborne and so wander around like some kind of helmeted lizard with a sleeping bag tail. Walkers realize that something interesting is about to happen and they suspend their activities to huddle in staring groups.

We go through the launch procedure; "Stand close, one arm round my harness and the other on my forearm. When I say *go*, run like hell. It's not too windy so we'll need a lot of ground speed to get off. " The glider is raised onto its 'A' frame and we take a hang check to ensure that the karabiners connecting our harnesses to the glider are secure and not twisted. With the help of a nose-man, the glider is positioned. Again we wait for 'the right moment', when a large cloud will be directly above the takeoff site, giving maximum upward suck of the air below it. With a few seconds to go I am totally focused on the flight. I am not worried because I don't have to make the decisions this time. It's all up to Steve to get it right and he is one of the best pilots in the business.

"Go!"

We run fast. The glider lifts off Steve's shoulders and accelerates, taking our weight as it gains airspeed and energy. The ground falls away and I am treading air. We are 1,000 feet above the ground. All is quiet and I savour the scene from my new vantage point. Steve stalls the glider to show how its response changes. We regain speed and swing right, along the line of a ridge. We are in sinking air according to the vario.

"If there is any lift, it will be along here." The vario bleeps in agreement and we feel a bump as we hit rising air. "Let's turn around and get some more of that."

The bar position is shifted and the glider responds by banking to the left then arcing round. There is a sudden jolt, forcing us to turn more steeply. "Did you feel the rising air as it pushed up the right wing?" After a number of turns we fly over the gorge we drove up earlier. People stop what they're doing and look up. Steve points out a flag on top of a building below. "If the wind's shifted then it can give lift as it hits the sides." Again we turn, circling over the gorge. What a view.

Still with over half our height to lose, we break for the valley. I can see clearly why we began by checking the landing site. Far below the trees and power lines pose no threat from this height and direction.   We glide perpendicular to the wind direction to lose some height. Steve points out that we have plenty of time at this stage to gauge our height and final approach. An air bubble, breaking away from the warming ground below, gives us an unexpected height gain.   To compensate we track further before making another 180-degree turn. "Ok, let's go for the long straight field rather than the other one." We complete a 90-degree turn to head us into wind and the final glide path looks perfect as we fly some twenty or so feet above the boundary wall. Now merely a few feet above the ground we skim over the grass. Steve skillfully bleeds off excess speed, the glider touches down and comes to rest.

I have a big silly grin on my face as we discuss the flight. I liked it. I liked it a lot.

Ol' George

Grant (Groundhog) Hoag

I was poised to launch my hang glider from the southwest Mt. Tamalpais site, and looked forward to picking up some lift over the redwood forest on the flight to Stinson Beach. Shifting my position, I felt an uncharacteristic crunching underfoot. I was standing on a pile of small white fragments mixed with gray powder.

"What am I standing on, eh?" I called out to Jim, who was holding my right wire.

Jim looked over, then down. "That's old George."

"Huh?" I replied, feeling less comfortable about the launch.

Jim explained: Old George had flown kites for many years on Mt. Tam, but had passed away recently. His last wishes were for his ashes to be scattered with the winds that had lifted his kites skyward. Two days previously George's befuddled and elderly buddies had heaved the contents of his urn skyward, but there had been no wind. Sadly, old George was left in a heap on the ground, and it was upon this heap that I was standing.

I stepped forward off George and launched. I did not look back, but I knew that I had been called. Groundhog was on a mission from God.

The next day I returned to launch armed with a battery-powered vacuum cleaner. My objectives were equal parts site maintenance and respect for my elders. After a few minutes of deft vacuuming, George was safely secured in a plastic bag, and the Mt. Tam launch was secure from spiritual distractions.

I taped George to a downtube and took off, descending towards Stinson Beach. Over the redwood trees on the hillside George and I parted ways. I was surprised to hear a pattering sound 100 feet below as the heavier fragments sprinkled upon the upper canopy of the trees. A more appropriate and pleasant finale to George's last flight.

Night Flight

EJ Steele

When I first started flying hang gliders it was all I could think about. I couldn't shut-up about it, either. I was always thinking of excuses to leave work early, and I did! I gave it so much attention that I never took a breath; at least that wasn't filled with hang gliding stories or lies. Then I met a few folks from the main circle of local pilots; *that* blew the lid off the cooker! These people were on fire! I'd go to the parties, and not only was everyone talking about flying, but the volume and intensity was so thick you could float a set of keys in it.

My main man, "Double-D" (I think it stands for "Dybbuk-Dave"), and I were out carousing on the town one night because we couldn't sleep. We were just wasting time, waiting for the sun to come 'round again. And that's when it hit us—Intermediate Syndrome!

"Come on! Why wait for the sun? Air is air; right? Light or dark these things still fly!" At first I couldn't believe what I was hearing; then I realized it was coming from my own mouth!

Of course it took me about halfway through 'Come on!' to convince that nut, Double-D. He was on it! He instantly produced a plan and a training regimen that "The Axe" would be proud of. We'd wait for a full moon and glide to the beach, we'd master the local micrometeorology to optimize launching conditions, and we'd rehearse the glide out on late afternoons first. Oh yeah! Before I was finished conceiving the idea, I was committed to a highly calculated plan of attack.

Things never turn out the way you plan them, and what we envisioned here would be no exception. We had every intention of following through with all of the preparations. We even did some rehearsal flights; all right, maybe one. But, late one afternoon, when I had just returned from a family vacation I soared the local ridge-lift spot until just after sunset. It was dark when I landed.

"Well, that was down right cheating," Double-D said jealously. "That's it! We're going... *tonight!*" I loaded my glider on his truck, and *Plan B* was in action. A quick call to the wind-talker would reveal no wind (well, okay, light over the back). Up the hill we went.

We arrived at launch to see the moon straight over-head; and by-God it was almost full. The city lights below looked inviting, but the beach still looked just a bit more than best glide away. I was so nervous I peed about fourteen times. The air was calm. We contemplated the no-winder for at least an hour. We checked, and quadruple checked, the glide using a slightly used, but carefully calibrated cigarette butt we dug out of the ashtray (I swear he has one of everything in that truck). Finally, in all our wisdom, we decided, "You can't fly, if you're not setup!"

We were never so meticulous with glider setup and preflight before. Once setup, and fourteen more trips to the bushes, we positioned ourselves one in front of the other, directly on the edge of launch. It was only appropriate that "Doyen-Dave" lead the chase, so he graciously took pole-position.

The adiabatic air slowly, but consistently, spiraled away from and towards launch. A small red strip of plastic that I scavenged off a crumpled Marlboro box, gently tied to my front wire, served as my windsock. It seemed as though hours would go by without a word said between us. Anything that was said was about how bright the sand on the beach was; and if we didn't make it, we'd always have the primary LZ just below.

It would take hours of sitting, silently, in our control frames, hooked-in before I heard The D-man scuffling about, raise his keel and crawl under the down tubes. "Oh my God, this is it!" I realized, so hard, that it echoed. I immediately jumped to my feet, just in time to see David's heels scrambling off of launch and into the darkness. As I stood in awe, I heard this incredible howl of freedom proudly pound through the canyon below.

He did it! Jesus! He actually did it...

I snapped-to. This was the cycle, and it might not last long. And, in a *lifetime-flashing-through-my-mind* moment I was running down launch, in a fully committed sprint towards the darkness. I can't say who or what took me away from the terrain; but when my control bar hit the windsock, down in front, I knew it was time to push-out.

I scanned the night sky for Double-D. I looked everywhere for a familiar hang glider silhouette against the lights below, but found nothing. I looked out to the city lights, and the full moon off in the distance. It was spectacular! I felt so much beauty, that tears ran down my night-chilled cheeks.

Slowly, I began to feel very alone, and realized just what situation I had gotten myself into. I flew over the primary LZ; that was a write-off. We waited so long into the night that the moon had past over too far, and was casting a huge shadow over the LZ; it looked like a big, black ink blotch. It would have to be the beach. My confidence wavered. I thought, "No problem." Then I thought, "I ain't makin' it! Why'd I do this to myself?" That only led me to,

"Look around dude, and enjoy. This may be the last you'll see this view." But, where the hell was Double-D?

During the final mile before the coastline, I saw a bright stream of light heading towards me from down below. I thought it might be the cops. Then the stream broke into distinct points. It was just some kids lighting off fireworks. To add one more anxious element, the east wind began to pick up. With only a few hundred yards to the sand—first over those pesky, 100-150 foot palm trees—I began to sink dramatically. My toes were pointed so hard they'd nearly break for the first half of the distance to goal. The second half, when I *knew* I had it, was a huge dive at the beach house and a crisp wingover into final. Luckily for me the beach house floodlights had been left on, and at just past four A.M. I had a no-stepper landing to end my first night flight.

I was so excited. I couldn't wait to pop open those beers we stuffed in our harnesses, hours ago, for the celebration on the beach. I shouted up and down the shore for Double-D with no response.

Quietly, a monotone voice said, "Hey I think your buddy hit a transformer." This guy had brought his date to the beach swing-sets (why, I don't know; to watch the hang gliders land?), and had witnessed the bright lights earlier. My mind raced in reverse to recall the *fireworks.*

Transformer?

I was nervous. TRANSFORMER! Images of electrocution filled my mind. I ran my glider, fully setup, across the street and stuffed it in to some bushes on the edge of a creek bordering an apartment complex. This night owl, co-incidentally named David, and his chick gave me a ride to the vicinity of the incident. I jumped from the truck before it could stop, and ran around the area calling for my bud. I was scared. "David! David!"

Just as I was about to lose it, I heard Double-D say very calmly, "Yes?"

He came out from under the trees, one of which he designated as his secondary LZ, and into the light. I swear the guy was floating about a foot off the ground. I ran to him and throttled him around the neck. I squeezed him so hard; I could barely hear him say, "That was a hoot." The guy was immortal.

We threw David's glider in the back of the truck, and headed back for mine. A Security Guard greeted us. I simply grabbed the glider and high-tailed it out of there! We shouted good-bye to the guard, and to our assistants, and ran into the darkness looking for a private spot to crack those beers.

Once we had the gliders both in the bag, we needed a secure hiding spot while we searched for a ride back to launch. We wandered about the local hotels looking for a proper storage rack. Like an answer from above, there it was; a huge pile of rolled up carpets! Perfect! I couldn't believe it. We rested our ships atop the stack, and I turned to Double-D and exclaimed; "God *is* a pilot."

We hailed a cab clear across town to where we'd left my truck. Some planning eh? I swear the cabby could see the aura around us. Of course he knew we were up to no good when we burst in to laughter at the thought of what we had just achieved.

David told me of his foiled attempt at the beach. He had turned back to make a play for a nearby golf course; power lines discounted that escape route. So, it was into the fluffiest tree available. Unfortunately, it wasn't robust enough to hold him. The wing rotated until it made the connection that started the firework show. The glider was then forced to rotate the opposite direction, just feet off the ground, and he landed standing up with the glider on his back. A no-stepper!

The adrenalin was capped off by the ride up to retrieve David's truck at launch. We rounded a spine at 1500' that faced us into the west just as we emerged above the fog layer that had sifted its way inland. We were facing the full moon, so beautifully lit up by the rising sun, setting in to the foggy blanket below. Without a word said, we turned toward each other, and knew that life is perfect!

Playing Tag at 3000 Feet

Peter Birren

This tale is about a single moment that made the previous 22 years in Pursuit of aviation worth every second of the cumulative effort. It's an event frozen in my memory.

The game of tag is mostly a children's game, phone tag not withstanding, one I thoroughly enjoyed playing when I was young. Never in my wildest dreams did I imagine flying a hang glider would present me with an opportunity to play this game with a hawk.

An August weekend in 1999 started out normally with the usual pre-flying phone calls to all the local pilots. It was my plan to camp at Bong Park in SE Wisconsin and get in a couple of days of flying. The weather wasn't fully cooperating as the forecasters predicted seasonable warm temperatures with lots of stable, high pressure clouds, so the call for Bong was a hard sell except to Igor, a new tow pilot, and Dan, a tandem instructor. Seems all the other pilots wanted to stay in bed. They know my attitude, "You never know what the weather's like at a site until you get there."

Igor wanted some practice but was only available for Saturday. My brother, Dave, and his son, Arnie, had been preparing for some time to each take their first tandem hang glider flights. Sunday, they were to celebrate Arnie's turning 17 by going up with Dan, so while the anticipated weather was a small bother, my personal flying was secondary. I wanted to help them have a good time. All that was enough for me to pack the camping gear and head out. I'd be tenting it alone, as my dear wife refers to the site as "Boring State Park."

With gliders assembled we started Saturday's towing, finding the air only a little buoyant. On my second flight, returning to the launch area and down to 900 feet, I found a shred of lift and turned to work it. A red tail hawk came into my thermal and we made a couple of turns together.

Hawks are undoubtedly the masters of the sky, able to do much more than we mere humans can with our dacron and aluminum ships. I've flown near them many times but they usually keep their distance. This particular Red-tailed Hawk, common at the park, looked a bit small and had every feather in place so I imagine it was a juvenile, not interested in the thermal as much as in this big, colorful thing in the air.

It wasn't with me very long, though it flew as close as 20 feet. Just curious, I guess. However, it did something I'd never seen—or heard—before. As it flew closer, it turned its head to look straight at me, then cooed softly, sounding much like a dove. Having never heard such a sound from a hawk, I tried to mimic the low call to perhaps keep it interested. With a single move that has me smiling as I recall it, the bird, the master of flight, looked to have an expression of surprise as it folded its wings, dove down with a bit of roll, and flew off with all capable speed. Guess my sound wasn't to its liking.

Igor and I each had several flights that day, which came to a close, as flying days always do, far too quickly. Gliders got packed and gear got stowed; Igor's for his trip home and mine in readiness for tomorrow.

Arnie was camping with his youth group on the other side of the park and I joined them for dinner. It was a group of older teenagers, including Arnie's sister, chaperoned by their mother who knew nothing about the next day's plans. We talked of the experience he would have on his birthday and told stories of his father's antics when he was much younger.

Sunday, as luck would have it, dawned overcast and gray, just as the weatherman had said. After Dan, his wife and driver Janet, and their son Ethan (my godson as well), showed up, I took my time setting up. For Arnie's sake I would take a tow to let him see a little of what we do. Janet did her sterling job of driving, pulling me off the ground like a child with a kite.

At about 1600 feet I noticed the car was no longer moving forward yet I was still climbing. This was most definitely lifting air, so I cut the weak-link and proceeded to gain altitude, making cloudbase at 3280. And still there wasn't a single ray of sunshine to be seen coming through the solid cloud layer.

Up and down, then back up again in what turned out to be very consistent lift, it was quite easy to stay up. I expanded my search to find other thermal triggers, netting a few that were as reliable as the first one, and I easily stayed above 2000 feet over the ground. The light south wind didn't present much of a barrier to flying into it, so I stretched my search to the south of launch after a while, to a farm a mile away that occasionally is a good source of lift. Flying very flat circles to conserve altitude I was disappointed to find nothing at all going up. Down to about 1600 feet I made the decision to head back to launch. I'd been in the air for well over an hour and was grateful for that, as all I had expected was a sled ride -- launch, fly, land -- to show Arnie what he could expect. This flight was a gift at this point and I wasn't about to push it.

Just as I was down to less than 1000 feet, Dan called me on the radio to say he had just spotted a hawk circling directly over the runway. Did I see it?

It took me a few seconds to find the bird because it was maybe 75 to 100 feet off the ground, camouflaged against the background of trees and shrubs.

But I saw its lazy circles and headed over to see if the lift would sustain me and my old glider. We had only 600 or so feet between us, so it was not difficult to find the thermal the hawk was using, and, indeed, I could use the lift.

With the previous day's flight with the red tail still fresh in my mind, I made sure to keep quiet in case this was the same bird. It looked different, however, but still I thought to maintain my silence.

Slowly, this feathered wonder gained on me, getting ever closer, until at 2000 feet and directly above launch, we were at the same altitude. Only then did I have a hint of an idea this might be a different type of encounter when the hawk lowered his legs a little so the extra drag would keep it at my level. We danced around the core of this thermal for several turns until this magnificent animal grew tired of trying to stay down so low, pulled in its landing gear, tightened its wings and immediately climbed 200 or more feet above me.

It obviously didn't think I was in the best air and headed north a quarter-mile, then stopped to circle some more. I took that move as a bit of a dare and followed. The hawk waited until I locked into the rising air, then headed north another few hundred yards, pausing to wait for me again. Obligingly, I again followed. By the third move out, I noticed we were getting beyond my comfort distance, a point where the landing zone was just out of reach of a single glide should I have to return. A cross country flight hadn't been planned and my relatives were now preparing for their tandem flights so I wanted to stay within landing range.

I left the bird's company and started the upwind leg back to launch, found a bit of lift and started circling. On the second loop around in the thermal I saw the bird; it was heading towards me! One hundred yards away and still a couple hundred feet above, the hawk incredibly lowered its legs and pulled in its wings, much to my amazement. This move brought it down to my altitude, but that wasn't all. It then tightened up and continued in my direction.

I watched continuously as it came closer... closer... and yet closer until it was a mere 5 feet below me, just off the corner of my control bar, when it turned its head and looked straight at me as if to say, "What? Don't you want to play any more?"

How can we know, or imagine knowing, what's in an animal's mind? It can be simple if that animal is a large dog, growling with its teeth bared. But what about a raptor? There isn't much in the way of facial expressions, except for what we can only imagine is there. But on this day, with this bird, on this flight, it became obvious the bird wanted to play. Who am I to refuse?

And so we played.

It flew away... I followed. I flew away... it followed. Each time we came together this beautiful Broad-Winged Hawk (buteo class Accipiter, as I later found out) would grow more friendly—some might say bold—but just short of letting me touch it, though it did get close enough once.

The dance at cloudbase lasted for well over 15 minutes, maybe 20, until at a closing it turned, looked at me, gave a call, then sped off to the east, perhaps back to the nest, perhaps to continue its hunting chores. But it most certainly left me with a soul-lifting memory, an encounter that can never be planned for, of a very special time with one of the true masters of the sky.

I landed after being in the air for almost 2-1/2 hours on a totally clouded-over day. Thermalling had seemed to be completely out of the picture yet here I was with a logbook entry that made all the others pale in comparison. The smile on my face was probably similar to the ones both Dave and Arnie had after their tandems. Dan was stoked as well so he offered to fly some more; Arnie had 3 tandems, one to 1850, and Dave, not really being the pilot type, got 2. I had wanted to show them a little of what to expect. We all got away with more than we bargained for.

Where were all the other pilots? Well, Bong isn't terribly good in east winds due to Lake Michigan, so they all went to other sites; I talked to one pilot on the radio, about 125 miles away as the hawk flies, and we had super-clean communication; even heard her driver in the car. Didn't hear a word about any good flights over that weekend, so it must not have been tremendous. But like I said earlier, "You never know what the weather is like at the site until you get there."

Tag. You're it.

In the Field Guide to Birds of North America, the Broad-Winged Hawk is described as "A woodland species, common and rather tame. Adult is easily recognized by the broad-barred tail. Immature, with characteristic buteo shape, has white underwing surface contrasting with black tips on primaries. It lacks the belly band of the much larger Red-tailed Hawk. Shape in flight is like a Red-tail's. Head-on, light cere suggests single, central "headlight." The Broad-wing hunts from a perch, flashing into action upon appearance of a large insect, mouse, or small reptile. It characteristically migrates in large flocks, forming "kettles." Call is a thin whistle suggesting Eastern Wood-Pewee's."

Potato Chips

Lyman Hart

Remembering my most memorable flight is like eating potato chips, *you can't have just one.* Each flight is unique in a way that only a true hang glider pilot can understand. Each is also unforgettable. Whether I'm soaring in ridge lift, thermalling over flat farmland, wing tip to wing tip with a beautiful bald eagle, or just competing with a gaggle of buzzards to be on top, each flight is a unique and unforgettable experience. Fellow pilots who share this same passion for flight make a flight more memorable.

If I could re-live one flight in particular it would be one of my early flights as a hang glider pilot. The people for whom I have the most respect, and to whom I attribute my learning, are in my fondest memories of flight. Among those people are the past instructors and tug pilots who were at one time employed by Kitty Hawk Kites. Rob Bachman gave me my first high altitude flights as Bo Hagewood flew the tug, what can compare to your first high altitude flight?

Well, maybe your first soaring mountain flight, and again I had the pleasure of flying with the Kitty Hawk Kite gang. It was November of 1995 on an overcast Tuesday morning and I had skipped work because the forecast was for a northwest wind at 10-15 mph, perfect for a flight at Woodstock. I thought that I might be able to employ the help of some wuffoes at the lookout tower for launch, as I was sure that no one would be on launch on an overcast Tuesday morning. As I neared the launch site I thought I caught a flash of color streak by the west finger of the mountain near launch. I blinked, refocused and saw what appeared to be several hang gliders riding across the ridge in both directions. Wow, someone to fly with! I hurried to the parking area next to the launch, grabbed all my gear, and headed up to the launch to see who was flying. Standing out front helping to wire everyone off was Bo! What the heck was he doing here? As it turns out, the group at Kitty Hawk Kites take a couple of weeks off in November each year to do what they do best, fly!

I shook Bo's hand and asked who was in the air and he began reciting names like, Bruce Weaver, Rob Bachman, Chad Elchin. It was a fresh pilots dream. I set up quickly, and Bo asked if I felt comfortable in the rather strong conditions. I, of course, said yes. There was no other answer, I had to fly; all my training had led up to this fantastic moment. Bo asked some of the local pilots to help him wire me off. It was that perfect moment when, with the help of the people you admire most, you commit to aviation. I listened as Bo gave me an assessment of the conditions. Then I listened to the wind, watched the tell tales on launch, and heard myself shout, "Clear!"

It was a perfect launch into a 600 fpm elevator above the ridge. I watched Bruce do a close fly by at launch and almost have a mid-air with a bald eagle. Someone was flying a Stealth past me like I was standing still. To my amazement the Stealth climbed up, up, and over in a smooth large loop; must have been Chad. This was fantastic! Smooth lift everywhere and some of the most incredible flying that I had seen to date, or perhaps since. We flew in each other's company for several hours, then one by one gliders lightly touched down in the LZ. I decided to land as well. I didn't want to be the last, especially if my landing wasn't, shall we say, *pretty*.

I left the ridge and started out over the valley, but I was still climbing. Over the LZ now, and still climbing. What the heck was going on? I dove left and dove right, 50 ft loss and 30 ft gain. This could take a while. I knew that people were watching the new guy and saying, "What's his problem, didn't anyone teach him to land? It's easy just quit going up!" Then I realized that this was the famous Shenandoah Valley wonder wind. This was great, even the wind was helping to make this day one that I would never forget.

After 20 minutes of diving my glider at the deck I was out of the strong lift and about 500 ft over the LZ. I could see that everyone was watching as I set up for my approach. I could see Bo waving me to a spot near the crowd. This was tense; I'd better do this right, only got one shot. I stuffed the bar, leveled my wings and headed toward Bo and the spot. The approach was good and I made a pretty landing, right in front of the crowd.

I saw the smiling faces of Bo, Rob and Sonny, I shook Rob's hand and said thanks. Rob complimented me and said, "I love to see people's dreams come to fruition." That pretty much sums it up, don't you think? The flight itself was just another potato chip, albeit a very tasty chip. But the people that I shared the flight with, my mentors, made it one of my most memorable flights. Many people were responsible for my training but some very special people stand out and will always be Sky Gods in my memory, most notably Rob, Bo and Sonny (who gave me my first 10 second dune flight). Thanks, wherever you are.

A Great Day In The Hills Of New York

The Finger Lakes

Bob Grant

Each May Wayne Bergman of East Coast Videos and many of his fellow pilots from along the east coast of Lake Michigan come to The Finger Lakes of New York State for a week of fantastic flying. 1995 was no exception and a group of about ten pilots showed up hoping for some great air. I live in London, Ontario, Canada, which is a five-hour drive from The Finger Lakes, whereas the Michigan pilots drive about ten hours to get there. We all meet at the Hickory Hills campground at the bottom of Mount Washington, commonly know as Hammondsport launch site.

For the first part of the week we visited many of the five sites within twenty-five miles of the campground. We had some decent soaring, but nothing spectacular. In this area of New York on light and variable days it is possible to try at least three of the five sites and the wind may be up most of them throughout the day. One day I flew two sites by four o'clock and then finally at five o'clock went to Mosey Banks, which overlooks the town of Bath NY. There I finally got lucky with the wind coming in at four or five miles per hour. It is best to try it at Mosey in the evening because the heat from the town breaks off and makes it soarable in some of the smoothest lift, often to four grand above the four hundred foot cliff launch. Mosey is an amazing place.

But, back to that week in May that I call *The Invasion*, because so many pilots converge on the area for that week. Friday rolled around and the forecast was for northwest winds at twenty miles per hour. We all drove to the top of the Hammondsport take-off, a seven hundred and fifty foot drop to the rolling landing area below. We arrived at launch at nine o'clock, and the wind was straight in but somewhat light. I set up and got ready because I don't like to rush at the last minute. By ten o'clock I was ready to launch, and Wayne, Rusty Beresh, John, Keith and others were almost ready. At ten-thirty the cycles were coming straight in at top speeds of 12 mph. I launched into a smooth thermal getting up nicely to five hundred feet over launch. The ridge at Hammondsport is about two miles long, so I cruised along watching the other pilots rushing with excitement to get into the air. Soon I found a good thermal and was on my way up to 2000' and feeling like this would be the day that I finally did a good XC flight. In the past years I have only made about six XC flights, the longest 21 miles. That doesn't sound very far now, but back then it was real exciting for me.

I saw Rusty Beresh take off and climb out nicely. Rusty lives at the south end of Lake Michigan and mostly flies the cliffs along the lake; he had never flown XC. Half-hour in the air, I was getting up to four grand and really enjoying the moderate thermal conditions. Rusty was also getting up, so I got on the radio and said, "Hey Rusty, looks like a good XC day, do you want to try it?"

"Gee, I don't know Bob, what do you think?" I coaxed Rusty for about twenty minutes before finally he said, "OK, let's do it." We headed down wind from 4500' above launch. The cruising was simply awesome.

I would take the lead, looking back to see if Rusty was still there. I could usually see him, but he was keeping rather far back and hard to keep track of. We were getting up to five grand and down to 2500' between thermals. As we passed the town of Savona, five miles east of Hammondsport, I was getting comfortable. The lift was more consistent as we traveled, and it was great having Rusty along so that we could gauge our thermals and take the best available. We passed the town of Campbell and were on our way to Corning, which we could see in the distance. I had flown to Corning on a previous XC, so I was hoping to beat my old record and looked ahead to see which side of the valley to follow.

There are small ranges on either side of Corning. I radioed to Rusty that I was going to fly directly across Corning and then use the lift which I thought would be coming up the 500 foot hills to the right of town. They appeared to be facing directly into the wind. I made a dash for the hills, but I was low. I made it to the crest but found very little lift. Within ten minutes, I was on approach into a nearby field with high-tension wires across it, making the landing a little tight. But I made an OK landing and that is good for me. I immediately radioed Rusty and asked him to relay a message to John Inkstrom as to my whereabouts. Fifteen minutes after I packed up John showed up with my van and we were off to another site called Hariss Hill near Elmira, NY. At Hariss Hill, it was very soarable and I had another smooth flight, gaining over three thousand feet and landing at seven PM for another two-hour flight.

Oh yes, I had a great day of flying and had at that time my longest XC of 28 miles. Even better, Rusty had taken the other side of the valley at Corning and continued on to fly into Pennsylvania for a total of sixty-five miles on his first XC flight. You should have seen that happy face and heard the stories when Rusty finally returned to the campground about eleven that evening.

If any of you would like to visit the Finger Lakes for some wonderful flying, check in with the Rochester club or visit my website at www.skynet.ca/~skydog.

The Mexican

Scot Trueblood

The chill that came over me was surprisingly strong but not unexpected; it was the cooling that sunburned, salt-crusted skin gets when the heat source has been removed. Dusk was giving way rapidly to full darkness, and in autumn the New Mexico desert at 4,500' gives the heat of the day back to the night all too willingly. I could have pulled some warmer clothes out of the harness bag at my feet, but a pair of headlights on the horizon had my full attention. In the last 45 minutes, only a couple of cars had been by, and they passed my outstretched thumb with the nervous anxiety so often exhibited by tick-tock, uptight types who smugly assure themselves that people on the side of the road in the middle of nowhere soliciting a ride are not in distress but rather are hopeless, unsuccessful bottom feeders who need another victim to dismember and dispose of in the desert. I just wanted, more than anything on earth, to get home.

Undoubtedly, I looked pretty creepy in the work clothes that I had flown in, and I hoped that the presence of my harness bag would lend an air of credibility to my inexplicable presence along the side of U.S. Highway 54 about 22 miles north of Carrizzozo, NM. Hitchhikers without baggage are especially scary; at least a backpack or duffel bag creates the illusion that you are a traveler with some agenda other than wanton killing. My situation was looking pretty bleak, and that was *before* the arrival of my new *compadre*.

Now, this fellow was a Mexican, from Mexico, and there was not a word of English in his vocabulary. Not only that, my new *amigo* was undoubtedly the filthiest human being on the face of the earth. No exaggeration, the *muchacho* was absolutely shit-caked from head to toe with grease, rust, dirt, blood, sweat, and no telling what else. If there was, or has ever been, a more begrimed human being on the face or the earth, they were dead or dying of dirt. And his only baggage was a set of cutting torches.

This seemed like a case of plain old bad luck. My prospects of getting a ride were already looking dim, and now I had a real-live horror-show character standing with me, in the middle of nowhere. In my best schoolboy Spanish, I nervously said, "Buenas tardes," to which he grinned a sporadically toothed grin and replied the same. Suddenly, I began to wonder if I was the one to be dismembered in the desert. I knew that, if I wasn't murdered, I was suddenly faced with the very real prospect of spending the night in the desert. I thought of my wife and children, the fact that they didn't have the foggiest notion where I was. And I just wanted to get home.

The day had started innocently enough, just a Saturday in Ruidoso, New Mexico, which required me to be present and productive in my woodworking shop. This Saturday had a twist though. I had, the evening before, been recruited to serve as a replacement player in a game of Ultimate Frisbee. Our team captain & fearless leader was my good hang gliding buddy and mentor Riker Davis. He knew that I had a pretty good Frisbee arm and would be gullible enough to be duped into playing against the fearsome Smoky Bear Hotshot firefighting crew. The fire fighters were in incredible condition from trotting around with 40 lb. packs fighting fires all the time, and usually made pretty quick work of our team from Sierra Blanca Ski Area. Game time was at 3 o'clock, and it hung over me like an appointment with the executioner.

A quick glance out the door of my shop at the 10 am break made my heart leap. The wind was blowing easterly and the cumies were already popping. This meant only one thing: Windy Point was ON. Windy Point is not your run-of-the-mill flying site. An east-facing scenic overlook on a state highway at 10,000' elevation means easy access, and the alpine scenery of nearby Sierra Blanca Peak at 12,003' makes it one of the most scenic flying sites in southern New Mexico. However, the prevailing southwesterly winds would usually send us packing down to Dry Canyon about an hour away in Alamogordo. When the winds shift to easterly, it is like a gift from God.

I knew by looking at the sky that the flying was going to be dynamite, but I couldn't just cut out on Riker and the Frisbee slaughter. I knew that the only solution was to make Riker guilty by association, a co-conspirator. By the time I called him, I had the whole sales pitch bundled & rehearsed. We should simply go up the hill and launch, then due to the incredible conditions, fly into town and land at the Frisbee field, where we would be greeted as heroes. Win or lose, we would be the stuff of legends, and the story would be told for years. The primary LZ at Eagle Lakes was fraught with hazards: very small, on a slope, between 2 lakes, deep in a canyon at 8'200', surrounded by trees. The entire surrounding area is industrial-strength forest and mountains, and flying to even the nearest alternate LZ involves flying cross-country. The flight to the playing field would require getting to at least 14,000' and making a difficult glide into the wind, something that, in 1984, had never been done. But I assured Riker that the day was ours, and that, just as surely as the sun rises, we were going to make it.

I should have known it was going to be an unusually good flight when my radio had no signs of life and new batteries did not improve the situation. Murphy's Law, as applied to hang gliding, assures that any piece of equipment which has ceased to function correctly will be the one most needed during the flight. This was back in the day when we flew with the old Radio Shack handheld CB radios; what marvels they were! Due to the befuddling phenomenon known as skip, one could usually hear truckers as far away as I-40 out of Albuquerque, but not communicate with one's own crew directly below. When my camera batteries were dead, too, I knew that I better at least dress really warm.

The usual crowd of tourists with the usual set of whuffo questions gathered as we assembled our gliders. Time was of the essence, so we set up without supplying the usual litany of canned answers. I ran down the steep slope off the road cut and easily into the air. Stepping into the Raymond cocoon, my gorgeous Comet 1-165 "Penelope" was like a frisky puppy as I began to work lift. Riker was a couple of minutes behind in his nearly-new Streak 160.

The flight was almost over before it began. The lift was patchy and turbulent, and soon we were both more than 500' below launch. We were working the heat from the pavement where the road switches back and forth up the face of the mountain but getting sparse results. The tall pine and fir trees were practically tickling my ribs as I scratched and sniffed; I was nearly flying behind them looking for lift, and Riker was about a quarter mile to the south doing the same thing. Looking skyward, the cumuli were too perfect to not be the result of good lift. Just as this thought registered, I flew into a thermal that had my sunglasses nearly pulling off my face from the G's. My old Litek Hummingbird was singing happily as the Altimaster 4 was clocking the vertical. Up we went at 800-1200fpm, and once above launch it was easy to move in over the summit to get in the fat lift wicking up the spines of the ridge. Climbing past 11,000', I realized that I didn't see Riker down below anywhere and quickly scanning the sky, spotted him in his own green patch at my same level, still about ¼ mile south of my position, climbing at my same rate.

The cotton-ball cumies were still much higher, and they were beckoning like an affectionate lover. The lift was easy to stay in and it provided a good opportunity to enjoy the fabulous scenery. Cloud shadows adorned the brilliant green alpine meadows like lace on sexy lingerie. There was a faint haze, which made the distant desert look a little fuzzy, like a slightly grainy photograph; but the dividing line between the inversion and the clear sky above was distinct. Between the blinding white cumuli, the dark blue sky above was like a window into space.

Riker was a bit above me now and still a little to the south, and we were both above 15,000'. I headed for the edge of the mile-wide lift as I figured that by the time I got to sink, I'd be at cloudbase. Flying south, on a heading for the Frisbee Killing Field, it was immediately apparent that we would be bucking a troublesome southerly headwind. After doggedly pounding into the surf for at least a half minute, I realized that this would be the stay of execution I needed. Surely everybody would understand that, if I missed the game because of an accidental epic flight, it was due to circumstances beyond my control.

Looking behind me, to the north, I could see the glittering blue of windswept Bonito Lake, the desert 10 miles or so beyond that, and clouds all the way to the horizon. The path of least resistance was clearly defined. With no radio contact, I silently said *adios* and peeled off for points unknown. My groundspeed was incredible as I flew back through the lift, and going out the turbulent eddies on the downwind side of the thermal felt like being shot out of a cannon. I drew a bead on the northeast corner of Church Mountain and hit cruise control.

The area below and in front of me was unlandable, but that only added to the excitement of the moment. I had the feeling of total exhilaration: plenty of altitude, a good tailwind, and open country in front. It was like riding a Harley in the sky, roaring along, shucking my responsibilities, not a worry in the world. I didn't think about the Frisbee game again until the next day.

Passing the corner of Church Mountain I was squirting through Indian Divide over the tiny town of Nogal like a slippery watermelon seed. Unfortunately, the seed was tied to a rock. I was squirting and sinking, sinking and sweating, and next thing I knew I was a few hundred feet off the deck well short of Carrizzozo. This was not what I had in mind and I knew the flight was not good enough to get me off the hook with Riker. I began to pray for lift, but still I was sinking; I resorted to making promises to God. At about 200' AGL I was above a dirt road through open desert with a couple of miles to hike to the highway, straight above a windmill that I was using to gauge the wind for landing. But I was still praying and making promises, and they suddenly began to kick in.

There was no ripping thermal, just a sudden absence of sink. Slowing down, I made some clumsy, tentative turns trying to stay in the lift. I was barely high enough to do a 360, and with no obstacles around I knew that if I fell out I could land anywhere. I had been in light lift for a fairly good upwind stretch so I knew that if I turned downwind I should be in lift all the way. It was at this moment that I had an epiphany: I realized that the power of prayer was very real.

Finishing several 360's I hadn't gained much altitude but was at least getting closer to the highway. Maybe this was going to work out after all. The thermal was getting stronger and I was up to about 500' by the time I crossed highway 380. It was only then that I realized that I could put my feet back fully in the harness and settle down again. The thermal began to really go vertical and was still drifting fast; I was back in business!

The area ahead was devoid of roads for several miles (or houses, cows, windmills, any sign of civilization) but I was climbing like King Kong. Passing several miles to the east of Carrizzozo, I was crossing the hinterlands of the O-Bar-O Ranch area. This was where I had learned to fly, and passing over the old training hills in the grasslands was a bit of a sentimental journey. More than 5 years earlier I had some of my finest memories down there; it has now been over 22.

Back to the Sky-Harley feeling again, I climbed and drifted for many miles with my thermal, and I still count that as one of my absolute lowest saves. Passing Lone Mountain, another old training site, I had finally leveled off and was roaring along straight over Highway 54. Gravity however, always has the last word with hang gliders and began to run the Harley low. It is north of Lone that the railroad track rejoins the highway, and the highway makes a change in heading toward the east, away from my drift.

At the confluence I witnessed a remarkable sight; dozens of railroad cars were strewn about, accordion-like, in the chaotic choreography of a derailment. I had read about this incident several weeks before, but hadn't driven this highway or seen the wreckage. The track was cleared but the 35 or 40 boxcars looked like forgotten old toys in the desert.

I was low again and it was getting late in the day. Crossing the highway to the west, I dribbled along in a succession of on-again off-again thermals. Down to about 500', I was about to give up and land when I blundered into a real corker. This thermal was climbing as well as the earlier low-save thermal but without the sweat. The drift was still strong and southeasterly, but the highway had changed its course and I was now drifting rapidly into no-man's land. Up to about 9,000'MSL, I was gazing into the distance; and there was nothing but distance in the distance. It was late in the day and this was true desolation, nothing but New Mexico map filler. Not even the faintest dirt road as far as the eye could see. With a heavy heart I turned away from my wonderful thermal.

Back-tracking into the wind, it was obvious that trying to cover more miles up the highway was going to require one hell of a crosswind run, and the apex of the highway where it met the train derailment was the best I could do. Getting back over the highway, I found a field next to a road that ran 200 yards or so into the desert. The wind on the ground was fairly strong and I set up a right-hand aircraft approach. On the downwind leg I flew through what was still kicking of that thermal, and had the scariest moment of the entire flight as the dustless devil trashed me very hard and spit me out in a severe nose down attitude downwind and very low. Cranking it around hard to get the nose into the wind, I fought turbulence all the way to the deck and had a no-step landing.

I quickly took stock of the situation: sun setting, no chase crew, in the middle of nowhere. The silver lining to this cloud of apparent doom was that nobody had ever flown this far from Windy Point. I hastily broke down and stashed the glider well away from the highway, and took my harness bag to the highway to thumb a ride.

Things were pretty quiet except for the wind. Watching the only cars on the road pass me by I began to realize that this wasn't going to be easy, but I remained optimistic. After all, I had hitchhiked my way across Texas in my youth; I could always get a ride, especially with a backpack at my feet. There wasn't a car in sight though, and I began to daydream. The derailed boxcars were only a couple hundred yards away, and the scene was a bit surreal, even spooky. The wind was blowing boxcar doors around and the wreckage seemed to be shifting, but could it be?? Still, strange noises were emanating from the tangled wreckage, and I stood transfixed, not sure if I was hallucinating. Suddenly, I was startled by the figure of a man, emerging from underneath a boxcar like an alien. He wandered slowly toward the road, staggering, seemingly confused. He was filthy dirty, clothes disheveled, looking like he's been under there for weeks. Was I seeing things? Could he have been a lone survivor of this catastrophe?

He was clutching something, half dragging it behind him, I couldn't tell what. He was walking straight toward me, and as he drew closer it dawned on me: he *was* an alien! An illegal alien from Mexico with cutting torches cutting up train parts for the scrap metal! He crossed the fence and walked straight over to me, giving only a tired & nervous nod as he turned to wait for a car to come. He was hitchhiking with me. Of all things! My slim prospects of getting a ride seemed to evaporate completely.

As the lone car on the horizon approached, I remembered my newly discovered belief in the power of prayer. Thinking of my family, I prayed only that I would somehow get to see them. Lo and behold, as the vehicle drew nearer, it began to slow down well in advance, almost before we stuck out our thumbs in unison. A large white van which was already too full stopped right in front of us and the side door slid open as though by appointment. In utter disbelief, I waited as my new friend threw his cutting torches inside behind the driver's seat, and I hoisted my flight bag into the floorboard ahead of one of the back seats. The smiling faces inside seemed too good to be true. It was a very large van with the first set of seats removed, creating a space between the driver's seats and the first row, and inside was a very large ranch family from Ancho on their way to Saturday night bible study and choir practice at the Baptist Church in Carrizozo. Most of them seemed to be teenage girls, dressed in their Saturday night best, with mom and pop in the front. The Mexican was up front with mom and pop; I had the good fortune to ride in the back with the girls.

The first thing pop said was, "You fellers looked like ya'd been workin' awful hard so we figgered ya needed a ride." It was the power of prayer at work. He spoke good Spanish so he and the Mexican had an animated conversation while I entertained the ladies with stories of my heroic flight. They were some of the kindest people I ever met, and despite their dressed-up appearance didn't give a hoot that we both looked like we had been living underneath that train. All they saw were two fellows on the side of the road who really looked like they needed a ride, and knew that they could help out.

My flight that day was 33 miles, a Windy Point site record that stood for a very long time. The lesson I learned though, was far more important: Never judge a fellow human by appearances only, for regardless of what they may look like, they may be your savior.

By the way, Riker couldn't penetrate the headwind and didn't make it to the Frisbee game either.

Yamaska, Quebec

Jim (Sky Dog) Palmieri

During the summer of 1999, I spent a lot of time boat towing on a large man-made lake in Virginia. Life was good, towing was great and all had fun. Late September, as we were winding down the summer flying season on the lake, I had an accident due to a premature release at about 100 feet. The result was damage to both wrists and two operations over the next 3 months and another 3 months in a cast. Needless to say, flying was out of the question for that spring and early summer. By August, my wrists were strong enough for gentle air flying; at least I hoped they were. My wife Maggie and I planned on visiting some pilot friends In Thetford Mines, Quebec for a week of flying. Not having flown for almost a year, I was a bit anxious about getting into the air again especially at an unknown site away from home. This was to be my final summer vacation before resuming teaching for the fall.

We left Roanoke, Virginia and made a 2-day stopover at Morningside Flight Park in Charlestown, New Hampshire, home of some of the nicest pilots anywhere in this country. Jeff Nicolay and Dave Baxter define the best in New England hospitality and should you ever get a chance to visit Morningside Flight Park you will not be disappointed. Morningside is an old flight park with huge training hills and a 450-foot almost cliff-like launch. A steep dirt and cement road leads you to the top where there is a small shed/clubhouse and a ramp. Below is a huge LZ with a spot-landing target. I figured a few flights off of the high hill would give me my confidence back and, more importantly, allow me to test the strength of my wrists in flight under a highly controlled environment. Even under strong 40-degree crosswinds at launch, all three of my launches and landing were good and the strength of my wrists was not a factor. Actually, the year layoff seemed like a day once I got into the air. The old feeling was back!

The next day found us under a low and wet cloudbase heralding time to depart Charlestown for Thetford Mines, Quebec. We had a great scenic drive through upper New England and Quebec Province. Thetford Mines is an old asbestos mining town with huge open asbestos mines and mountains of asbestos debris dotting the landscape. Large mountains could be seen on the horizon, certainly a haven for hang glider pilots. We were met by 3 local pilots, Marc, Daniel and Francois. We spent a week in the upstairs of Marc's home and were treated to hospitality that only natives of Quebec can offer. The food and the Canadian beers were the best, but the winds were not favorable to flying. Finally after 5 days of waiting we departed for Yamaska Mountain, about 60 miles out side of Montreal.

Yamaska is a big mountain and it sits like a loaf of bread out in the middle of the flatlands. The mountain is beautiful, as is the surrounding countryside. I think there are 7 separate launches at the top of the mountain, supported by two competing clubs. When we arrived, the air was filled with both hang gliders and especially paragliders. Pilots can load their gliders on an old truck and for a small charge get hauled up the mountain. Instead, we loaded our new red Ford F-150 with gliders and pilots and attempted driving the road up the mountain. After several wrong turns on roads not made even for a donkey, we made it to the top. The wind was strong and cross but the air was clean and warm.

The Southeast launch consists of a tight parking area with a small climb on a dirt path to the launch area. The launch is rather tight; trees and shrubs surround the set-up area, which is about 6 feet lower than the ramp, making up a rough bowl area. If gliders are arranged properly, 5 to 6 could be set up and still protected from the wind. The ramp is rather large and covered with carpet, at least in places. Paraglider pilots were setting up closer to launch. There were three in our group setting up to fly. Daniel, a skinny light pilot, was flying a sensor 610 F2 with 150 squares, putting him on the lower end of the recommended weight range for that glider. Daniel was the first to set-up and to be off the ramp. The wind was strong and cross at launch and as soon as a straight in cycle crossed the ramp, he was off and up. Certainly he was on a soaring machine, especially with VG off and flaps pulled on. The sky was filled with paragliders, and at the time Daniel launched, he was the only hang glider in the air.

The landing zone was to the far left of launch, and out of sight. The countryside around Yamaska is relatively flat and in August, all the fields looked the same, either tall with grass or hay or brown with cut hay. There were power lines that would have to be contended with on approach should some of the unofficial fields be used as an LZ. There was a small river to be crossed to get to the official landing area.

Marc Laferriere and I were ready to launch 30 minutes after Daniel. Daniel was 800 to 1000 feet over the mountain and well above even the slowest flying paraglider. Needless to say, I was a touch nervous if not puckered about launching from this mountain. A combination of a year off from flying, a new site and a ramp with cross wind and strong thermals ripping through did not really put me at ease. Marc, being the gracious host, was not going to launch until I was off and up.

Before continuing with this story, I need to tell you about Marc Laferriere.

Marc is probably the number one pilot in Quebec. He's been flying for over 20 years and swears by his Sensor. The whole club in Thetford Mines consists of Sensor owners. Marc and I first met through the Internet. Marc is an artist. He paints hang gliders and paragliders. (A tour of his web page **http://www3.sympatico.ca/marc.laferriere/Gallerie.html** is a must if you enjoy hang glider art.) I asked him to do several paintings for me and one, which is my favorite, shows me flying in an Airborne Sting above Marc in his Sensor. Marc has an unusual Sensor, he has painted the under sail to look like flames as one would see on an old fashioned hot rod. From this association, we have become good friends and I always joke about me flying an intermediate glider above his Sensor. His reply is always the same... *"Yes you are above me, but only in the painting!"*

Back to the story. After a hang check, and with the help of my wife Maggie and Marc, I carry my Airborne Shark up to the ramp. The wind is very cross and the wings never feel balanced. To compound this, the afternoon thermals are moving across the ramp like a locomotive. They are large and fat. After watching 4 or 5 cycles, my wings load fully and I am off. I make a right turn and within a short period of time I am 500 feet over. To my right, about a mile down the ridge, I see Daniel. He is high and back over the end of the mountain taking advantage of the crosswind conditions. I work my way towards him, but not knowing the mountain, I am shy to go too far. Not knowing the exact location of the LZ has added to my apprehension, effectively putting me on a short leash. As I venture toward the left of launch in hopes of spotting the LZ, I lose the lift and encounter rough air because of the crosswind rotor on that side of the mountain. Finally on my 12th pass to the left, I spot the LZ as a paraglider pilot lands. I head toward Daniel. The leash has been removed and I leave the paragliders below.

I have been in the air about 30 minutes and Marc has not left the ramp due to wind conditions. Finally, I see his glider slide off the ramp and watch Marc struggle to find lift. It takes Marc about 5 minutes to work himself high enough above launch so he can venture out to find lift. I am looking down on Marc who is about 600-700 feet below me. I know he will want to get above me because of the ongoing joke we have about the painting.

I find a great thermal and core it as slowly as I can, taking full advantage of all the lift available to me and to put as much distance between Marc and myself as possible.

Marc sees the thermal and heads over. He begins to work the thermal and when he is about 400 feet below me, I yell down to him, "Who is that below me? Could it be a Sensor on fire?" As soon as Marc hits the core of the thermal, and it is a big thermal, he begins to rise. I watch him climb as if he were on an elevator. The Sensor with VG off and full flaps is certainly doing what it was designed to do. I try with all the skill I have to continue the climb, but he reaches me and looks over and smiles. And in his best English with a strong French Canadian accent, Marc says, "Hello Jim, how are you? Good bye!" And up he went.

For the next hour we played in the sky, moving out into the valley and working thermals together in the buoyant air surrounding the mountain. Neither Marc nor I ever got to within 200 feet of Daniel. He was the top of the stack and it was going to stay that way all afternoon. We had become those little boys again, playing in a friend's back yard and we celebrated our friendship in the air. It was an afternoon of flying I will always remember.

Finally, when the fatigue of the day and the trip began to surface, I headed out to the LZ. The wind had switched 90 degrees making what would have been a landing in between rows of cut hay, into a landing across the rows of cut hay. The day was meant to be one of fun and the landing was perfect. Within 20 minutes, both Daniel and Marc headed for the LZ.

The day had been a great one, and we were comforted by a warm afternoon sun and friendship. That evening we celebrated the day with spouses and other pilots at a local restaurant, putting the finishing touches onto a most memorable flight and fun afternoon. Life is good.

The Magic Of Tobacco Row Mountain

Marc (MAX) Laferrière

On the 31st of March 2001, I left Quebec with five of my friends and fellow pilots for what was to be a dream hang gliding vacation in Tennessee. After 24 hours of straight driving we arrived around the dinner hour in the Sequatchie Valley, home of the Tennessee Tree Toppers. The conditions were good to make a small investigative flight. The wind was very light but even a small sled run was heaven after such a long voyage by car. It was not history making but it was a much needed flight. From that point on, weather conditions deteriorated for the remainder of the week. Canadian pilots are known as great lovers and great beer drinkers, but our wives were home and even Canadians can only drink so much Budweiser. We had an open invitation to stay with Maggie and Jim (Sky Dog) Palmieri and fly one of their sites in Virginia. We decided to return to Quebec but not before stopping off in Virginia since it was along the way. We were a bit heart broken not to fly the Sequatchie Valley as much as we wanted to or as much as we had in our dreams when we left Thetford Mines, Quebec.

After 7 hours of roads and a good night of sleep we all woke with hopes of a full day of flying. The sun filled the sky, and after a week of rain it felt good. Also, I knew that the heat from the sun would certainly make for a good day for flying. We followed Jim and Maggie to Tobacco Row Mountain, a site where I had a great flight two years earlier. Tobacco Row Mountain is a massive mountain with a launch ramp 1800 feet AGL and a landing area very, very far away... very far in front of us. I am still astonished to see this beautiful and even a little wild environment, far from any the great urban centre. After arriving at this big mountain, I saw that conditions were good and we made the decision to fly. Although my legs were tired, I began to unload my Sensor from the car. Everyone was silent as the pilots began to assemble their wings. While assembling my hang glider, I listened and concentrated on the thermals as they cycled through in fluid sheets across the trees above me.

We watched for about an hour as the conditions built with the day. The wind was directly out of the Southeast, light but straight in at launch. There were thermals cycling through but the sky was without many clouds. Danny Fortin was the first to leave the mountain. The conditions did not support ridge lift and Danny moved away from the mountain in search of thermals. He worked the air with intensity, but too quickly he had to head in to land. He communicated with us by radio and reported that the conditions were very rough and difficult and that it was necessary to keep both hands tightly gripped to the control bar. We were a little disappointed at that report from our fellow club-member.

François Gilbert launched next and headed out toward the landing field, working a few bubbles, but ended up with only a 20-minute flight. His flight put pressure on me to be the one to get above the mountain! With the launch at 1800 feet I was beginning to think that it was possible to climb at least up to 2,400 feet... 600 feet above the mountain. Serge Prévost launched next, and like Danny he had to work very hard before landing. François Dussault launched aggressively, he could taste the flight before it happened... he wanted up! Immediately, he turned and climbed up to the level of the launch. The conditions were beginning to get better as the day progressed. I moved immediately towards my wing, hoping to get into the air quickly and fly with my buddy. I would be able to test my new, all yellow, harness, a *WP Race*. It makes me stand out in my Sensor, and the combination is perfect. I moved toward the ramp and I asked where François was, but the Sky Dog told me that he was making his final approach into the landing field.

I am undecided. The conditions seem to me to be good! I concentrate once again and I listen for the wind and the thermal cycles but it is my heart, which resounds in my helmet. Now there is no decision to make other than to visualize a good time to take off. On launch, my wing feels like it weighs 200 pounds, and I have difficulty stabilizing it. I look to the sky for the locals flying (soaring birds) and I bid the mountain a fond *adieu* and launch with energy as if I were to propel myself 300 feet above the mountain. I zipper up my new *WP Race* and have the energy as if I had just squeezed a case of Gatorade to lemon. I am full energy. I see a bird soaring to my left and pull on the VG all the way. It is now time to get going. The vario tells me that I am in a tight thermal and I screw the thermal upwards very, very tightly towards my left. I have no time to look at the landscape. On the points of my feet, I take myself up to 300 feet over the top of the mountain and I head over to Jim and Maggie and Marco Levasseur. At once I yell, "Bye-bye," as I am hit with another bubble that lifts my left wing.

I respond instantaneously as I core this thermal with an energy that surprises me. My vario awakens; it cries, it howls. I again hear the beats of my heart, which gives me the rate and rhythm I want to roll up this tiny thermal. I nevertheless continue to work even though my butt is tightly puckered! My eyes are fixed on the tip of my wing. I see the landscape whirl around me. After a few minutes, my vario is quiet again. I decide to take a breather, a little rest, because it seems to me that the 10 minutes I spent coring this thermal passed like a minute, but I am tired. I leave the thermal to rest my arms a little. I look at my altimeter. It indicates 4,400 feet, and that to me is a climb in record time. In a few moments I find myself at cloudbase, which looks more like a wet Kleenex. I am just within a few feet of the top of it. WOW! I release and observe the landscape, so filled with beauty. Although my vario screamed in agony throughout the ascent, it is quiet now, and I enjoy it. I fly for one hour before I am back down at a level with launch.

The air is filled with energy, but I decide to go to see my buddies who are stuck on the ground. Beers, music... beers... open hang gliders, more beers. I knew how they felt about my magical flight after they yelled up to me, " Fuck You, Max," when I was still 2000 feet above the landing area. I can hear them, and I smile. I decide to make a test to see if my new harness... now known as the *Banana Flambe*, will open. Ayollllle!!! I am not able to move my hands from the basetube! Aouch, where is the master key? The thermals were really strong today.

Where did I get all my energy for this flight? Ha yes, it is true; it is because of my chums who were stuck on the ground. Yes my friends were all grounders so the yelling to me was necessary for them to save face, for we are the *Sensor Team!* I continue to exercise my arms throughout the descent. I take advantage of the sink even though the approach to the landing field is peppered with lift. My feet are tightened like a ballerina's.

My vario begins squawking again. Do I follow the cloud and the lift? If I do, I don't think I would have the strength to do it all over again. The temptation is great, but I make the decision to keep the peace with my chums. I decide to land as quickly as possible. I fly over the landing area and relax my arms and release the tension in my legs. François indicates the direction of the wind and I prepare my approach and landing. I start to open my harness at 500 feet and finish at 200 feet. The muscles of my arms are filled with fatigue and pain and they make me suffer all the way down.

All my buddies come to see me; their faces filled with smiles. I knew they were my close friends because they did not shout, "Congratulations Marc, great landing!" But rather, "WACK!" We laughed. One of the guys took my harness, the other my wing, another offered me a good cold bottle of beer and we turned towards the other wings, which were still open. There was music in the landing area and it had the feel of a festival. This was a beautiful intense day, just as I like them!

I write this history a few days after the flight and I still have the muscle soreness. It was my first thermal flight of the year and a most memorable flight. It is the second time that I have flown this Virginia site, *Tobacco Row* , and I make a point of thanking my friends Jim and Maggie Palmieri for their great hospitality and their great generosities. I have been flying hang gliders for over 20 years and it is not my highest flight, nor is it my longest flight but I will remember it as one of my most beautiful flights.

Flying With Sandhill Cranes

Wayne Kerr

I can't remember a time where I wasn't thinking about flight, about flying or about things that had the ability to fly. As a kid, I used to dream about gliding and spent hundreds of hours drawing airplanes and gliders. My parents had a good friend named Phil Eastman who was a private pilot with an interest in motorless flight. The first time I ever handled an airplane's controls was with Phil. It set me on a path that I don't think any influence could have knocked me away from.

My first mentor was a glider pilot named Calvin Devries. He helped me learn to fly sailplanes about 10 or 11 years ago. He was obsessive about clean flying and helped to instill in me a strong respect for fundamental aerodynamics. It is amazing how many students don't understand very basic principles about the movement of air over and around the surfaces of their wings. Calvin also showed me how to fly a glider with the air instead of just through the air, staying involved in an ongoing exchange of energy throughout the climb and glide. I mean to say that he taught a few of us to fly with an awareness of relatively minor variations in vertical speed in different areas of a thermal, and to use these differences in lift strength to maximize climb. Optimized climbs are not perfect circles at steady angles of bank and airspeeds. Likewise, optimized inter-thermal glides will vary from side to side of the most direct course as the pilot searches for and "bumps" scraps of lift. In nature, a pilot will never see migrating redtails, climbing cranes, or foraging vultures locked into autopilot mode while coring a thermal. They are always alert and adapting to micro-changes in conditions. Learning to fly like the birds has helped me over the years to see and feel subtle changes in the air. Often, being a pilot gave me the key to understand the detailed intricacies of what was taking place with birds in flight.

My good friend Carl Hiebert broke his back in a hang gliding accident a decade and a half ago, permanently losing the use of his legs. He doe not blame anyone for what happened to him. The accident never stopped his love of flying or anything else about life. Flying is the way he expresses what he sees as beautiful to other people. It is a way for Carl to share his unique perspective about life. I've learned a tremendous amount about safety from Carl and have really appreciated his quiet counsel when I have been tempted to do stupid things in the air, especially when a project deadline is looming. He helps me say NO when I need to. He is so much fun to fly with that it helps me remember that even if the work I am doing isn't necessarily fun, the reward at the end of it is. There must be time to just get back up in the air and just play in the air with family or good friends. Many people I have worked with seem to forget this.

The first time I ever flew away from the home field was very memorable. Deliberately turning my nose away from the wide grass runway and gliding out of range was nerve wracking but incredibly rewarding. The sure knowledge that I was at least one thermal away from home, and then two, then three, etc., somehow boosted my sprits and made flying very exciting. Everyone should push off and fly cross-country, even if they just get a few miles away.

In 1995 I was working on a project to see if we could teach Sandhill cranes to fly with our trike. The Sandhill cranes were a research surrogate for Whooping cranes, a species just too rare to risk conducting research on at that time, especially with an untried method. Sandhill cranes are essentially soaring birds and have a very light wing loading. They are just lovely to look at. I used a tiny single-seat trike that weighed nothing compared to our modern two-seat trikes. It had a huge 240 square-foot wing and it felt like I could thermal it on just a bee burp! After several weeks of experimentation, the birds were flying with us just fine and we seemed to be accepted by them as a member of the flock. We knew they loved to play in lift, and my thermalling skills had been getting a bit of a welcome workout, which was of benefit to me. We decided to fly them 50 km out and return and test their cross-country skills both under power and in gliding mode.

We departed early and flew above the convective layer on the outward leg. As we descended through the inversion at the stopover, we could tell the day was really going to cook. We waited a few hours for the day to develop and then launched for the return trip home. We set the throttle for a constant 200 fpm sink rate, thermalled for altitude gain and glided our way back home. The birds seemed to love it and I was as thrilled as could be. I remember working lift down low, maybe at 750 feet. I was looking down my wingtip as we circled around and around. One of these incredibly beautiful birds was climbing with me, keeping perfect station off my wingtip. It was a view that almost nobody ever gets and I felt almost drunk with exhilaration. As it turned out, the day was over-developing to a point where I felt marginally unsafe, and we made a precautionary landing at about 40 km. It was the most exciting XC flight of my life.

There was a flight that occurred in Northern Ontario in 1998 that was pure magic. We had been struggling for months under trying conditions, trying to see whether we could teach trumpeter swans to fly with us well enough to induce a migration, yet still preserve their "wildness" so that they could be safely released. We were badly under-funded, tired and stressed out. We had equipment failures and I was nursing a painful injury. At the end of a perfect high-pressure day on the Canadian Thanksgiving weekend, it all came together. We were able to convince all five cygnets in an experimental group to take off and fly with the trike out of our protected bay and into the main body of the lake. We climbed several hundred feet. I had an incredible view of the rugged ridges and lakes all set off by the autumn foliage at peak color change and compounded with an incredible northern sunset over a black, glassy lake. After about ten minutes, the flight broke up as we lost one after another cygnet due to exhaustion. I was soon reduced to only one bird. This bird was strong but we were far from our home base, and with the sun already below the horizon. As she sank towards the water I could tell from her wing beats that she was ready to land, which frightened me. She was so low that tiny splashes marked each stroke.

I flew as low as I dared and slowly eased the bar out until the wing was buffeting, creating a big, well-organized vortex to try to encourage her. In the videotape, it was clear when the vortex reached her, as you could see it spreading across the water. Her wing-beats picked up to the point where she stopped splashing. I added just enough power to hold the attitude and we cruised back home that way, with her hitching a ride on my wingtip vortex. This was a magnificent feeling.

The
Wandering
Dog

Ready To Hit The Air With My GhostBuster

Mark Poustinchian

There I was, on what seemed to be the final glide at about 1500' agl, 161 miles away from Quest Air and thinking that I would miss breaking Florida's state record again. Damn, I needed seven more miles! Despite the late afternoon magic air, it seemed unlikely to happen. It was 5:30 pm, the sky was blue, and I needed one more thermal. I desperately looked around for that last thermal trigger or any sign of a thermal. All of sudden there it was, half a mile away...

On Tuesday, April 11th, we started to get ready early. I had a feeling that it was going to be a good day. Two days before I made a big mistake on the best day that I have seen in Florida. I am still kicking myself for making such a huge mistake, which had put me on the ground at 95 miles early in the day. That day it was so good that I felt I was unsinkable. I was staying high, perfect clouds, and great thermals. I tried to go west to avoid the obstacles to the north. Conditions were so good that I was planning where I needed to be three hours ahead of time. I was planning to fly north to Georgia over friendly fields late in the afternoon for my first 200-miler. Before me was a big blue hole that I felt I could cross. My GPS was showing 45 mph groundspeed and I was over 6500' agl. It seemed there could not be a blue hole big enough to put me down. That's what a good day can do to a soaring pilot; it sets the conditions for big mistakes and bad decisions.

I flew into the blue hole and was doing great until I lost a few thousand feet. All of a sudden the cloud street on the other side looked much further away. The wind was changing. The lower I got, the slower the glider's speed. My ground speed was dropping rapidly; the GPS was showing 20 mph instead of 40+. I knew I had made a big mistake; I should have continued north instead of jumping the blue hole on the west side to get to another cloud street. I landed into a 10 mph west wind at 95 miles and knew that I messed up big time.

On the same day, Bo Hagewood, one of the local X-C pilots at Quest Air flew 155 miles on his Fusion for his first Georgia landing and a personal best. Campbell Bowen flew his GhostBuster 146 miles from Quest Air for his personal best. He landed just five miles shy of the Georgia border, in the last possible field in the middle of nowhere. From the air he could see Georgia, however he didn't think much of the prospect of a tree landing. Davis Straub flew 154 miles from Wallaby on an Exxtacy for his longest flight in Florida. Steve Kroop from Flytec flew his GhostBuster 116 miles from Quest Air. Armen from Canada flew 114 miles from Quest Air on his Fusion for his first 100-miler in Florida. All of them were reaching top altitudes of 7,500-8,000' or more.

April 9th had been a spectacular day and I had blown it. I was determined to do my best on April 11th. Conditions were not nearly as good, but small cumies started to pop early. I was ready to go by 10:30 am. You should have seen Bo running for his harness as soon as he saw me putting my glider on the tow cart. For the first time I was going to be in the air before he was.

A $3000 prize was on the line for the first 200-miler on a GhostBuster or an Exxtacy from Quest Air. Everyone was going for it, or at least for a new record, every chance they got. There are some hard-core X-C pilots at Quest Air and we were also having an informal contest to see who would have the most 100-plus- and 150-plus-milers at the end of the year. On the eleventh, I was in the lead with five and three for the year. But, the pressure was on every flyable day; it's a tough job, but some one has to do it.

Winsor, the good-looking tug pilot at Quest Air, towed me up at 10:45 am, and I was on my way. As I was drifting away, I saw Bo in the air behind a tug. Damn, he sure didn't waste any time. I had no idea that I wouldn't be landing for another eight hours. Florida is a land of opportunity for pilots who want long flights and great thermals, and lots of mosquito bites.

The first 50 miles was a piece of pie. I spotted a big fire northwest of Ocala, and decided to go for it and get really high. I was a few miles away, but was not expecting the massive sink that was waiting for me before I reached the fire. Before I knew it I was too low over places where I should not be landing. Steve Kropp from Flytec once told me, "When you are flying around Ocala, try to stay away from fields that have really fancy fences. Most likely they have one of those million dollar horses in them." All I could see were fancy wooden fences, some of them painted white, surrounding fields that looked like golf courses. Very fancy indeed. I had been so sure that I would climb out when I reached the fire that I hadn't been paying attention to the surrounding area.

Damn, I got so low so fast that I did not know what to do. I was too low to glide out of there, and too afraid to land. My luck, one of those horses would break or twist an ankle, and I would end up with a million dollar lawsuit on my hands. The ground was in shadow below me and it had been in the shade for a long time. The air felt very smooth and that horrible sinky feeling was all over the place. I unzipped the harness and picked a field that seemed empty of horses. My watch was showing 12:30 pm; I could not believe that I was at 400' and getting ready to land. I felt I had blown it again. Suddenly two horses emerged from under the trees. They had spotted me and were spooked, running across the field like crazy. I got very religious then and had the biggest incentive to climb out of there.

My prayers were answered. Two birds flew off the trees below me and started to turn in a very light thermal. Another bird joined them and all of sudden I had three birds below me, climbing slowly. A few seconds later I hit the bubbles; it was a very light thermal. The shadow was drifting away below me and I knew that if I could just hang on in light lift for five or ten minutes, I might have a chance to climb out. I gained only 500 feet in that thermal before it fell apart. I could see another large field a couple miles to the northwest, which had some cows in it, and no fancy-looking fences. It was a far better choice for landing, and I was more than happy to go for it.

I hit sink immediately and had to go back. I did not have the glide to the next field. Meantime the running horses had triggered a good thermal, and I was able to get back on track. After that I was very conservative and did my best not to get so low again.

I believe that if one can stay in the air until 2:30 pm, there is a good chance to be able to fly until very late in the afternoon. I was a very happy camper when I was high and it was after 2:30. I had a chance to view the scenery, and what a nice view it was. The clouds were very small and very far in between, however the air was getting very nice and the big sink was gone. There were many horse fields, and so many lakes. Golf courses and small airports are all over the place. Small residential areas are very nicely sculpted among the trees. Oh yes, life for the rich and famous is definitely here.

Arkansas, where I come from, has many chicken houses and the thermals usually bring the smell of the chickens with them, which we gladly sniff for the best cores. We may see a golf course once in a great while after many miles of cross country flying, but nothing like Florida. Arkansas landing fields have chiggers that get on your feet and start digging into your skin. Florida landing fields have mosquitoes that are ready to gladly eat you alive. You feel the burning pain right away when mosquitoes bite. However, the itching pain related to chiggers has a later effect, like when you take your socks off to go to sleep. I have been known to scratch my feet for hours before finally falling asleep; damn chiggers. But you know what? I sure miss Arkansas, and my old flying buddies. I'll plan to go back for a visit at the end of summer to see and fly with the pilots who taught me to fly. They shared all their tricks with me.

I was closing in on 100 miles. My radio was not working due to a bad connection. I could hear all my flying buddies from Quest Air not far behind and could hear Samantha asking them if they have heard from me.

"No we haven't Samantha, he could be down on the ground close to Quest Air" they replied.

"Well, I'm close to Gainesville [about 90 miles from Quest Air], should I continue driving north or go back?"

"I don't know what to tell you, it's your call." Oh no, this could not be happening; I was only 10 miles away from her at 5000' agl. Shortly after that I heard Samantha, "I think I'll go shopping in Gainesville". All right, that's my girl! I'd rather she go spend some money rather than driving back. I replaced the battery in the radio, but still could not transmit. I wiggled the connection wires and found the problem. I was back on the radio again.

To everyone's surprise I was still in the air—and ahead of them! Three hard-core X-C pilots from Quest Air were not too far behind. Bo was the closest. We were all flying GhostBusters and going for the prize money. Bo was sure having a good time on his and making good ground. Campbell Bowen started after everyone, but that didn't stop him from trying to catch up and pass everyone. He does this often, and does it quite well. They were all putting the pressure on me. Steve Kroop was close to Campbell. Way to go guys, they were doing great. All four of us had passed the 100-mile point.

I could see Highway 10 on the horizon. Perfect planning! Highway 75 was far to the right and there were fields to the northwest and north as far as one could see. The clouds were gone, however I could see the haze domes forming and dissipating very quickly. I flew over Highway 10 at 4000' agl and 150 miles from Quest Air. I needed only 18 more miles for the state record. The wind was becoming southerly with a slight west component. Wind velocity was also diminishing and the thermal's drift slowing. Decisions, decisions! Do I stay with the light thermals, killing a lot of time for a couple hundred feet and a couple more miles, or do I go on glide looking for a better one? The choice would be crucial. I opted for the glide in search of a better thermal.

I was flying over Highway 75, which runs to the northwest, and decided to continue north to go with the little tail wind that I had. I could see the town of Jennings to my right and the field just to the north of town where I had landed a few weeks previously when I had my personal best flight of 163 miles. During that flight I crossed the Georgia border, but flew back because of a fence line at the middle of the field. I landed in Florida ¼ mile short of the border. Everybody gave me a hard time, suggesting that I should have crashed into the fence, if necessary, to log the interstate flight.

I was going to cross the Georgia border again, and this time I would not return. Reality check! I was down to 1500' at 161 miles. This was not good, I knew I could land in Georgia, but I needed seven more miles to break Florida's hang gliding distance record. The next possible fields looked very far away, with lots of trees in between. I needed one more thermal for the state record. And there it was, waiting for me. Joy joy! What a feeling! I radioed that a new state record would be set by *at least* one of us, pulled in the base bar, and went for it! Over the middle of the trees; no going back now.

Two birds were climbing ½ mile away, over the trees. I reached them at the same altitude and yelled, "Thank you, I love you!" I have a Double Yellow Amazon Parrot as a pet and have a very close relationship with birds. I think they all know how much I love birds and are always there to give the old man a break. They have rescued me and shown me the way when I needed them the most. The thermal weak, less than 100 fpm climb. But I gladly worked that thermal for 25 minutes to gain 1800'. I was 3300' agl and could not feel any better.

I had covered 165 miles and was on the brink of a new record. Sure of myself now, I announced that I would be breaking the state record in a few minutes and going on to try for 200 miles. I heard the cheers on the radio, especially Samantha. She was looking forward to some of the $3000 prize money, which I promised her; she is a great driver and full of encouragement.

I went on glide, passed 168 miles, and screamed as loud as I could in celebration. Suddenly, I felt a disturbance in the air. Could there be a big one nearby? It sure felt like it. I was at 2100' agl and full of anticipation. The glider was talking to me, and I was listening very carefully. I had heard this message before. The wind started to roar in my ears and I could feel the glider speeding up. Boom! I hit the edge of a strong thermal at 5:40 pm. It took me to 5578' msl.

It was getting close to 6 pm and I was at 5000',closing in on 170 miles and thinking maybe I could make 200 miles. The tail wind was almost nonexistent. I needed just a couple more thermals. Unfortunately there was only one more thermal on my flight path. I worked it for about 1700' gain, then nothing. I glided until I was down to 200' and turned to set up a landing over some huge fields northwest of Lakeland, Georgia. I landed at 192 miles after 8 hours, 1 minute and 10 seconds of flying. This was a new personal best X-C for me, and the longest time that I had stayed in the air.

How do I know all the details? My Ball GC shows me everything I need to know when I download the recorded flight to my computer. I love technology, and these instruments are great. My Garmin eMap showed me all the highways all the way to the end. I have 50 counties loaded on it, including all the counties in southern Georgia and had a detailed map during the entire flight. I told Samantha I'd be landing 2 or 3 miles northwest of Lakeland, and she was not far behind. We have a laptop set up with an old Garmin 45 and she uses the Delorme Street Atlas software. I called Samantha when I landed to give her my exact GPS coordinates. She drove down the dirt road and got to me before I even had a chance to pack the glider. To top it off she had cold water; I finished all my water four hours into the flight and was very thirsty.

Driving back, we wondered how the others had done and whether anyone had made 200 miles. We stopped in Gainesville for dinner, and as we turned in to the restaurant we saw Campbell's truck, the retrieve vehicle for the other three. We surprised everyone when we walked in. The atmosphere was full of joy and celebration. I had the flight of the day; not only had I broken the Florida distance record, but the East Coast distance record as well.

All four of us had flown our personal bests on our GhostBusters. Campbell Bowen did a great job of passing the other two and landing in

Georgia for the first time, a 162 miles flight. Bo Hagewood landed at 156 miles for his personal best, just shy of the border. Steve Kroop flew 138 miles for his best flight ever. This had been a very special day for all of us.

I want to thank Flight Design for a wonderful glider. My GhostBuster has made my life full of joy and has rewarded me with many miles of great X-C flying. I want to thank Quest Air and the crew for the wonderful job that they are doing, especially Winsor, my tow pilot. Samantha, thank you so much for all your efforts and miles and miles of driving and giving me the much-needed encouragement. You have been a big part of all my long X-C flights.

Double Jeopardy

Mark Grubbs

A few years ago, during one of my personal hang-gliding milestones, I had the opportunity to combine and experience two dangerous activities in one day. I believe I showed good, mature judgment in both cases.

My first 100-mile cross-country flight (a milestone in any hang-glider pilot's career) was in the Owens Valley, a 100 mile long corridor of high-desert located about 150 miles northeast of Los Angeles. This 20 mile-wide valley is bordered on the west by the Sierra Nevada and on the east by the equally tall White and Inyo Mountain Ranges. Flying in this region is "extreme" hang-gliding; turbulent, gut wrenching thermal lift that allow climbs to 18,000 feet and beyond. Temperatures range from 100-plus degrees near the desert floor, to sub-zero conditions at high-altitudes. Pilots who choose to experience hang-gliding at its most demanding equip themselves against the dangers of airframe structural failure, dehydration, hypoxia, and hypothermia.

The usual route for these adventures involves launching from Walt's Point, at 9,000 feet in the Sierras and just south of Mt. Whitney. While many pilots attempt to fly beyond 100 miles, an obvious mileage marker is well known to pilots worldwide, for it is precisely 100 air-miles from launch, and provides an enormous dirt airstrip; making late afternoon landings in gnarly desert conditions much more forgiving.

The airstrip and landmark are collectively known as "Janie's Ranch", the first in a series of well-used brothels that are strung along Highway 6 as it passes through the California-Nevada border. Years ago, Janie's was so popular with patron's from the LA region that they built the dirt runway to accommodate their more wealthy and adventurous customers. These days, business is slow due to the panic over AIDS, but Janie has always had a friendly policy towards hang-glider pilots. It's the only safe place to land near the 100 mile mark, and pilots are encouraged to visit the brothel, even if they just need to use the pay-phone inside, or avail themselves to the full-service bar to celebrate a good day of flying. Janie's other comforts are always an option.

My first journey to Janie's took me a little over four hours, considered pretty fast in those days. Conditions where very turbulent and demanding, even for the Owens Valley. The strong tailwind and fast climb rates allowed me to race well ahead of my chase vehicle, even though they were following me up Highway 395 at 65 mph. I got so far ahead of them that we completely lost radio communication. The weather conditions were radical, but damn it, I was going to fly a hundred miles!

As I neared the end of the valley, I noticed a lot of thunderstorms, squall lines and extremely dangerous weather to the north. If I continued over Montgomery Pass and kept going northeast (the usual route for 150 to 200 mile attempts) I would be putting myself in a life-threatening situation. If I survived, I would be forced to land where there were no telephones. The only certain, reasonably safe landing site was at Janie's.

I flew away from Boundary Peak at the end of the White Mountains and arrived over my intended LZ at 11,000 feet; 5,000 feet above the desert floor. I spent the next half-hour doing wingovers and loops in the buoyant air; partially as victory maneuvers to celebrate my first 100-miler, and partially in an effort to loose altitude and just plain *get down* before the radical weather moved in.

Eventually, I got low enough to where there was more wind than lift, set up an approach, zoomed through the wind gradient and flared to a perfect landing on Janie's runway.

I de-rigged my glider at the edge of the runway, then carried it over to the entrance. I realized that it would be several hours before my flying buddies would be able to get there, and that I could spend that time celebrating my personal-best at Janie's bar. Almost as quickly came the reality-check. There might be hidden dangers; the place could be so well used that the inside could be full of airborne HIV.

OK, that was a little *too* paranoid. I decided that I'd just go inside, assess the environment, and make my decision based on observations.

The inside was air-conditioned and empty, except for an older woman who I naturally assumed to be *the* Janie. She greeted me as soon as I entered. I briefly explained my situation, and she happily offered the use of her phone. When I was done with the call, secure in the knowledge that I would be picked up in a few hours, I walked over to the bar and ordered a beer. My hostess, as she was taking my money, asked me if I would like to celebrate my 100-miler and "take a look at some of the girls".

I turned around. There were three "employees" dressed, or undressed, in lingerie, standing in a line a few feet away. They were all smiles.

But none of them had a full set of teeth.

They all looked well-used. Being alone in a dark room with one of them, and paying for it, didn't seem like a smart thing to do. I made some polite excuse about being broke, and explained that I'd just wait for my ride outside.

I took my beer and went back outside to my equipment. Under the hot desert sun, I made a pillow out of my harness bag, sat down in the dirt, leaned back, and opened the can of beer...tilted it sideways...and poured it over my head.

It seemed a safer way to celebrate.

Ants in the Pants

David Giles

Early in the workweek, Dean Funk and I started planning a three-day-weekend trip to Lookout Mountain, Georgia, hoping for some big XC mileage. Friday morning we woke up in the LZ to a decent sounding forecast. To make a long story short, Friday was good for some nice ridge soaring, but we never got high enough to go anywhere. We both had fun flights, but I landed in stinking hot, mid-day, no-wind conditions, and took out some aluminum with a badly timed flare. Later in the afternoon, the ridge really turned on and many pilots got all the ridge soaring they could stand. I went back up and flew again, and Gary Engelhart and I made an enjoyable run to the point and back.

Saturday dawned with an even better forecast than Friday. I went up top early to set up before the heat and crowds became oppressive. Dean decided to tow up out of the LZ, where his glider was still set up from the day before. Judy Hildebrand and Buddy Cutts were also set up in the LZ, ready to tow up and go XC with us. Greg Westbury showed up on top, and we were ready to go. While waiting for good conditions, we talked about possible routes, flying strategies, and how cool it would be to see the skyscrapers of Atlanta from the air. Greg had brought along an employee of his, Jason, to be our driver. Jason turned out to be a great driver. He was good with the radio (not too much talking), knew his way around Georgia, and was an all-around nice guy.

Dean towed up first to check things out. He wasn't exactly specking out like we had hoped; but Greg and I were hot and tired of waiting, so we went ahead and launched. Buddy towed up and joined us, and the four of us tried to get up to the few clouds that were beginning to form. A street was building nicely across the valley, coming straight at launch. We worked the ridge, and we worked the valley, but for about 45 minutes we struggled to get high. Judy was wisely hanging out in the LZ, conserving energy, waiting to see if it would really turn on, and Buddy had gone out to land and try a different glider.

After an hour, Dean, Greg, and I finally started getting better and higher climbs. Eventually we got to 3,500' over the plateau, under a building cloud. Dean was higher and further over the back than Greg and I, but when he said he was going for it, Greg and I followed. Dean must have been in a really sweet spot as he continued to climb higher while Greg and I struggled just to stay even. As we cleared the backside of the plateau, we were joined by another glider. I didn't immediately recognize the pilot, but I was pretty sure it was a Pulse. It turned out to be fellow Alabamian, Mark Ogle. He did an awesome job of helping Greg and me find the good stuff. Greg, Mark, and I finally climbed to Dean's level, 6,000' MSL. Mark flew beautifully, but his radio gave out, and he landed intentionally to make retrieval more convenient. Greg and I caught up with Dean, and for the next 30 miles, we had classic, street-running XC conditions. Greg and I had an awe-inspiring, but nerve-wracking encounter with a cloud that took us to nearly 8,200' MSL. Dean got low at one point, but made a valiant save and joined us back near cloudbase. We also heard on the radio, that Buddy and Judy were in the air and coming over the back behind us.

Dean, Greg, and I each had our moments as leader of the pack, but for the most part we flew as a team. At 50 miles, we began to see the cooling towers of a nuclear plant in the distance, our cloud street running right over them. But what was beyond worried us. This was new territory for all of us, and as we approached the cooling towers, we saw the massive expanse of forest just a few miles ahead. Gary Englehart (local XC record holder—157 miles) came on the radio. He was at home listening in on our radio chatter and wanted to give us moral support. Since we were coming up on what looked like a possible dead end, he pulled out some maps and told us what our best options would be. What could be better than this: 50 miles downwind on a great day with a couple of buddies flying nearby and a seasoned pro on the ground, cheering us on and helping out with navigation?

We crossed over the cooling towers; the forest was trying to intimidate us into landing. The cloud street we had been following had withered somewhat and didn't look too promising. Greg, being the wiser, more mature pilot, decided to land here where there were plenty of safe fields, rather than venture into no-man's land. I, being the aggressive, more stubborn type, was unwilling to give up just yet. I told Greg I was going on, and he said, "Good luck, you're going to need it!"

I decided to venture a little ways over the forest, making sure I had the glide necessary to back out. I had good altitude at 7,000' MSL, and could now see a few landable fields sprinkled around the forest. The clouds were beginning to re-form and the street was coming back together. I was gliding downwind at best glide with a groundspeed of over 50 miles an hour, and had gained several hundred feet in straight-ahead flight. I made a smart-ass comment on the radio about one of us regretting our decision, and that seemed to put the ants in Greg's pants. I looked back to see Dean and Greg flying at me like angry hornets. Glad to see I wouldn't be alone, I slowed and climbed in the widespread lift. We got back together and enjoyed more great conditions for the next 15 miles.

With the forest nothing but a bad memory, we were cruising along when Greg said, "Hey David, look over to the east." I'm not sure how I had missed it, but there, plain as day, was the skyline of Atlanta. We were ten times higher than the skyscrapers, so they didn't look as big as I expected, but they were an impressive sight! What impressed me more, was the big clearing just to the south of Atlanta—Hartsfield International Airport.

I looked up and straight overhead was a massive jet on its downwind leg into Hartsfield. A few seconds later another one followed right behind. They were several thousand feet above us, but that was too close for comfort. We were outside the TCA, but still it made us nervous. We poured on the speed to get out of the traffic lane. The cloud street was getting weaker, but what was left of it was heading straight into Hartsfield airspace. We had to abandon the street and head due south. The lift was getting spottier and the sink more abundant. We had spread out some, Greg to the west, Dean to the east, and me in the middle. Dean pointed our attention to some water towers he said were three miles from his house. He had accomplished a long-time dream of flying home (and beyond) from Lookout. Greg said he was struggling and might have to land, but a few minutes later he was climbing back out. Next I was struggling and trying to figure out where Greg had found the lift.

We heard Judy on the radio talking to our driver with retrieval instructions. She had decided not to go over the forest alone, and landed after 65 mile. Gary was also on the radio, trying to locate us. We were almost out of radio range, and we later joked that Gary seemed a little over-anxious about our progress. We envisioned him at home, monitoring our progress, watching the clock, and calculating whether his record would be safe. (Unfortunately, it was.) I was trying to ask Greg where he had found his thermal, but with all the radio chatter, I couldn't hear him. I finally saw the field he was climbing over; he had already specked out. I came to the field at 1,500' AGL and start searching. I was 82 miles out, and didn't want to land, remembering how incredibly hot it was near the earth. I hit several teaser bumps, the kind where you lose more than you gain trying, before I hit the real thing. WHAM! It was small but powerful, and I kept a close eye on my climb versus drift, since the field below was my only landing choice for a couple of miles. As I topped 6,500' MSL I saw Greg ahead in the distance. Dean was below us, struggling at 1,800', but seemed to be getting back up.

With that altitude, and the extra miles I figured the 100-mile mark was a sure thing. But there's no such thing as a sure thing, and I began to realize this as I sank again towards the last good landing field before a large stand of trees. I reached the field with 3,000'. I could see one more possible landing field a mile downwind, but I couldn't tell much about it from that distance. I was over a massive farm with great landing areas. For reasons I won't go into here, I was highly motivated to have a good landing in the glider I was flying. I ran a search pattern hoping to find something, but found nothing. Dean radioed that he had just landed in winds gusting over 20 mph, and to be careful. I like high-wind landings, and other than the weird, helicopter-like descent, it was a good one. It was 5:00 p.m. eastern time, and Greg had somehow avoided the sink cycle that grounded Dean and I, and said he was still doing well. I knew that if conditions held, he might have another hour of good flying. My GPS indicated 96.1 miles from Lookout Mountain. Dean, further to the east, had stretched his glide to 97.1 miles. The farmer in the field where I had landed got off his tractor and came to check on me. He was as friendly as you could ask for, and even offered to drive me back to I-20 for easy retrieval. Once I was picked up, we went to get Dean, and then on to Newnan, Georgia to find Greg. He flew 116 miles and landed at an airstrip. He said that the lift was still good, and another cloud street was in reach, but he was worried about getting into the Airspace of Warner-Robbins Air Force Base. Besides, he had clearly spanked Dean and I, and had the bragging rights. He chose the easy landing and retrieval option, which we appreciated. Along with Judy, who had been picked up earlier, we all wearily piled into Greg's van. A three-hour drive back to Lookout gave us plenty of time to high-five each other and share our flights in minute detail.

When we picked up Greg at the airstrip where he had landed, he was seen *adjusting* himself quite vigorously. On the return drive, he seemed to squirm a little more than usual. When we stopped for dinner at the Cracker Barrel, he excused himself from the table and was gone for some time. Back at the table, he finally had an explanation for his strange social behavior (I mean above and beyond his typically strange social behavior). He had been carrying a passenger for some time; a small black ant had been trapped in his shorts and bit him every once in awhile just to remind him that it was there. Dean and I decided he deserved it for out-flying us. It was a hilarious end to an awesome day!

I've had lots of XC experiences, but this was the first time I'd gone over the back at Lookout, and it was truly awesome! This flight was 6 miles short of my personal best, but it will probably take first place on my favorite flights list. The highlights: fantastic conditions, close team-like flying with two good friends, the skyline of Atlanta, no radio or equipment failures, great retrieval crew, safe flights. Dean and Greg doubled their previous personal bests, and who knows, if Greg hadn't had to stop for restricted airspace, Gary's record might have been in danger after all!

Venezuela

Daniel Gravage

February 19, 1985

The *General* was relaying the weather data he had just received from the Air Base to interested flyers, and those who could understand Spanish, at the daily pilots' meeting. We were on the Loma Lisa launch site overlooking the town of La Victoria. Near the end of his talk he also spoke in English, making sure that everyone gathered closer and listened as he repeated his message that it is forbidden to fly in the area around the Air Base. It was well marked with a thick red line on our maps. No excuses, no exceptions.

Apparently the week before the competition began a local pilot had flown his glider into the area and was attempting a low save, directly off the end of the main runway. Meanwhile, two *F-14* fighter jets sat impatiently on the deck, burning valuable fuel, while waiting for the hapless glider jockey to clear the take-off zone. It would be interesting to have heard the conversation between the jet pilots.

The incident led to the closing of the area. Not that any sane pilot would want to drift in there anyway. Jet wash is nasty stuff I've been told.

Conditions on launch were consistent with previous days, a nice breeze straight up the hill with regular thermals busting through, and nice puffy cumuli forming along the course line to the west. This will be our fourth flight, and the second day of competition. There had been two practice days to allow pilots to get familiar with the sky and topography, and the retrieval process.

My first flight was the shortest of all my flights in Venezuela, and the retrieve took longer than any other. I was on a dead end road that the Pepsi retrieval truck failed to check, just past the village of Zuata. Being lost in a foreign country with limited language skills is a challenge, but at least the locals were curious enough to figure out where I needed to get and led me back to the hotel on a bus.

I commandeered a car and driver from the hotel and went back to get my glider, only to get lost on the way. When we finally reached the area where I had left my glider, it was gone. We drove up and down the village hoping that I would recognize one of the fellows that had helped me break down the glider. My driver asked a couple of kids if they had seen the *icaro*, and they pointed to the house next door. There was my beloved Comet 2, up on the roof. They had transferred it there for safekeeping, or for keeping forever maybe, I'm not sure. All told it took four hours to return from a 10 kilometer, one hour flight. I did much better on all subsequent retrieves, and usually had a good time as well.

On this first trip we did not employ a driver (retrieves were included in the entry fee), and we learned that getting back to the hotel could be every bit as much a challenge as flying in the competition.

After one flight I was picked up by a big army troop transport truck (arranged for by the General), and then guided the driver a few more kilometers down the road to where Barney had landed. The driver deposited the two of us at the next small town while he continued on toward some pilots that had reportedly landed way out in the boonies. We were more than happy to wait it out in the comforts of a tavern.

Since the competition was taking place during Carnival, festivities were occurring in every city and village we came to, and this little oasis was no exception. After indulging in numerous *cervesas*, we wandered out to the courtyard behind the tavern to see what all the excitement was about. There was a crowd of kids and teenagers around a tall, greased wooden pole that was decorated with steamers and balloons. The object was to somehow shimmy up as high as you could and grab a balloon. I doubt that those attempting the feat would ever wear those clothes again; this wasn't cooking grease, it was axle grease.

This did not concern Barney, however, and after numerous bottles of bravery and strength, he proposed to give it a go. I joined in the chorus of kids and encouraged him. His first attempt got him only half as high as the lowest balloon. That balloon marked the point where no one had been able to reach yet. But the kids loved it and wanted to see more, and so did Barney. Up he went again, this time managing a technique that defied the grease. With a mighty pull, he reached the balloon, and the crowd roared. That must have invested him with even more power, because he kept on climbing and reached the next balloon. Now the crown had grown larger, and everyone was cheering and yelling as Barney grabbed the second balloon from the top, and a streamer. By now he'd had it, and slowly slid back to the ground, but he had made history. As I understood the bartender, no one had ever climbed so high. He was a hero, the *Americano,* and we basked in the glory and free beer for quite some time until the troop truck returned for us.

Knowing the retrieves would be interesting, and the conditions at launch were good again today, I was anxious for the flying to begin. You just knew that not long after take-off, the wing would be carving a spiral path toward the clouds that formed directly overhead.

The atmosphere on top of the mountain was a bit of a carnival, too. Adding to the mix were lots of spectators, media, Army personnel (yes, with guns), concessions, and of course a plethora of multi-colored wings. The

Germans were in their area attaching the latest instrumentation to the control bars, girls in minimal clothing surrounded the Colombians, and the British were quietly planning on leaving us in the dust. There were also pilots from France and Chile. The Venezuelans were always willing to share their knowledge with anyone, and most of them spoke very good English. They were excellent hosts, and very entertaining.

Soon the thermal cycles became more frequent and a little stronger. If there is anything I've learned about flying competitions, it is wise to get off as soon as possible to avoid large gaggles over the launch area. Today I had made sure all my gear was ready before the pilots meeting. As soon as I watched five or six gliders climb consistently I worked my way up to the take off zone and was gone.

One of the risks associated with launching early is that there are fewer "markers" out on course in front of you. I could see two wings down low only 2 or 3 kilometers west of launch, and another pair climbing in a thermal beyond. I couldn't see any other gliders beyond those, so this meant I would have to find my own lift. It's much easier to be able to race to the next thermal when you can see other pilots mapping out the lift. The pilot that flew into the cloud above me suddenly appeared again, 500 feet higher and slightly in front. We cruised about 5km before circling in lift again. By now I was looking at Zuata and the dead end valley ahead. The hills to the west of it looked like the next area of potential lift, but crossing that small valley had been difficult the first day, and I would hate to have to land there again, especially on a gorgeous day such as this. Clouds were popping everywhere along the course ahead. A more beautiful site a glider pilot will not see!

I didn't know the pilot that was hanging with me, except that he was a Venezuelan. We ended up scratching the hills above Zuata together, as well as with 4 or 5 large black vulture-like birds they call *Zamuros*. These birds were very common; sometimes we'd see 50 or more circling in a thermal. Little did I know then that they would guide me on a flight that turned out to be the most memorable of my hang gliding career. Their wingspan is equal to those of our Golden Eagles, about 5 to 6 feet. First encounters with birds this size can be somewhat intimidating, but in all my experiences I have yet to see any sign of aggression. I have heard tales of talons shredding dacron, but believe that somebody just came too close during mating or nesting season.

The lift we had hoped for was not materializing, and our situation was getting desperate. The only consolation was that we were beyond the spine of the hills that circumnavigated Zuata, and I would not be landing in that wretched little hole. However, a landing near Cagua, was just on the west side of the foothills, looked imminent. At least it was on a regular retrieve route.

Then my new buddy found something, and I was able to zip in under him and locate the ragged beginnings of the thermal. It was small enough that only half of a circle resulted in any altitude gain. We were zigging and zagging, cranking and banking, determined not to let our last hope drift away.

Finally, a full circle resulted in a climb all the way around. The highway below was vaguely familiar. I dug out my map and realized I was a few kilometers into the *Forbidden Zone* that the General had warned us about. I think my thermal partner was considering our location too, because he seemed to hesitate a bit and circled wide upwind, falling out of the lift. I took this opportunity to climb above him for the first time on the flight; we had been in the air a little over an hour. He rejoined me and we continued to climb. We had to make a crucial decision: leave the thermal and fly back upwind and an almost certain landing, or continue climbing and hope to gain enough altitude to cross the Zone. To the north were some foothills, the next chance for finding a thermal. Ten kilometers to the west was Lago de Valencia, a huge body of water that could not be crossed from here (and full of Piranha, I was told). We were drifting northwest, directly toward the airbase. I circled and waited to see what the other guy would do; he circled, craning his neck, waiting to see what I would do.

We were 3,000 feet above the ground, a couple of thousand below cloudbase. Finally, the other pilot bailed out, and the last I saw of him he was on a track to the southeast.

For a split second I felt victory, but then reality smacked me and I took note that I was nearly dead center of the large no-fly zone. I spotted the air base only about 7 kilometers west. The main runway was huge, and I envisioned the first wave of attack jets scrambling to come and blow my sorry ass out of the sky. I could see the area off the end of the runway where the glider pilot had been working the thermal. I topped out in the lift,. I turned away from my parallel course with the base, and proceeded full steam ahead to the northwest boundary of the Forbidden Zone, toward the city of Maracay, 10 kilometers away. So far no heat-seeking missiles had penetrated my much-puckered toosh; still, the risk of being caught was very real.

Nothing feels as good as lots of altitude, and I had as much as the day would allow now. Maracay marked the edge of the Zone and I would make it easily. The foothills beyond the city looked inviting, with numerous cumulus clouds forming. Would I have enough height to glide over the city? The closer I got, the further the other side of the city seemed to retreat. Carumba, this was one large city! Maracay is where our favorite cervesa, Polar, is brewed. The Polar brewery buys their barley from a Great Falls granary. I've probably driven right by the Montana barley field that ended up in my beer glass in the middle of Venezuela.

The flight resembled an action-adventure movie. Just when you think the hero is safe, up pops another bad guy. I didn't have the orbs to cross the city; not a single safe landing area in sight if I reached the halfway point and was too low. I traversed back and forth along the eastern edge looking for another thermal. Nothing. I was down to 400 feet and drifted over a large field that I expected I'd be standing in soon. Then, just like in the movies, a flash of hope. I spotted a flock of 20 *Zamuros* take off from the trees and start climbing. All I had to do was center over them, and there was the lift! It didn't take long for the vultures to catch up to me. What an exciting moment, surrounded by a flock of big black birds and climbing toward cloudbase again. The thermal was going up steadily and getting larger, and was drifting right out over the center of Maracay. I had never been in the air over such a large city before; it was an awesome sight. I snapped photos of the bullring in the center of the city, and then proceeded to head for the hills. The birds had slowly peeled away and I was flying solo again.

The next challenge was to get to the foothills, 10 kilometers to the north. These hills gradually gained altitude and formed the main mountain range that separates the coastal area along the Caribbean Sea from the inland plains and hills where we have been flying. Spectacular ridges perpendicular to the main range formed numerous barriers to my intended flight path. I had been in the air for two hours and I was feeling great. But for the last hour I have been traveling almost 45 degrees away from the rest of the competition pilots. Since the day's task was open distance, I was happy knowing whatever distance I achieved would count.

Maintaining good altitude, I was enjoying the sights below. Little villages were tucked into all the drainage's and scattered along the hillsides. I worked some lift over the mountain ridge near a freeway tunnel. The lift was spotty as the wing drifted up the spine, further into the mountains. The clouds above me were fewer now, but were still forming. The top of the divide was covered with a thick cloud that seemed to be rolling down toward me, an optical illusion I decided. I needed more altitude to cross the spine and into the next narrow valley. I surveyed the terrain ahead for the next likely thermal trigger and saw a large bare hilltop, a big black slab of rock. Very promising indeed. A well-beaten path led up the hill from the village below to a huge wooden cross. It was obviously some sort of shrine, and I was hoping it would be another "savior" thermal source.

As I came blazing over the top of the cross, not more than 150 feet above it, a most incredible event occurred. The entire area around the shrine came alive with an enormous explosion of the black vultures! Hundreds of them! At that very moment the nose of the glider pitched up hard as it entered the thermal. Wrestling for control of the wing, the sky had turned into a surreal vortex of feathers and dust and dacron. The lift was broken and varied; add to that the exhilaration of seeing so many vultures taking flight all around my glider, and you could say it was mayhem. There were easily more than two hundred birds in the area around the shrine, and within moments not one was left on the ground.

Numerous gaggles formed, mapping out a large area of lift. The Zamuros again showed no fear of the glider, constantly buzzing quite close. I reached for my camera to get a close-up shot of a bird, but the rough air preempted my attempts. The first order of business was to stay in the thermal. Half the birds drifted away from the lift and disappeared in the first thousand feet, but the rest were intent on climbing high with the new kid in town. At times I would observe birds in another core of lift climbing faster, and I would alter my course and join them. After two thousand feet, the lift consolidated into one large thermal and the climb was much easier. I could enjoy the scenery and try the camera again. The lift was so widespread that the birds had drifted away from good focus, and the resulting photos showed only a few birds at a distance.

The lift carried me to a four thousand foot gain, respectable compared to most of the previous week's gains. I was circling in wisps of the clouds, not afraid to make a few turns up into the white; I was quite sure there were no other gliders in the area. As I exited the cloud I was at least two thousand feet above a very dense cloudbank that covered the spine of the coastal range, and it *was* in fact pouring down the inland side. The cumulus clouds I was under were fed by thermals rising from the valleys and fields at the base of the range on the inland side. The nimbostratus clouds coming over the top stretched all the way to the sea. Any view of the land or beaches was completely obliterated by these clouds that were formed by the cooler sea air meeting the warmer air above. A truly spectacular panorama indeed! For miles in front of me the same conditions existed, and the flight path was obvious.

All that was required was to race to the next cumulus and climb up to it. They were only about 5 kilometers apart. There was a small set of clouds over every valley ahead. Hours of hard work were now paying dividends. I continued on this westerly course for 30 kilometers, which by now added up to about 75k from the launch site. Paralleling my course was a major highway for easy retrieval. But the sun was getting very low, even though the lift still seemed plentiful.

I arrived at a point where the highway took a turn north, through the mountains to the beach. I could continue west for another 10 to 15 kilometers into a sparsely populated area with few roads or turn south the same distance toward the city of Valencia. Valencia would be into a slight headwind and I would not gain any distance. I decided to just float around and set down where I was. For 20 minutes I searched for a suitable landing field, and by the time I located one I had drifted 5 kilometers back east. I touched down to a graceful landing in a large green field just as the sun set behind the range.

For the first time in four landings I was not mobbed by a slew of kids. I came in unnoticed, and would enjoy a solitary moment to reflect on the day while I took the wing down. The field was completely surrounded by a solid wall, 5 feet tall; maybe trespassing was not tolerated. By the time I had the wing folded and bagged it was dark. I carried the gear across the field to a house and knocked on the door. An old man answered, and I used my best impersonation of Spanish to greet him and introduce myself. I had planned on asking permission to stash the wing while I went to a phone in the little village down the road. I knew that he wouldn't have a phone; nobody in the country did. The only phones are located in the Plaza (city center) of each town. His dialect was much different than any I had heard. I wasn't prepared for my inability to communicate, but I was able to convey that I wanted to leave the glider by his fence and he seemed agreeable.

Not far from his house was a large community building with some sort of gathering in progress. I thought I might get lucky and find a phone there. A young girl came to the door, and as soon as she met the tall, pale looking gringo with the sunburned face she ran back inside. Her mother arrived at the door and began speaking in the same odd dialect as the old man, then suddenly closed the door. I realized that I was in the middle of one of the Portuguese communities that I had heard about. Their version of Spanish was so different to me that I gave up and headed down the road to the small town I had seen from the air.

It was a long walk, but it was a pleasant evening and the folks I passed along the road were friendly. A small car pulled up alongside and asked me some questions, wondering if I was the *icaro*. They gave me the thumbs up as they pulled away, but no ride.

As I got closer to town I could hear the sounds people and music; it was easy to find my way to the Plaza. The police station (*La Policia*) and the phones were right across the street. For the first time in Venezuela I had trouble making a connection back to the hotel. I enlisted the help of a policeman, but had no better luck. A lovely young woman walked by and overheard my predicament. She spoke perfect English and had me on the line with the hotel in no time.

The man at the desk would not believe me, asking over and over if the location was correct, so I gave the phone over to the young lady who confirmed my whereabouts. He told me to stay put and someone would be directed to pick me up, but it might be a while.

In the meantime, Gabrielle and her family invited me to join them over at the Carnival. Only a fool would refuse such an invitation. It was Fat Tuesday, the final day of celebration before Lent, and the place was hopping! They bought me a hotdog and a drink, and in return I told them of the day's adventure, and all about the flying competition. They introduced me to some other fellows who spoke English, and they saw to it that I had a rum in my hand at all times. Some of the townspeople had been to the United States, so we had lots to talk about as we walked around the Carnival. After several *Cuba Libres*, I had forgotten all about watching for my retrieval. I had no idea who I should be looking for, and besides, how would they ever find me in the middle of a thousand partygoers? Another refreshing beverage eased my worries.

And then suddenly I had four familiar faces standing right in front of me. Larry Tudor said I was easy to spot in the crowd, as I stood at least a head taller than anyone else. The Venezuelan pilot and his retrieval crew were all smiles at their successful retrieve. They were surprised that I was so far away from the rest of the competition, and wondered how I had gotten here. I told them the story, except for the part about crossing the Forbidden Zone. I was drunk, but I knew enough not to admit to…well, whatever.

These folks could see that there was no need to hurry and leave this little piece of paradise, so we continued to enjoy the festivities well into the evening. It was a long drive back to La Victoria that night, probably 120 kilometers by the highway. We were the last ones back to the hotel by a long shot, but it did not matter, we had more fun. At least *I* did!

I placed my pin in the map and I ended up with 80 kilometers, a distance I was quite pleased with but not enough to place very high. Some pilots, like Larry and Eric Raymond, had flown over 150 kilometers. I don't know whether they recall much of their flights, but I had such an amazing adventure that day that every turn, every thermal, is forever etched in my memory.

Portrait from Above!

Scott Rowe

Light easterly winds were forecast for Memorial Day and as the thermal activity on Saturday was quite abundant with comfortably unstable air at Mossy Banks, my bet was that Harriet Hollister would be the site to fly. Although some pilots shy away from the park because of its shallow launch and subtle double fall-line landing zone, I favor it for its cross-country potential and incredible view of the Finger Lakes. I have to admit its close proximity to Rochester doesn't hurt either.

I recall flying cross-country in easterlies at Mossy Banks one time, and some fifty miles to the south of Harriet Hollister experiencing a desperate and panicked hitch hike ride from the back hills of rural New York! I had accepted a ride from two locals and one bottle of whiskey in a beat up old Rambler. I remember placing my gear bag on my lap for protection in case that old rust bucket found a tree under the less than sober guidance of its driver who appeared to have popped the caps of one too many beer bottles, by the looks of his teeth! Actually if memory serve me correctly that's why he was drinking, to quell the pain from tooth decay! True story, although admittedly an exception to my cross-country hang gliding adventures! Let's just say I figured that flying the easterlies downwind at Harriet would put me in more hospitable terrain for landing *and* retrieval!

I awoke early Monday morning to calm winds, around six in the morning, and opted for a quick ski on the glassy waters at the south end of Irondequoit Bay just minutes from the house. My water skiing buddies, Jim and Skip, had both skied a couple runs when a breeze started to kick in from the north off of Lake Ontario. I glanced to the south and there already were beautiful puffy cumulus clouds starting to form. My thoughts were immediately transfixed on duplicating Saturday's flying success, where my buddy John and I had cloudbase gains of five thousand feet at Mossy. I immediately exclaimed to my friends how my arms and blistered hands were too fatigued for another set and now the increasingly choppy waters dictated we return to shore (and to flying). Later, my wife, Kim, would chastise me for leaving the boat uncovered, but how do you explain that tingling feeling in your gut that interferes with rational thought, to someone who hasn't yet felt the tug of a strong thermal under her wing? Oh don't get me wrong, Kim flies alright, and even gets plenty excited about it, but her thermalling days are still ahead of her!

Returning home, there already were two let's-go-flying messages to which I immediately responded. The car, still packed since Saturday, shifted into autopilot and I arrived 45 minutes later at Harriet Holister Spencer Park. On my ride down from Rochester I closely monitored the conditions expecting them to improve farther south, away from lake effect. The clouds were forming nicely and did not seem in danger of over-developing, yet the winds appeared a bit light. At launch the wind exhibited a light easterly component, but light enough so as to not worry about rotor from the lower ridge immediately in front and to the right of launch. But where was everyone? I proceeded to set up and began to think that I was at the wrong site, but there was no time to drive to Italy Valley. This was prime launch time!

Harriet Hollister has a limited set-up area just to the right of launch with room for only three gliders, more can be setup on the road just over the guardrail but as it's unpaved it can get pretty dusty. Being first allowed me the luxury of a choice setup spot where I could glance out and monitor the wind etching its direction on the surface of nearby Honeoye Lake some 1200 feet below and time thermal cycles rolling up the slot as well.

My Moyes XS went together quickly and with each snap of a batten bungee the tingling feeling in my stomach radiated, culminating in a heightening of my senses so important in detecting the shifts in wind, felt on the skin of your face and the sound in your ears. Even the changing air pressures on the wing are telegraphed to your arms and shoulders as wind flows and eddies around the wing tips. Sometimes the glider suddenly seems to take on tremendous weight as downward forces from a wayward thermal-eddy finds the top surface and causes the top wires to suddenly go taunt and the crossbar to shift.

As I pulled my harness from the car Mark and Brian showed up followed shortly by Bob. Maintaining my heightened readiness I didn't spare too many words with the boys, as my plan was set.

I tested my grip on the smooth down tubes and snugged my shoulders up against them for control as I eyed the sky above for red tail hawks or turkey vultures, usually a sure indication of the air's potential. Sometimes if you're lucky the raptures circle in big fat thermals just in front of launch. The thermals often rise up out of a deep ravine that is hidden just beyond the bowl under the treetops of hemlocks, maples and oaks. Once, flying too low over the ravine, I encountered a blast of thermal air that radically tipped me up onto my wing tip. It was only my years of experience and a huge adrenaline rush that prevented me from stalling headlong down into the deep chasm.

The treetops in the bowl out front started moving as though God had an invisible paintbrush and He slowly drew it across the treetops, causing the leaves to move about. Like falling dominoes they all flip over and reveal their undersides, usually a much lighter shade of green. The tell-tails in the launch slot came to life, flickering slowly at first and then straightening nicely as the wind strength increased. The fluorescent surveyor's tapes, tied to tiny maple saplings, were equal in their reception of the wind; signs that this thermal cycle was square in the slot and coming towards me.

"Clear!" I yelled to my wiremen. They quickly dropped back to allow the glider free access to the air. I launched cleanly at 12:30 p.m. after momentarily wrestling with the glider a bit in the strengthening thermal wind.

I tested the bowl out front briefly for lift and turbulence. There was a hint of bad air there and I cautiously moved to the north towards Honeoye Lake and away from the potential rotor caused by the front ridge and crossing air. My first thermal took some nurturing (I sometimes talk to the thermals out loud as if to encourage them) and I soon spiraled skyward. With each 360, my view of the valley below me grew, I could see Neil and another pilot just arriving at launch, their van winding its way into the park.

Closing in on cloudbase with Honeoye, Hemlock and Canadice Lakes now clearly in view, I gave the VG cord three good pulls. It's always an awkward movement, reaching across the body to grab the tensioning cord while flying with the other remaining hand on the control bar. With each successive grab the cord bunches around your hand invariably entangling it. A quick shake of the hand frees the excess cord and the wing tightens.

With my wing now even more efficient and taut, I punched out of my thermal, heading west over small Canadice Lake. The lake is strictly regulated and reserved for canoes and kayaks, a small lake where only berries, nuts and water are allowed in one's lunch basket. How they enforce that I'll never know, but Rochester gets its drinking water from this glacial drop in the bucket, so I don't mind! Not too many years after this flight I would take my boys, Skylar and Keaton, for a paddle and look up at the sky as I was now looking down at the water.

I was at 5000 feet, plus or minus a few. The sink between thermals was considerable, 400-600 ft/min, and I pulled in to minimize my time in the sinking air. The likelihood of finding a thermal over the small lake was slim, but I knew I had plenty of altitude to cross and certainly would find lift on the other side! I usually like to try and drift in a thermal over these narrow bodies of water but this was early in the flight and I was less conservative than usual.

I made it safely across and was heading toward the south end of Conesus lake. I was getting low and feared the worst. I banked my Moyes XS toward a familiar landing area, a golf course that I visited by air a couple years back. I recall getting a big kick out of yelling, "*Fore!*" as I flew over a group of golfers, and their surprised looks as they gawked skyward. I also recall being thankful I was wearing a helmet as at least one golf ball came my way! Yes, another good reason to always wear your helmet! But my trusty Afro vario sang its sweet tune and I again rocketed upward and drifted with the thermal towards the eastern shore of Conesus Lake. It was a nice day and there were many boats out on the lake. I relaxed and watched the activity; sailing, tubing and water skiing down below me. Everyone was enjoying Memorial Day festivities, including myself!

As I sailed over a familiar patch of water, I remembered teaching sailboarding here in the late seventies, when sailboards were known as windsurfers! They were simple, one board and one sail. I taught in a Speedo swimsuit! No doubt a desperate attempt at seeking coolness and perhaps revealing my earlier influences of being raised too close to Quebec, in a small town called Champlain. As youths we used to laugh at the tourists from Montreal in their brightly colored Speedos. But I've long since left that border town, and it's safe to say I wouldn't be caught dead in a Speedo now, nor would I look the same!

I recalled a windsurfer race on this same lake where a gust front suddenly came down on us quickly from the north. Looking down the course, one by one every sailor was flung from his Windsurfer. Rescue boats had to retrieve many of us as our large 60 square foot sails were simply too much for the winds. There were winter excursions, too, where windsurfers became ice-surfers and unseen pressure cracks would send us ass-over-tea-kettles, skipping like stones on our backsides! Crazy? Yes!

I continued on my westward heading past Conesus and could now see Route 390, vehicles swirling south and north through the Genessee Valley. I expected and got more lift as I flew over the valley, working to the south of the town of Mt. Morris. I got really excited as I neared the Genessee River west of town. I enjoyed a wonderful aerial view of the Mt. Morris dam and Letchworth Park, but realized that I was again getting low and my landing-out options were more limited here. My strategy required a bit more attentiveness.

The Genessee River looked swollen. It meandered its way to the dam, a path it has been carving out of the valley for millions of years as evidenced by the high cliffs surrounding it. I scanned for kayaks or rafts in sediment-laden waters, but spotted none. Either the cold water or high water volume had kept die-hard boaters away to enjoy Memorial Day picnics and barbeques.

My variometer found another thermal and I specked-out again, passing Warsaw and the north end of Silver Lake. How many bodies of water was that? Canadice, Hemlock, Conesus, Genessee River and Silver Lake; cool! I got dangerously low near a huge radio tower. I half expected some radio interference with my variometer, but luckily did not receive any. I unzipped my pod harness to prepare for what seemed to be the inevitable landing. I scanned the surface for a good LZ, perhaps one with a huge gathering of people sympathetic to my retrieval situation. There was a gathering of families both to my north and south on either side of the road. Who were the best candidates? Can you tell from the air? It's hard. One group spotted me and they became the chosen ones. But alas another thermal, a weak one at first, and then I was cloudward bound. I continued my journey west.

The most spectacular site came to view, Lake Erie and the Buffalo skyline. I started mentally celebrating, envisioning interviews from the Buffalo newspaper, maybe a television spot with women gawking and requesting my autograph. It would at least be a pioneering first for a hang glider. I thought I could make it; the lift had been so reliable. It was a premature celebration.

I sunk out in Strykerville, at the small country farmhouse of John and Marilynn Smith. I set up over a freshly mowed alfalfa field; the radiating heat felt good on my skin and the fresh farm smell was pleasant to my nose. The crop was gathered neatly in rows to dry. I spotted John and Marilynn weeding in their garden and yelled out to get their attention. My throat was so parched and my ears plugged from the quick descent, that my yell didn't sound like my own voice. They looked up, and I landed while eyeing two flags, one American and one Canadian, fluttering in the breeze and showing me the proper approach.

I landed safely with a perfect two-step landing (hey, who's to know differently?) and exchanged pleasantries with the Smiths who were as awed to hear about my aerial adventure as I was to tell it! I called my wife, Kim, and begged for retrieval. She could tell how excited I was and didn't give me a hard time, even though it was easily an hour and a half away. On the way home we bumped into Neil, who excitedly told of his equally noteworthy flight. He expressed surprise at having landed so close to me as he felt his flight path over ground had zigzagged quite a bit! He also mentioned that he had maxed out in his thermals and found cloudbase at six grand! Gee! If I had only waited out those extra thousand feet before departing my thermals I could have been sipping ice cold Gennies on the beautiful shores of Lake Erie!

I landed at 2:50 p.m., two hours and twenty minutes away from Harriet Holister Spencer Park, some forty-seven miles away! It wasn't a world record, not a personal best, and not even a regional record, but it was a new route and a spectacular aerial adventure that had me reminiscing of adventures past the whole way and simply left me in awe of nature and the wondrous geography of the Western New York's Finger Lakes and Genessee River Valley.

How to Set a Hang Gliding World Record

The Zapata Record

Davis Straub

Gary Osoba, at his home in Wichita, but still very much connected to the World Record Encampment, sent in the following early morning weather forecast for Wednesday, the 9th:

10 am: Should be cumulus at about 2,000' agl. Light but workable lift, better than yesterday at this time. Last night it looked like today could be at 2500' to 3,000' by 10 am but more moisture than predicted came in overnight. You might wish to re-examine your leaving height and weigh the trade-offs between abundant clouds with possible organization or some cloud streeting and the safety net. This will give you more time on course (of course). If I had the choice of adequate clouds at 2000' or blue at 3000' I'd take the clouds every time. Today, more than the other days, it will benefit you to get off earlier. I'm seeing a better air mass definition as you move toward Laredo...as you enter it, you'll just be swept up into a superb flight path along the ideal route. At 10 am in Laredo the cloudbase should be 500' higher than your launch, the lift will be stronger and better organized, and the winds will be stronger and from a better direction. Expect winds at cloudbase to run about 5 mph stronger (20 mph plus) and from about 155-165 degrees. Get up there as soon as you can.

For your launch, winds at the surface about 135 degrees at 12 mph. Winds at cloudbase about 150 degrees at 15-18 mph.

1 pm around the region of Catarina: Very good-looking lapse rates. Should be strong lift, nicely formed, there's a reasonable chance for some organization and cloud street here and there. Cloudbase around 6,000' agl and get this... winds aloft from an average of about 180 degrees. Running about 15 mph. If you have good clouds, race, race, race.

4 pm around Uvalde and the Hill Country: Nice, strong thermals. Well formed and big. Winds aloft shift a little more easterly to about 160 degrees, just right for the route up Hwy 55. Should be running about 12-15 mph. Cloudbase over the hills at 7500' to 8000' msl, so you should be able to cover the terrain nicely.

Late afternoon & early evening above the Edwards Plateau: Good, well-formed lift should continue late. Winds back southerly about 180 degrees at 12-15 mph.

Cloudbase around 9000' to 9500' msl (7000' agl). You have a very good chance of streeting here. Looks much better to me than the day Dave made the clouds.

Pretty soon after you sense that the lift is starting to back off (but not die), you might need to dial down your racing with a higher proportion than S2F would dictate. Hopefully the racing will still consist of organized, cloud streeting runs. I would be careful to stay really high, with the goal of getting all the length you can out of the day and all the winds have to offer. Certainly by the time you climb in the last real thermal of the day, you want to hang with it at the top of the climb forever. To continue to core even 50 fpm down makes more sense than leaving it if it is late and there are no more real climbs out there to be had. If you misjudge this and there's another climb to cloudbase, fine...you can just repeat the tactic. Of course, depending upon sunlight, etc., you may get another modest "climb" or a level drift or two way down the altitude scale...just try to hang forever in the last real one that goes to cloudbase. You should be able to extend your final glide 30-50 minutes if this is the case, and can cover lots of extra ground during this time period.

Some chance of over development all along the course to about Uvalde today, but not extreme. As you move north of Catarina, you might see some beautiful, long-winged Open Class ships from the Nationals to help spot the better thermals for you. I would not conclude that because winds don't average above 20 mph over the course, you couldn't do it today. With the way things are shaping up, it could be a much better day than the record day during the first encampment. We'll just have to see.

Gary is obviously very excited about the day and is doing every thing that he can to encourage me. I really appreciate it, but wonder if he isn't overstating things. The windcast for surface winds shows a lot of easterly component:

The wind direction is supposed to become more southerly as I head north to the west of San Antonio. The center of the high pressure is still too far north, so that there will be predominantly southeasterly winds instead of south winds. The problem with a southeasterly wind direction is that there aren't any paved roads that go in this direction. That's why we like the fact that the winds are supposed to turn to the south, so I can go up the northerly route – highway 83.

But the 7 pm windcast shows a more easterly component to the north as I get there later in the day. The windcast predicts that the winds will increase during the day.

At 8 AM, the cu's fill in fast at Zapata, it is almost dark from all the low level cu's by 9 AM. They are thicker than any we've seen so far. When we drive to the airport, their shadows are running almost as fast as the truck (40 mph), but it is mild on the ground. The cloud base must start off at about 1,500'.

My ATOS is all set up, and as we are out at the airport by 9 AM. I have been flying with the stock round base tube and my wheels here in Texas. The wheels saved me once again the first day I flew here and landed downwind into a rocky field. I figure that my carbon-fiber aero base tube is just a bit too wimpy for Texas. My steel aero base tube would be fine (same as the one Dave Sharp flies with), but isn't as comfortable as the round one.

With the glider set up all we have to do is haul it on the little two wheel cart that Dave Sharp, Dustin Marin, and Gary Osoba built, out to the south end of the runway. This is a delicate process, as you have to pull the semi-secured glider first into the wind (no problem) and then downwind (you hope that the wind doesn't blow it over into the truck). You go fast enough downwind to keep the wind from blowing over the glider.

Unfortunately, the rope that holds the nose of the glider down comes lose, and the keel falls to the runway. I'm riding my bike and holding the wing tip to level the glider, and as soon as the keel hits, I go over the handlebars. Minor scrapes. The glider is fine and we continue.

When we get to the end of the runway, I notice that one of my super thin spoileron wires is kinked and has one broken strand. I decide that it is good enough for the day, but will have to be replaced before I fly again. There is really very little force on the spoileron wires.

I'm ready to go a little before 10 AM, but when I first start to take off, I've got one of the lines of the bridle under my arm, instead of over my head. I have Belinda stop the truck after a few feet, and fix the problem. So far, not a great start for the day. I'm sure hoping that I don't obsess during the flight about the kinked side wire.

The winds are over 10 mph on the ground (as Gary predicted) and right down the runway (130 degrees), so it is very easy to get into the air and climb well on tow. It really is a testament to this launch site that we can pretty consistently get up early in the morning from 700'-1000'.

There are clouds over the runway, and I find a light thermal right at the center of the runway. It's going up at about 200 fpm, and I pin off leaving the rope right on the runway. This is a sign that the winds are at 130 degrees (the runway direction), so I will be pushed to the northwest toward Laredo and its airport.

The clouds are streeting and it is clear that I will have to follow the streets at least until I get far enough away from the airport to be able to get out from a landing area without having to call the Sheriff to unlock the gates. Cloud base is 2,600' MSL (2,200' AGL) so when I leave at cloud base, I leave lower than I would like. Still there is a nice filled-in street in front of me, and I just stay under it.

I cover the first 15 miles in twenty minutes without having to turn more than a turn or two. My ground speed is between 50 and 55 mph. The lift is light, but so is the sink. At this point, I start hopping cloud streets to the east, in order to get around Laredo. I need to be five miles to the east of the airport, or over 3,000' AGL.

Here I'm jumping to the northeast to get into the next cloud street. Cloudbase is rising and by 11 AM I can get to 3,800'. I'm an hour and a half earlier than what we've been averaging as I'm almost to Laredo. Dave and I left the Zapata airport at 11:45 AM on the day that he set the record.

I get down to 1,500' AGL 10 miles southeast of the Laredo airport, but find my first good lift of the day – 500 fpm. There are plenty of clouds, and I've been hopping a couple of streets to get to the east, so I'm pretty confident. Still up. After going down at 100 miles the day before, I'm careful to take any lift when I get below 2000' AGL.

I'm able to get far enough east of the airport and climb high enough that I stay well out of controlled airspace. This is not only a legal consideration. The Laredo airport is very busy because it is the port of entry for goods coming from Mexico (think NAFTA). I definitely want to stay away from any air traffic.

With the winds out of the southeast, I'm forced to jump to another street to get lined up with highway 83, which branches off of Interstate 35 north of Laredo. I'm running between 3,500' MSL and 2000' MSL. I've switched to MSL on my Brauniger variometer, because I know that the ground is climbing. It starts at 400' at Zapata, and is probably 700' north of Laredo. It will climb to 2,400' at the Edwards Plateau.

The Brauniger gives me readings of the wind direction and speed. It varies between 120 degrees at 12 mph, and 150 degrees at 15 mph. It appears from the wind lines on the ponds below to be about 160 degrees. Thankfully highway 83 goes a bit northwest at this point.

I'm not getting any strong lift. It is usually between 300 and 400 fpm in the best thermals. I work 200 to 250 fpm if I get at all low. Soon after I start up highway 83 at 60 miles out, I have to be sure to get up enough to feel safe about crossing a five-mile stretch of Mesquite. I haven't been getting that high, and cloud base is now 5,000' MSL. With the strong winds I figure I'll try to get up early before I'm carried over the Mesquite patch. Still, the winds also help shorten up the patch.

Twenty miles of Mesquite start at 70 miles out, broken only by three ranch airstrips (well, almost). With the streeting, and consistent, if light, lift I'm able to stay comfortable at above 3,500' MSL. I'm running pretty fast, but not averaging 40 mph. I'm way ahead of any previous time on the course.

Catarina is about 100 miles out on the highway, and the site where I went down on the previous day. I'm there at 12:30 PM, half an hour before Gary's prediction, but he's darn close. I decide to cut the corner on the highway as it jogs northwest a bit here to Carrizo Springs, and I head for Crystal City.

I'm down to 1000' AGL five miles south of town, feeling out the lift. So far I've really enjoyed the air, and there have been few "chunky bits." I had told myself that I was tired of having long flights that weren't enjoyable, and I was only going to do this if it was fun. So far, it has been.

The nice moist, soft thermally air that comes out of the Gulf, was a big draw for me to come to Zapata. I loved the fact that it was low, so that I didn't need oxygen and I could dress lightly. I hate feeling like a snowmobile operator when I fly. I didn't wear gloves, had on my shorts (and thin little Converse All Stars that can fit in the pod), a thermal undershirt, and a fleece sweater.

The day had started relatively cool with all the clouds. I had even forgotten to put on my hat when I first got to the airport, something that would not have happened here on any sunny day. So I wasn't too warm in my sweater while flying.

I find a bit of lift south of Crystal City and get in a nice soft but light thermal. It is large enough for both me and the hawk that joins me. We stay at the same elevation (with respect to each other) for the next 4,000' of climb. It is the most pleasant thermals of the day, and gets to about 500 near the top.

You can really tell by the track of the thermal in the lower portion of the figure that the wind is blowing from the southeast. I'm beginning to think that now is the time of day that I should start making some better speeds. I'm still averaging below 40 mph, although my inter-thermal ground speeds are now between 55 mph and 60 mph. The climbs are slow, so that adds up. Also, I can't get very high, so I have to take a lot of climbs. I don't have as many options to just take the big lift (as though there were any). Still, I really appreciate the relative lack of hard bounces and broken up air, so the trade off is worth it.

I'm scooting toward Uvalde and have already decided to take highway 55, which takes a more northwesterly direction than does highway 83. I have a declared goal at highway 277 and Interstate 10. 55 will take me there, so another good reason to go this direction. The winds continue southeast, in spite of what the windcast shows (Uvalde is west of San Antonio).

I'm past Uvalde at 170 miles at 3 PM. When Dave and I took this route before, we were here at 4:30 PM. I'm just hoping that the day lasts as long. I get my first strong thermal of the day at 1000 fpm on the averager for about two minutes before it drops back a bit. I'm wondering if the day has finally picked up (it doesn't).

I'm still following the cloud streets, but they've been full of potholes since Laredo. They are still there, but there is no running underneath them and not turning. They are also cocked a bit to the west, so I do have to jump from one to the next, every so often.

At 190 miles out, I'm by Camp Wood and low again. This is where I went down on the previous flight, and I'm wary. I have to run way to the west to get out of the small valley and over to the cloud street to the west.

I get low enough to sweat (1000' AGL) as I work a bit of junky lift off some hills and rocks. It doesn't stay together and again I'm running low north up the narrowing valley trying to get under a cloud. It looks bad, as I drift over a field and check out the landing possibilities. They are getting fewer as the road starts climbing up to the Edwards Plateau.

I will work anything, and I find a bit of lift off the dry riverbed that drifts fast to the north. In spite of its weakness, I vow to stay in it no matter what, to at least 6,000' MSL. I have to go back and find it a few times, but I hold to the promise and even get to 7,000' MSL in 400 fpm near the top.

The thermal has taken me up onto the plateau and I'm looking out at Rocksprings. There is a cloud street on the eastern side and one on the west, and I take the eastern one first. I then have to jump over to the western one over Rocksprings and climb out from 2000' AGL over town.

At this point, 220 miles out from launch, highway 55 heads off to the west. Dave Sharp had earlier taken a more northerly route along ranch roads, and I decide that I should do the same. I'm trying to line up with the winds and head at about 340 degrees.

In the main I have to follow the clouds. The roads are a secondary consideration, but then I do want to get picked up if I go down. The ranch roads are definitely there, but just how one gets to them is not quite clear as I skip between. I think I can make it to Interstate 10, forty miles to the north.

Some upper layer clouds have come in. Gary is following the weather at work and notices these clouds also. There are actually two layers of clouds above the cu's, so it is completely dark on the ground now to the north of Rocksprings.

Still, I was able to climb to 8,400' MSL (6,000' AGL) at Rocksprings, so at least I'm high as I venture out into the dark and poorly roaded area. There are still thin cu's under the higher clouds, and I have to get to each one to get lift. The streets are still there, but they are mostly potholes.

About thirty miles out from Rocksprings, I work myself further west to get back out into the sunlight. The high clouds don't take up all the sky, so I'm able to get just to the northwest of a still smoldering burnt-off field, and under some better cu's.

I get a bit disoriented, and find myself going more west than north and come in south of Sonora and cross highway 277. My goal in taking what I thought was a northerly route from Rocksprings was to keep to the east of highway 277 and maybe get the declared goal at Sonora as I drifted to the west just north of Interstate 10.

Now, given my confusion, I'm eight miles south of Interstate 10 and west of Sonora. I take a right turn and fly north. I get low and have to scoot to the southwest of Sonora to get under a cloud. At 800' AGL with Mesquite all around, I pick up 200 fpm in a small thermal, but I hang on because there really isn't anywhere to land. I'm sure not excited about going down at 260 miles so I do whatever it takes to stay in the air.

I'm five miles west of highway 277, which goes north to San Angelo. There are no roads to the northwest, only Interstate 10 to the west. Still, there are some cultivated fields now under me so I head north, trying to stay within reach of 277.

The cloud streets are generally tending to the north and not the northwest. I'm staying under the cloud streets and staying high.

My wife Belinda tells me that there is a parallel northerly paved road about 30 miles to the north, so I should be able to see it at some point. I'm moving along well, and I'm now getting over 8,000' MSL. It is a bit cold up there (in the sixties), so I am shivering in my light clothes. The thermals are smooth, but they are now getting stronger, 500 fpm. With a good southerly component of the wind, I'm moving along.

The clouds are quite a bit different than earlier in the day. I'm back out in the sun, the cu's are quite high, and the streets are back, but sparsely. You can really feel that you are in lift now and the cu's are darker and more sharply defined.

I'm ten to fifteen miles west of San Angelo, when I run out of roads. I take a dirt farm road going north, but it doesn't look like it goes that far. I figure I'm going to land at about 320 miles out, good enough to have the new record.

At the last moment, I decide to glide across some unlandable hills (no roads either) as it looks like I can make it a few more miles and land near another farm. I have plenty of tail wind and I'm just floating, so why not.

I make it to the farms at about 1000' AGL, and low and behold, I'm under a cloud. Pure luck. I start working up and getting Belinda back on the radio to tell her where I've gone. She'll have to detour around to the east to get a road to the north. I can see the divided highway that goes out of San Angelo to the northwest. It's really the only choice I have, so I climb out slowly and then just go on final glide down the highway. All the clouds are gone by now (it is almost 8 PM) and the air is glassy smooth. There is still plenty of wind and heat on the ground, and I glide 20 miles before landing at 8 PM at a farm near Sterling City. I want to be sure to have a few witnesses, so I cut the flight a little bit short at 347 miles.

Is 400 or more miles possible here in a hang glider? Oh yeah, no problem. You just want a bit better weather conditions. You want the Bermuda high a bit further to the south, so that you have south winds instead of southeasterly. You want stronger winds, maybe 20 to 30 mph, and better lift (unless it gets too rough). Whether you get all that in the same package is a bit more problematic, but it should happen fairly often.

Gary Osoba is the person most responsible for making it possible for me to set this record. He did all the hard work of finding the right spot to fly. He really loves this stuff, and I'm very sorry that he broke the under carriage of the Carbon Dragon on his first tows at Zapata. Since I was driving the tow vehicle, I feel a little responsibility for that.

Gary talked to me a year ago about going to Texas, and I could hardly wait. I'm sure glad that I got Dave Sharp to come; he was a great encouragement, especially when he set the record first.

The ATOS flew perfectly, not a single spin. Thanks to Felix and Berndt for building a fun glider to fly.

I couldn't have flown this flight without Belinda driving. I had thought that I would stay in Zapata when Belinda left to visit her brother, but I knew that another driver wouldn't really work out. I needed the confidence to know that she would be there if I got lost.

The people of Zapata have been great to all of us. Bob McVey, the local newspaper publisher, shared his house with all those pilots and drivers without a mobile home. He was also my official observer on some earlier flights. He called the Sheriff and got Dustin out when he went down behind locked gates. He wrote us up in the newspaper.

Charlie, the airport owner/manager, has been very helpful. He gave us the run of the place, and just asked us to have an aircraft radio to keep out of the way of incoming planes. We loved being in his big hanger and using his airport.

July, at the Zapata Chamber of Commerce, got us free RV parking at the Lake Front Lodge as well as free meal tickets from McDonalds and Subway. Thanks to her and the helpful folks in Zapata.

Thanks to everyone who made all the equipment that I flew with. It all worked, even the pilot tracking system (which is sometimes problematic). The Rodger Hoyt's Gate Savers were real handy. Heiner Beisel's heads up device worked on my neck for 10 hours.

To Kagel...Well Almost

John Scott

It's the Sunday after by birthday and the weatherman has given me nice post-frontal conditions as a present. I just got off the phone with, first Tom Truax, and then Tony Deleo. Tom has scheduled an 8:30 am meet time at Parma Park, Santa Barbara's main LZ. Since it takes an hour and a half to get there from my house in West Los Angeles that is too soon for me. Tony and I decide to meet at Bailard in Carpenteria at 9:00 instead. Two weeks earlier I had a nice 38 miler from this same site, but I didn't have a driver and I was left along the side of the road for 3 hours; it's nice to see that Tony has brought his brother along. We load into Tony's Subaru because it has the proper racks for his new Atos. By 10:30 we're set up at launch and ready to go. You could tell it's supposed to be a good day because some of the local hang glider pilots were already at launch when we first arrived; normally we beat them there by an hour.

Tom's crew of PG pilots started launching about 9:45. They were soon at cloudbase. Because of a little bit of east flow Tom calls Painted Cave near the San Marcos Pass as a turn point before an open distance task toward the east.

Sorry, Sundowner, my plans are for open distance – I need those Michael Champlin XC Challenge points - and so I'm not going to waste an hour or so of non-airsick time chasing around a turn point.

At 10:50 I'm east bound, or so I thought. I didn't get up at launch or the Thermal Factory and so now I'm limping out to the front points. *Amateur!* But, no reason to panic. The Antenna Farm, as it is called, is usually a reliable thermal generator, and a PG pilot is topping out at about 2k higher right in front of me. *I knew there was no reason to panic.* But as I look back at the Factory in the middle of my climb, I see that the clouds have dissipated, and the gliders that were beneath them, are now sinking out toward me.

The day is not starting out as I had hoped, but I see Jeff Ross turning circles behind the power lines at the base of the Factory so I head over to him. The lift is nothing to write home about, but it keeps me in the ball game. Scott Angel is with us.

Well, this isn't working; I'm going to fish out front above the power lines. More scraps, but at least I'm gaining. Hey you in the blue paraglider, can't you see that I was here first circling to the right? What's with the figure eights?

Yee Ha, the west finally pushes through and I'm in the convergence, or at least so I thought. Regardless, as I make my way toward the building cloudbase, I can see all the other guys that were struggling on the Factory do the same. I'm still out front so I make my way back to the top of the spine. I come in just as E.J. Steele tops out and heads on course towards Montecito Peak. The race is finally on!

E.J. is already climbing out at Montecito as I go on my glide. Scott Angel is on my tail after first staying back to reach cloudbase. Upon arriving at Montecito I struggle on its SW spine so I quickly beeline it for the east spine. Looking back I see Scotty connect with something that takes him to cloudbase again. E.J. is already turning circles on West Ramero to the east. *Oh well, third place.* The east spine works well enough and soon I'm at cloudbase, giving chase. From the road cut at Ramero it is a quick climb to cloudbase again.

Tim Riley is 25 yards off my tail as I'm about to glide in below the road cut. Above me on the turnout, a dozen mountain bikers stop to watch our progress. As I hit the lift above the spine I crank the glider on its ear. Before I can finish my 360, Tim is doing the same. Two thousand feet later, I go on my glide, passing the bikers along the way. Tim is still 25 yards off my tail. Looking back I can see that the bikers haven't moved; for a brief moment, I would have changed places.

Leaving Ramero I can see Scotty and E.J. out in front struggling to get established on Castle Ridge. As Scotty and E.J. fall off a little further east with Scotty taking the lead, I luck out and connect with something on the spine that they just dribbled off of. Below me a group of dirt bikers stop to watch our progress. I can hear them hollering with approval above their engine noise. Now at cloudbase, I easily pass E.J. Scotty is just ahead of me, searching for lift.

Casitas Pass, just a few miles ahead of us, is our main XC obstacle, but this little section here requires the most patience because of its proximity to the ocean. Because of the cooler air of the marine influence, cloudbase can be as much as 1k lower than anywhere else along the ridgeline. Scotty and E.J. prove the point, but I feel like I'm on the leading edge of the west pushing through. I'm able to take the lead halfway through the section. On the radio I can hear pilots back in Santa Barbara complaining about a strong SE wind.

Southeast? What the hell are you guys talking about? I'm east of you and I'm feeling a west push.

Apparently the SE wind was wrapping around Rincon Point and coming onshore; we were lucky enough to be in its eddy.

At Noon Peak, the start of the Casitas Pass, I'm in the fish mode. The SW spine didn't work, and now I'm limping off the SE spine. If I don't find something soon, I'll have to call it a day. *Oh well, at least I'm in a position to glide to my truck at Bailard.* But I can do without that kind of convenience, I'm sure I'll find something; the day is too good. And I do find something. As I turn circles in the light, broken lift, Scotty flies in right below me. Soon we are both high enough to step back to the main spine. I can see E.J. gliding in below. On the main spine the lift is strong and smooth and I can just tell at this point that it will take us high enough to make a play for West Divide Peak, the most critical decision point in the pass. Generally, if you don't find lift when you first arrive at West Divide, you head out. Getting high on Noon Peak is critical. For some reason Scotty leaves our thermal early. I stay back and work the thermal to cloudbase before going into the pass.

At West Divide I come in a hundred feet below the top of the spine, which is almost high enough to keep on going if I don't find lift. Scotty looks like he is low enough that if he doesn't get up he won't make the glide out. At West Divide I tuck the glider in close and scratch my way up the spine. *East wind my foot, I'm drifting right across the face of the peak.* I see Scotty is back in the ball game and E.J. has caught up and has now joined me in my thermal. With its strong eastward drift, the thermal that E.J. and I are working deposits us right on top of the spine of East Divide. Normally, if you can get above West Divide Peak you can glide all the way to Whiteledge, the eastern side of the Casitas Pass; East Divide provides a little skip, but you generally don't have to stay around to work it. On this day, however, East Divide is on, and soon both E.J. and I are racing to cloudbase. I pick a better core and beat him there by 500 ft.

Back in the lead, I head over to Whiteledge. *What a beautiful sight!* First of all, I made it through the pass, and so I'm just happy I won't be missing dinner because of a long hike. But this really is a special place. Whiteledge gets its name from the steep granite wall that makes up its SW flank; it compares to anything in the Owens Valley. At the base of the mountain is Casitas Lake, a well-known bass fishing spot. Beyond the lake, separated by the coastal range, is the Pacific Ocean. To the north lies Pine Mountain and the other snow-covered peaks of the San Rafael mountain range. Toward the east, lies the beautiful Ojai Valley, which is where I'm heading.

Whiteledge works well enough but cloud base has dropped below the east side of the ridge. Fortunately, we are way out in front of the main ridgeline so going through the cloud for a brief moment won't provide much of a hazard. I pop out the east side of the cloud and beeline it for my trusty thermal trigger, a mile west of Rt. 33 on the main ridgeline. Normally, this is a reliable quick 2k gain, but today the lift is weak.

Where are those other guys? They must have turned back for Santa Barbara; I must be on my own. Oh, wait, there they are.

Scotty comes in about 1k below me and starts turning circles. E.J. keeps on going and passes us both to work the last point before 33 and the start of the Topa Topa mountain range. I give up on the stuff I'm working to join him. I come in higher than E.J., but the lift he is working doesn't seem to be worth stopping for, so I continue on. On the first point beyond the Nut House spine east of 33, I'm down to 1700ft. and hanging on for dear life. E.J. flies in to join me. The scraps turn into a sweetie, and it doesn't take long for me to be on my way at 5k. E.J. bails out below 4k to regain the lead.

What is it with these young guns, always in the race mode? There is a certain satisfaction being in the lead, but…why force the issue?

Heading over to Nordoff Ridge, the place to be when it is blowing Santa Anas, I can see E.J. flushing off the east spine. Scotty is behind me working the back ridgeline. At Nordoff I connect with something that takes me to 5500 ft and cloudbase. E.J. is now at least 3k below me limping over to Three Stooges. We're at the 25-mile mark from Santa Barbara and I will take the lead for good. The rest of the way through Ojai is pretty straight-forward: up to cloud base at Twin Peaks, continue to work the front points of West and East Repeater, and then step back to Boyd's. From cloudbase at Boyd's, I head directly over to Santa Paula Peak without stopping at the Rocky Bluffs, the last mountainous terrain of the Ojai Valley.

I'm a bit lower than I would like upon arriving at Santa Paula Peak, but I see three birds soaring up the NW spine. Soon I'm sharing a ratty thermal with them, out-climbing one of them.

Jeez, what are those funny numbers on their wings? California condors. This is the second time I have had the pleasure of soaring with these magnificent birds.

John Greynald's Santa Barbara site record is 74 miles. Generally, if you can make it through the Casitas Pass, chances are you can make it to Santa Paula Peak; the race for the site record, however, starts here. The top of the ridgeline is in the clouds, but I am able to turn the corner and dribble along the face until I fall off the eastern-most spine toward the town of Filmore. Above town, and just short of Oak Mountain, I find some weak lift for a thousand-foot gain. But in the foothills to the east, less than a mile way, a nice flat-bottomed cloud is forming; I give up my weak lift and head directly for it. Nothing. *Come on, what's feeding this?* I have no choice but to fall off to Highway 126 and the middle of the Santa Clara river basin. I'm now at the 50-mile mark, and down to 1500 ft. I report on the radio that if I don't find something soon I'll be landing near the town of Piru, tying my 53-mile PR from Santa Barbara. Above town I fumble into some weak lift that takes me back to 3600 ft. Above me clouds are beginning to form, but I just can't seem to get up to them. And again, just to the east, a nice big flat-bottomed cloud in the foothills is within gliding distance. Again, nothing. And again, I have to fall off towards 126. This time, however, it is all she wrote, and I'm on the ground shortly thereafter.

Woulda, shoulda, coulda…Why didn't I stay back there at Piru, searching a little more?

Ten minutes after landing, E.J. comes limping in and puts it down right next to me; 15 minutes after that, Scotty follows. It is the longest flight from Santa Barbara for all three of us, 57.5 miles; there are high fives all around.

For the other pilots, Tom Truax landed in Filmore (adding the turnpoint, his mileage matched or slightly beat ours). Everyone else was scattered along the course line, with some having their own personal bests. For me the flight marks three times in a row since November that I have been able to make it at least to Santa Paula from Santa Barbara. I have had flights of 53.5, 38.3 and 57.5 miles respectively... not bad for the time of year.

Just another 15 miles or so and I'll make it to Kagel, my longtime goal.

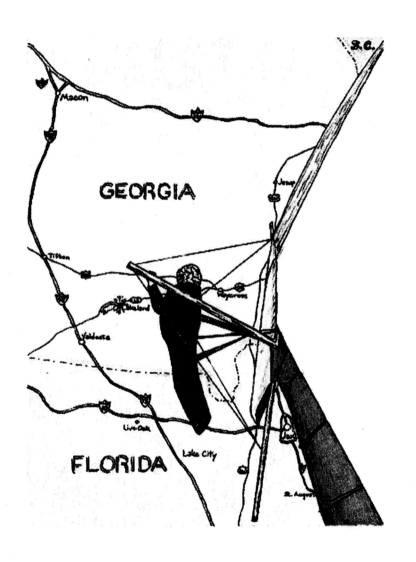

Pulling In The Flaps

Mark Poustinchian

On Thursday, March 8, 2000, the wind was from the east about 5 to 10 mph. Despite the crosswind three Quest Air X-C pilots decided to go north and see what happens. Bo Hagewood flew 100 miles and, due to the blue sky, turned around and landed a few miles to the south to make the retrieval easier. Campbell Bowen flew 125 miles and landed close to highway 75. I flew 133 miles and after 6 hours and 6 minutes of flying landed north of I-10 close to highway 75. The Ball GC was showing anywhere from 0 to 5 mph tailwind and also 0 to 5 mph headwind. It was slow going and all the miles were due to glide, no drift. I hate it when that happens, it takes forever to get some miles, especially when the thermals are far apart and not that strong.

On Friday, March 9, due to all these long flights from Quest Air Mark Gibbo came to Quest Air to fly with us. Mike Eberly from North American Flight Design also was here and he added a little incentive of $1000 cash for any pilot flying a GhostBuster to Georgia. The race was on!

At 11:30 am we started to get airborne. The wind was from southwest at 10 mph. Being the chicken that I am, I started flying over highway 75 where there are big landing fields. I got low several times crossing blue holes. The lowest save was from 400' agl. The cloud streets were lined up from southwest to northeast. At one time I flew 15 miles to the west into a 5-8 mph head wind to clear some bad areas, damn. That slowed me up big time.

It is true when they say, *"no guts no glory."* I should have had enough courage to go downwind to the northeast to the part of Georgia that comes down into Florida. However, there are too many lakes and too many trees to the north and northeast for my type of flying. That is what Gibbo did and flew his GhostBuster 140 miles and made it to the Georgia's finger into Florida. He did a great job and took the direct route. I flew my GhostBuster 6 hours and 14 minutes and landed at 135 miles from Quest Air about 40 miles to the west of Gibbo. In Florida you usually land just before dark and you'd better be prepared to be eaten alive by the Florida mosquitoes. I don't know how many sucked my blood when I was breaking down the glider. All I know was that I was slapping myself all over the place and at times had to run to get away.

What a great set up Mark Gibbo has for X-C flying. His dad is a great person and a great driver. He flies hang gliders and is able to give Gibbo great information on the radio. The battery on my radio was low and I could not transmit anymore; however I could hear well. "Dad, tell me which side of highway 75 has the best-looking clouds."

"West of highway 75 is looking much better right now, clouds to the east are far apart and dissipating."

Damn, here I was on the east of 75 and getting way too low, 400' agl to be exact. I would have given a $100 bill for that information 20 minutes ago when I was high and decided to go to the east of 75.

When Gibbo was crossing the border at the Georgia's finger, his dad was already there and checking out the possible LZ's and giving him all the information about the wind direction, power lines and fences which again I would have given another $100 bill for. According to Mark, the possible LZ's are small and far apart. Anybody looking for a great X-C driver in Florida should try to talk Gibbo's dad into driving; he is great.

Saturday, my new mission: make it to Georgia. Again the wind was from the south and going southwest further north. Well it seemed that I would have to fly crosswind again and try to go to Georgia the hard way. I have fallen in love with highway 75, and it seems that these days I end up following it regardless of the wind direction. However a driver like Gibbo's dad could change all that.

People at Quest Air have been giving me a hard time; they say that I have been cheating when I tell the tug pilots to tow me downwind and drop me off down wind. I try to release downwind to eliminate the option of landing at Quest Air if the air is marginal. I figure that if I can't land for another tow, then I am going to give it my best to get up and go. It's also more economical for a cheap guy like me, only one tow.

This day I hit a nice thermal that put my glider about 75 feet above the tug and I figured I better release and take it up before it broke the weak link. I was about 1000' agl and about ¼ mile to the east of Quest Air. That thermal got me to about 3200'. After that I stayed below 2000' for 40 minutes, getting angrier by the minute. I was dealing with small punchy thermals. Damn, *where's the beef?* I could not climb, no matter what I did. I flew over several landing options just a few miles north of Quest Air. It was not a good start and I was tiring fast. I drank half of my water supply in the first half hour due to dry mouth; I hate it when that happens

I was at 20 miles with a southwest wind of 5 to 10 mph. Considering how much I love highway 75 due to big fields and easy retrievals, I had to fly crosswind again and go northeast and get the miles the hard way. One of these days we will have 10 mph southeast wind for the 200 miler. Anyway, I had to fly a long ways with a 2-3 mph tailwind and had to cover many miles. The thermals were punchy and there was bad sink between the thermals; I was not a happy camper.

My girlfriend had offered to drive for me, however I told her to wait for a while and hit the road about 2 hours later. I wished Mark Gibbo's dad was there to give me the great info about what was happening ahead with cloud formations, spacing and duration. All I know was that it was not easy to and I had to work my butt off to stay up. When I passed the 100 mark, I talked to my girlfriend on the radio. She was 15 miles behind. I was glad that I wouldn't have to wait long for retrieval. However, she has been known to disappear in the past, nowhere to be reached on the radio. Of course, this usually happens when I am getting low. She'll decide to go shopping and disappear without warning. Sure enough, half an hour later there was no response. Damn, she did it again!

I was getting close to I-10. The air was smooth and the thermals were as big as football fields. Ah, how sweet it was, I could stay high after 4:30 pm and enjoy the view for a change. The bad sink was disappearing and the air started to fill with small bubbles. It was not so easy in Arkansas. This was all new to me; I love Florida.

I was on the west side of highway 75 and shortly after that it started to run more westerly on the north side of Florida. I was getting to ugly parts - woods and woods and more woods, damn. They are pretty, however they are also my worst nightmare. I could see some fields to the north, 10 miles away; however it looked very ugly after that. I had been dealing with a cross wind during the entire flight and now it was going to get worse. The Ball GC was showing a tailwind of about 3 to 5 mph and when I turned more westerly it went to zero tail wind. Oh well, there was nothing that I could do.

Flying a few more miles over highway 75 to northwest, the view to the north got very interesting. I believe I was somewhere southeast of Jasper. It looked like a nuclear bomb has exploded in this area. The ground looked like another planet; very interesting, and not a great place to land. There was 10 miles of Mars-land, no trees, white-sandy colored ground and big holes in the ground. No thanks; I think I'll just follow 75 for a while.

The sink rate had fallen to about 100 fpm and the air was as smooth as glass. The sun was already down and I was at 5000' agl. Two days earlier, Campbell Bowen landed around 6:20 pm after a 125-mile X-C flight and I just could not believe that it was possible to fly so late. The tailwind was close to zero and I had to do some crabbing to stay on 75. After gliding for 30 minutes I came to the end of the world again. At 2500' agl it looked like the trees had trapped me again. There was a big field about 2 miles to the north. As I turned the glider north the GhostBuster suddenly started to cover ground as if I were in a small airplane. The Ball GC vario was showing a tailwind of 12-14 mph. Damn, I have been missing most of that tail wind component during the entire flight.

Samantha was still nowhere to be found and I knew that I would have to get a hold of her by cell phone soon after landing. I landed at 6:22 pm after 6 hours and 36 minutes and after 163 hard-earned miles. This flight broke my own record of 155 miles for Quest Air and also my personal best record, which I got about two weeks ago. I recorded the flight on my ball GC with a Garmin Map attached. After downloading the data and GPS flight path, it can be seen that I crossed the Georgia border when I was getting ready to land and flew about a quarter of a mile into Georgia when I was about 1500' agl. Due to a lack of landing zones I landed a quarter mile south of the border. But I had crossed the Georgia border! I was only 4 miles short of a new record for the state of Florida as well. But, it is just March, it gets better in April!

I love flying out here, about 19 hours of flying in the last three days. Life is just too good. I gave up my professional job as a senior structural engineer at a nuclear power plant to follow my dreams of flying. All my dreams are coming true and I think giving up my job was the best thing that I have done. My little cubicle office was beginning to feel like a prison, and I needed to be free to fly like a bird. What a great sport this is and I am so lucky to be a part of it.

I love my GhostBuster and in less than three months it already has over 100 hours on it. I have flown it over 1300 miles. I would not trade it in for anything out there. I have had my personal best flights here with my new glider and I want to thank Flight Design for creating a wonderful glider. They should not change a thing, this wing is just awesome the way it is.

The GhostBuster is more of a handful than the Exxtacy, but what do you expect? There always has been a tradeoff when you give up some handling for performance. Give me performance and you can keep the handling, because performance is what I want. All these years pilots have been trying to fly from flight parks in Florida to Georgia and nobody made it until the GhostBusters showed up around here. Two days in a row the GhostBusters made it to Georgia. And 100-milers are a piece of cake with a GhostBuster.

Next mission: break the Florida state record and try to go 200 miles. Just give me a 10 mph southeast wind and a good day and get out of the way because the GhostBusters are flying through. You can push out all you want, I'll be pulling in with the flaps retracted and going for another record.

Breaking the Arkansas State Record

Mark Poustinchian

Well, what did you expect? I am flying the best X-C hang glider I have ever flown, my sweet-flying Exxtacy.

On July 29 I broke the altitude record for Class II gliders in Arkansas. It was from Magazine and I got to 9,030' agl over no-man's-land between Mount Nebo and Mount Magazine. I landed at 50.4 miles near Jerusalem.

Then, on July 30, I broke my own Arkansas X-C record of 104 miles. On that day I flew from Mount Magazine into northeast Arkansas and made it to Newport, a distance of 137 miles. It took four hours and 14 minutes and I landed at 5:48 PM in a soybean field less than 50 miles from the Tennessee border.

Believe it or not, this was easier than my 104-miler. I got up in a 1,000-plus fpm thermal after launching with Jim Kerns. I climbed to more than 7,500' AGL, and turned the glider northeast toward Russellville, making it over the Whataburger LZ in Russellville with over 5,500' AGL in less than 40 minutes. Whataburger is about 30 miles from Magazine. I probably made fewer than ten big, fat turns while the lift was 1,000-plus and I was below 6,000' AGL. Definitley my fastest time to Whataburger. There was a cloud street perfectly lined up all the way to Russellville at over 8,000' AGL. I reached my highest altitude southwest of Greers Ferry Lake at 8,520' AGL. After passing Crow Mountain I struggled for a while and got to 1,600' AGL. But not long thereafter I found a 1, 600 fpm boomer that took me to 8,400' AGL and I was on my way again.

There were no hills, mountains or extensive tree-covered areas to cross, just a terrific view of the flatlands and Greers Ferry Lake to my left, and fantastic cumies everywhere. There was no sign of over development. I only wish we had had a good tail wind; it was about five mph from the southwest. With a 15- to 20-mph tailwind and no blue hole at the end of the flight I would have made it into Tennessee, more than 200 miles away.

I made a mistake that left me short of 142 miles, which is the Oklahoma record set by Bruce Mahoney in 1985. There was a lot of shade under me as I approached 6,000' AGL and the lift got weak, only 100 to 150 fpm, so I left the thermal to get to the shadow boundary ahead of me. Unfortunately, that was my last thermal and there was not a single bump thereafter. There were a lot of green farm fields for miles and miles, and no sign of any clouds ahead of me, just blue sky. If only I had stayed with that thermal, gained another 1,000', and drifted a couple of more miles....

Jim Kerns doubled his best X-C distance that day, landing at over 75 miles on the south side of Greers Ferry Lake. Ron Sewell also made his best X-C distance, landing past Atkins at about 42 miles from Magazine.

Life is way too good these days. If the forecast calls for 100+ temperatures and a 20% chance of thunderstorms, and the thermal index predicts good thermals with cloud base over 8,000' AGL, drop everything - and I mean everything - and go flying in Arkansas.

Weekend in Owen's Valley - 1997

Grant (Groundhog) Hoag

Thursday 3 July: Didn't pack the truck until after work yesterday, so arrived in Tuttle Creek Campground in Lone Pine at 1 a.m. Awake at 6:30 when the sun hit the tent, instantly raising the temperature to 90 degrees. I'm seeing double; a desert mirage? Nope, just groggy from lack of sleep. The Trout Wagon lumbers by the tent, filled with the week's delivery of stocking trout. Grab the pole and follow the wagon. Catch a limit of dazed trout in 20 minutes. Cancel flying for the day and instead hike up to 10,500' in Cottonwood Canyon to get acclimatized to altitude. The pines are dropping so much pollen it looks like a big fire, instead of the forest love fest it actually is. Mosquitoes eat me alive. In the evening retreat to Tuttle Creek for trout bake.

Friday 4 July: Independence Day. It's already crowded at Walt's Point by 9 a.m. Site-monitor John soon arrives with more pilots who immediately jam into the remaining sites. Tom is the first to launch, seeking a record paraglider flight. A quarter-mile in front of launch he suffers an end-cell collapse. One, two, three revolutions down. Where's the reserve? Much too late he throws it. Wham! Tom hits the canyon rocks 2,000 feet below launch before the reserve deploys, and John moves into rescue-coordinator mode. Two guys take off down the canyon to locate and assess Tom's condition. Others follow with first-aid kits, radios, neck brace, water, body board, ropes etc. Rock fall is a constant problem.

Tom is located and stabilized with unspecified back injuries. With six pilots lifting the body board and 6 pulling on ropes, Tom is hauled sled-dog style back up to launch and into the ambulance. Flying resumes. Later that day Tom is released from the hospital.

Rescue finished, so flying goal becomes the town of Independence, where the annual BBQ and fireworks display is happening. Land at the airport, fold up and go to the town park. While in line for an $8-plate of ribs with all the fixin's, Jim keys up on the SHGA frequency. Seems he landed out away from the road after launching from Black Eagle, and his driver isn't responding. Damn - the smell of the ribs is very attractive, but Jim's plaintive calls are heart rendering. Consider turning off the radio, but instead leave the festivities and head out into the trackless waste near Mazurka Canyon. With Jim in the car, head up the road towards launch. Jim's driver calls! Radio was accidentally knocked off frequency, but now the car's got a flat on Black Eagle Mine Road. Drive up the mining road, change the flat. Jim's driver suggests that chase isn't much fun at times. Back down the hill, it's too late for the BBQ, so go back to Lone Pine for showers and "We Toss 'Em, They're Awesome" pizza. Yum.

Saturday 5 July: Drive up to Walt's Point to learn that yesterday Kamyar flew to Tonapah (155 miles). He's an animal. Today winds are switchy, but we launch anyway. Westerlies happen early and it's rock and roll, Owen's Valley style. Fly over to the Inyos from Whitney Portal, but can't make the crossing and land at Mazurka Canyon Road. Very hot day. Temperature peaks at 99 degrees, with 6% humidity. Thankfully it's a lot cooler above 10,000'. Our chase driver insists on running the car's a/c at all times. Seems reasonable, since the Toyota never overheats. After flying, organize a BBQ party at the campsite. Libations.

Sunday 6 July: North winds. Go hiking, with mosquito repellent. Listen on radio as everyone flies 50 miles to the South. The Big O is consistently unpredictable.

Monday, 7 July: Local pilots are excited. Conditions seem great. No inversion, humidity is up, wind direction variable. Tandem team declares goal for new world record. Nobody wants to launch first, and winds are cycling up launch with 15-mph gusts. Scary. Visiting pilot cannot resist, and takes off at 12:45 AM. Immediately he sinks out. I launch next, aggressively thermal in the saddle, get up and head north. Winds are very light. My Afro vario goes nuts. In smooth air the needle swings from pegged up to down. Very annoying, and not useful - turn it off. Ten minutes later it acts normal. Weird.

North of Onion Valley sink to 10,500 feet, but catch a weak and thin thermal with 100 fpm up. Work it, work it, work it, and slowly the thermal gets better; 400 fpm, 600 fpm up. Altitude 12,000', 14,000', 17,000'. Getting cold, boost oxygen flow rate. Temperature 20 degrees, and Camalbak water tube frozen. Plenty of time to admire the view while climbing. Pull out the disposable camera and take some shots until fingers freeze. The sky darkens and Fresno becomes visible to the west beyond the unfolding Sierras. Oops! Gone above 17,999! Jump out of the thermal and dive North for thicker air. 16,000' over Klondike Lake.

Fly to the White Mountains under a big cloud street. No need to thermal, so fly straight for 20 miles to White Mountain Peak without losing any altitude. Yodel at a lone hiker near the peak. Radio comes to life with an alert of strong gusts 9,000' below on the ground in Chalfant Valley. Am startled to witness a classic microburst of air crashing into a plowed field near the racetrack. Dust fronts moving at 25 mph fan out to the north and south simultaneously from the field. A pilot on the ground begs his chase to help him control his glider in the winds. It looks scary. Am glad to be high.

Pass through a band of virga at 12,000'. BIG mistake! Gentle lift turns to massive sink. Am hammered by 1,000-fpm downdrafts, and have to run west to Chalfant Valley. In 10 minutes have lost 7,000', and am down to the valley floor. Pray to reach the highway before having to set down. Face into the wind with zero forward penetration. 40' above the ground fall out of the sky in the wind gradient. Wham! Plow into a (soft) sagebrush. Unhook and secure the glider. Wow. 85 miles in 5 hours. Hear that the tandem team has set a new world's record today!

Tuesday 8 July: Go fishing in Onion Valley. At 1:30 five gliders slip silently north, high overhead. One bounces in and out of cloudbase; just another day in paradise. Five minutes later an F-117 Stealth Fighter Bomber flies past overhead on the same path, but below the gliders. A vision unfolds in my head of newspaper headlines in Baghdad: "Hang Gliding Hero Honored Posthumously for Downing Stealth Bomber." Hum. Better stick to my fishing today. The trout are delicious.

A Spuds' Eye View

The Day the *Spud Club* Was Formed

Doug Johnson

What is the 'Spud Club'? Well, I'm glad you asked. The 'Spud Club' is a small group of hang glider pilots who have flown their craft from Chelan Butte, WA into the state of Idaho. The border between Washington and Idaho is 140 miles at its closest point from Chelan. Any pilot who takes off at Chelan Butte, and lands in Idaho, automatically becomes a member of 'The Spud Club'. Being a 'Spud Club' member has some great advantages and perks; one of the best is 'Bragging Rights', which, when combined with two bucks, can get you a cup of coffee just about anywhere!

Let me give you a little background about Chelan and my experience there. Many pilots have claimed the Washington State XC crown since the Butte was first used as a cross-country launch pad. Many of the early ones were from Minnesota and Wisconsin and I heard all about the place at our local flying sites here in the Midwest. Danny Uchytil and Lee Fisher had moved to Seattle. They were more than willing to drive the three and one half hours to Chelan for the great flying conditions on the weekends. They had lots of fun trying to outdo each other, both in the air and on the ground. Jerry House, Jon Solon, Kevin Bye, Buck McMinn, and Larry Majchrzak would make the move to Washington over the next few years.

In 1979 most pilots who were going to Chelan went there because the conditions allowed them to get really high and stay up for long durations. Only a few pilots were experimenting with Chelan's XC potential. Those few pilots would get very high over the Butte and then fly east toward the wheat fields of Eastern Washington. But before they could get there they had to get past the first major hurdle, the Columbia River Gorge. Getting across the gorge was quite a feat in those days; the darn thing is five miles across and 3000' deep! There's no lift to be found anywhere while crossing, it's all sink until you make the other side. The Butte is 3800' MSL and the far rim is only 700' lower. How high do you want to be before leaving? Get as high as you can! 4000' AGL or more would usually get you there. For those who were willing to attempt the crossing, the rewards on the other side were great. The first thermal you find on the eastern rim is a major relief after being in the sink for so long.

Eastern Washington is relatively flat with a few lakes, and lava flows breaking up the monotony. The average altitude is 2000-2500' MSL. Dust devils dance across the wheat fields as they start to release their heat in the late morning. As you look from the Butte towards Mansfield, these dust devils are a good indication that it's time to launch. There are few roads to follow. However, there is a major road running straight east from the gorge, through Mansfield, to Simms Corner. Beyond Simms is Banks Lake. Banks is at the 35mile mark on your XC journey. This is a major obstacle. Pilots must be very high, depending on the speed of the westerly wind, in order to make it to the other side. 7000' AGL is usually enough. Banks Lake also forces your driver to make quite a detour to the south. Getting low on the east side of the lake, with your driver going around the end of the lake, twenty miles to the south, could mean a long walk to a phone. Over the years, as glider performance improved, the Banks Lake crossing became less scary. Information was exchanged between pilots about communications, chase routes and strategies and this obstacle and others were overcome as the limit of XC flying was extended eastward.

The next big problem on XC flight was the forested area between Creston and Davenport. This is about 80 miles from launch and about seven to eight miles across. The area just past Creston is covered with rough lava and trees. If there is an area without trees that is big enough to put a glider down in, I'll guarantee that it is very rough ground. Bad place to land! Eventually this area was overcome as well. Spokane, WA is another area of concern with its TCA and suburbs. The final barrier is the Bitterroot Mountains in Idaho. "Houston, we have a BIG problem!"

In 1980 Dave Little set the new state record by flying almost to Simms Corner, which is 33 miles from the Butte. The following list will give you an idea of how the XC record got extended over the first 15 years. These are the longest flights recorded for each year:

1981: Gerry Uchytil	39 miles	
1982: Gerry Uchytil	91 miles	
1983: Gerry Uchytil	80 miles	
1984: Joe Evans	107 miles (first hundred-miler from Chelan)	
1985: Kevin Bye	122 miles	
1986: John Woiwode	131 miles	
1987: Mike Neuman	157 miles	
1988: Kevin Bye	125 miles	
1989: Howard Osterlund	155 miles	
1990: Stew Cameron	85-mile triangle	
1991: Lionel Space	91.5 mile triangle	
1992: Paul Gallagher	151 miles	
1994: 8 female pilots	declared 100 miles out and back	

(Butte to Almira, WA to Chelan airport during a competition)

There are pilots who held the state XC record for a short time, but because another pilot bested their mileage before the end of the year, they didn't make the list. I know Lee Fisher and Kevin Bye went back and forth in the lead during the summer of 1985. There were probably others. All of the flights listed above are from Chelan. Jeff Kohler holds the current state record of 189 miles. However, he flew south from Tekoa, near Spokane and landed in Oregon.

Because a very large number of my flying friends had already moved to Washington, or were thinking about it, and because there was such great flying at Chelan, I just HAD to get out there. So, I loaded up the car and headed west. I first flew at Chelan in July of 1982. I was flying a Raven 229 at the time and had a total of 29 hours in my logbook as a result of three years of effort. Now I was looking for hours and lots of them. My first flight in Chelan was July 12, 1982. In my first vacation there, I logged 8:15 hours. I flew nine out of ten days! Wow! Chelan really was living up to its reputation! My first XC flight in a hang glider occurred there on July 26, 1982. It was a one-hour flight, which covered all of 12 miles to the town of Waterville, WA. A mile before I landed I was down to about 1500' AGL when I spotted a large swirl in the wheat. I had been cautioned to steer clear of these violent disturbances. Well I wasn't very far from this thing and the next thing I knew I was going up! I made a few 360's and gained a few hundred feet. I was also getting my butt kicked! I had had enough of this abuse and decided that it would be the right thing to do if I would just give up on it. As soon as I left the thermal I lost the few hundred feet I had just gained faster than I had gained it! I turned toward Waterville and landed next to a house with a swimming pool. The people who lived there were very hospitable. They let me use their phone and offered me food and drink. I thought, "This XC stuff is great fun!" I was hooked. When I talked to other pilots about the thermal in the wheat I was told that some of them were having success getting really high in them. But be careful! They seemed to mark an area of strong lift, strong sink, and turbulence. I would end up driving out to Chelan eleven times in the next fourteen years.

In 1983 I bought a new glider, a Progressive Aircraft 'Pro Star II', and went back to Chelan after a trip to the Owens Valley with Danny and Gerry Uchytil. During my second year at Chelan I flew in the Classic. I was encouraged by taking seventh place out of a field of twenty-two in my first competition. I flew a total of 72 miles in the three-day long contest. Now I was sold on Chelan. This place will make a pilot out of you. I made lots of new friends. Jon Dawkins. Larry and Tina Jorgenson. Mike Daley. Scott Ruttledge. Paul Clocke, John Elliott, Dave Little, Marilyn Raines, Jeff Kohler, Gene Mathews. Of course, I got to see all of my old midwestern friends, too. Once again, I decide that I'd be back for sure!

In 1984 I bought a new Airwave 'Magic III' and immediately noticed a huge difference in performance. Word was getting around about what a great XC site Chelan really was. The field for the Chelan Classic was starting to grow much larger and the pilots more experienced. With so many good pilots around, I was learning this XC thing on a fantastically steep learning curve! I finished 12th in the Chelan Classic that year but was not disappointed at all. Just try and keep me away from this place!

One of the regular Chelan pilots, Lee Fisher, a 'Skydog' transplant from back home, went down to Crestline, CA and won the Sport Class at the '84 Nationals! Here's one of the guys I really looked up to (just kidding Lee) winning his class at the Nationals! Lee was always there to push everyone a little harder with his flying and practical jokes. He was always close by whenever anyone had a great XC flight. Lee and I chased Joe Evans on the first 100-mile flight from Chelan! Mentor.

By the time the 1985 Nationals were held there I had about 750 miles of XC and over 150 hours under my belt! What a difference a couple years, great friends and a great site can make! I was ready for more! When the competition was over I wound up flying 482 miles and logging 30:05 hours in 7 flights! My friend and 'Skydog' founder, Gerry Uchytil, won the 'Sport Class'. I took 6th place! I got to fly with, and learn a lot from, World Champion John Pendry and former champ Steve Moyes. Chris Bulger, Jim Lee, Dennis Pagen, Pete Lehmann, and Randy Adams. Ben and Alegra Davidson. Jim Zeiset, Rich Pfiffer, Gerry Charlevoix, and Tip Rodgers were there also. The list is almost endless. Everyone who was anyone in the sport was there.

I did not come out of this meet unscathed though. I destroyed my glider by ground looping my landing in the fifth round. Although the tailwind I had had all day was light, it had switched around 180 degrees when I landed. Goal was the eastern end of the runway at the Davenport, WA airport, which is 90 miles from launch. I made it to the western end of the runway. The next morning I rebuilt my glider with spare parts that Ken Brown and Chris Bulger from Airwave had on hand. It took about four hours in the city park with the help of Buck McMinn, Bill Cummings and Larry Majchrzak. I was able to fly that day, which was the first 100 mile task ever called in a US Nationals. Buck lives in Chelan and was my first instructor back in Minnesota. I'll never forget the first thing he said to me on the training hill; "If you could see the air, you probably wouldn't fly." Great instructor! Mentor.

In 1986 I headed out to Chelan and another Nationals. Yep. Two years in a row of Nationals at Chelan. I represented Region 7 by winning the Regional Championship. There were quite a few pilots better than me at the Regionals, but I got lucky. In the Nationals I improved to 4th place in the 'Sport Class'. By the end of 1986 I had flown 235 hours and 1400 miles of XC. There was still nothing called the 'Spud Club' but people were starting to talk about it. John Woiwode had flown 131miles from Chelan to somewhere north of Spokane. Now the record was close to Idaho, but still, not quite there. Idaho was calling.

Though this may seem more like the history of Doug Johnson than the story of XC in Chelan, my point is that the two are related. Chelan was making every pilot's logbook fat. We were all getting better and setting new PR's all the time. That's what Chelan does to pilots. It challenges them to get better. The town of Chelan even encouraged us by erecting a cherry wood, carved eagle statue in the city park. On it was a plaque that listed the best flight of the previous year. Most of us were trying hard to emulate the pilots whose names were on the plaque. I'm tellin' ya, this was hang gliding heaven!

The 'Spud Club' was born on June 30, 1987 when five pilots from all over the United States flew into Idaho from Chelan. What a day it was! It was hot. It was windy. It was a Tuesday. Conditions had been kind of iffy the day before with a north to northwest wind of about 5 to 10. Most of the regulars from Seattle were on 'the Green Side' working. So, only about fifteen pilots flew that day instead of the usual 30-40 on the weekend. About half of those were 'Skydogs'. We had planned to all get together and fly when we could have the Butte pretty much to ourselves. We all made our way to the top of the Butte by 10:00 AM. The forecast was for west wind, 10 to 20, and high temperature of 100 degrees. It was a perfect day for XC, maybe a long XC. So get out your road atlases and follow along!

I launched at 1:10 PM about 15 minutes behind Gerry Uchytil. I always watch what Gerry does very closely. My best flights have all been on the same days and from the same places as some of his best flights. Mentor. The first indication that the day might really be good was how high I got above the Butte. Cloud base was at 10,000'MSL! That's more than 6,000' over the top of the Butte. I had also drifted half way across the gorge. There would be no waiting around. It's time to go XC.

I crossed the gorge and found some light lift on the far rim. I gained only 1500' before I saw a good dust devil getting organized at the power lines. The dust devil was about two miles out in front of me and I got drilled trying to get to it. Finally the nose of my glider started to lift and I found 750 FPM lift on the upwind side of the dust. I climbed back up to cloudbase. I was halfway to Mansfield (20 miles) in really good shape. I heard Gerry talking to someone on the radio. We were using CB's at that time. I had a big advantage over most other pilots with a really good dipole antenna, and it helped me to know how the other pilots were doing, arrange retrievals, and pass along messages from pilots to their drivers. Gerry was at least ten miles in front of me, as usual, but was always nice enough to let me know where he was and always offered encouragement.

It was a great day by Chelan standards. There were lots of dust devils and clouds to mark your next move. I was making 10 miles on every thermal. Next thing I knew, I was crossing Banks Lake, 35 miles from launch. Cloud base was getting higher and the drift was getting stronger. I had dropped my car off at the junkyard. We had an agreement between us that if anyone didn't get up after launch and landed in the junkyard, he would be a chase driver. I tried to find out if anyone was on the road yet. I got no response.

When I got to the Almira area (50 miles) I heard Gerry on the radio saying he was at 11,000' MSL, everything was going great. He said "Dougy, can you believe how fast we got out here? I'm at Wilbur and I've only been in the air for two hours!" I responded with equal amazement. Again, he encouraged me, "Keep it up buddy, this is going to be a big day." Mentor. He and I had landed at the Wilbur airport (60 miles) in 1983 after four hours in the air! At the time, that was my longest flight. I tried again to contact a driver. Still, no response.

We continued along and passed over Creston, 75 miles out. The barrier of woods and lava between Creston and Davenport didn't seem to be as big an obstacle today as in the past. We were getting close to 12,000 MSL (about 10,000 AGL!) and the drift was incredible! As I flew over Davenport (90 miles) I could see Reardon out in front of me. I was really excited, I was pretty sure I was going to make Reardon. This beautiful little town in eastern Washington was the magical 100-mile mark. I had never done a 100-miler before! I was going to do it today! Finally! It's hard to describe how I felt as the town drifted by a mile and a half below me. With a hundred miles behind me now, I topped out in the next thermal at 12,500'. I was planning my route around Spokane when my radio cracked to life. Dan O'Hara was driving my car and he was looking for me. It was the most beautiful thing I think I have ever heard; I already had over 100 miles, *and* I had a driver in *my* car. We agreed that if we lost contact we would both call Buck's house in Chelan to coordinate the pickup.

Dan 'Flair' O'Hara's day was spent flying, first his glider and then my car. He flew from the Butte to the first turn in the road going to Mansfield. He got low and the lift was the same as when I was there. Broken by the wind. He decided to work his way back to the junkyard and land. He took a quick swim in Lake Chelan, stopped at the Municipal Liquor Store where he filled my cooler full of post-flight refreshments, then headed for the Chelan Falls Bridge. Good move! He figured that by the time he got up through McNeil Canyon and out into the flats of Eastern Washington, there would be pilots down everywhere.

When he got out to Mansfield, he hadn't seen anyone yet. Somewhere between Mansfield and Simms Corner he found a pilot on the ground. The pilot had a hand-held radio with a big antenna. They made a call and Gerry came back on the radio saying he was already at Creston, 75 miles out. He said he had seen three or four other pilots out in front of him as well. Now 'Flair' knew why he hadn't found too many pilots yet. He was 40 miles behind! Driving 70mph he headed for Coulee City, about 40 miles from launch if you go that way by air, and the southern end of Banks Lake.

When he got there he stopped and tried the radio. He couldn't raise anyone, but he knew we were out in front of him. He raced eastward at 70-75mph. When he got to the rest stop between Creston and Davenport he pulled over again. This time he got out of the car with the mike in his hand and noticed that the foldable antennae was still down. He stood it up and finally got us on the radio. We were already in the Spokane area. He was still 30-40 miles behind. He drove (flew) my little Toyota wagon as fast as it would go toward Spokane, trying to catch us.

The ground speed on this flight was incredible. We were averaging 30 mph! I started to veer more to the north to take advantage of some good clouds and also to avoid the Spokane International airport. I was staying in a narrow altitude range between 9000' and 12,500' MSL. I knew the top of the Spokane TCA was 8000' so I was pretty sure I would not have a problem there. In the time I spent between Reardon and the northern suburbs of Spokane (130 miles) I saw a B52 and a 'heavy' (commercial passenger jet) come in from the north and land. They were nowhere near my altitude. They were so low in fact that I could see their shadows on the ground as they approached the airport. I would have to pay attention here. My flight path was taking me at least 10 miles north of downtown and I would have to correct to the southeast after I passed the city. The freeway to Coeur d'Alene, ID, looked like the best route for retrieval. Gerry was still out in front of me, heading that direction and doing well. He was getting to 13,500'MSL. He had told me that one of the axioms of XC flying is to get as high as you can late in the day because the lift gets weaker as the sun gets lower. Use the altitude to really pile on the miles.

A couple of CB guys with powerful base stations got on our channel. Their chatter went on for several minutes and finally our driver, Dan O'Hara, breaks in and says, "Please clear this channel. There is a world record hang gliding flight in progress and they are using this channel. Please clear this channel." I start laughing like crazy! Well, bless their little hearts. They were very nice about it and got off! Upon further review we concluded that our driver had been emboldened by that fact that he had gotten quite thirsty on the 3 hours, plus, of chase. It was 100 degrees and there was no AC in my Toyota! He was just being 'Flair' and I'm sure not complaining.

Gerry was at the Bitterroot Mountains with nowhere to go. He actually went up into the mountains because he had so much altitude, but could see no place to put it down. He saw a glider in the air to the southeast, which turned out was Mike Neuman, but could not see that there where any landing areas over that way. He came back toward me and landed at a high school track a couple miles north of downtown. I was not finding any lift. I was getting low on what was to be final glide and, sure enough, I lost contact with Flair. I could see the field where Gerry said he would land. I glided as far as I could, trying to get there, but wound up putting it down on two miles short. I had been in the air for 4 hours 55 minutes. A man came over from a business across the road and signed my landing witness form. On it he wrote "Doug Johnson landed at Inter-State Concrete, Coeur d'Alene, Idaho, June 30,1987 at 6:05 PM. Clear and Windy". The concrete place had closed so I walked about a half mile over to the Wal-Mart and called Buck, "Hey Buck, I landed in Coeur d'Alene."

He said, "You and Flair are playing some kind of game, aren't you?"

"No Buck, I'm serious. Where's Flair? Has he called?"

"Come on now, where are you really?" "I'm in Coeur d'Alene! Gerry landed about two miles further than me!" *Then* he believed me. If Gerry was out here, I had to be serious.

He said, "You *are* serious, aren't you?"

"Hey man, you saw the conditions today. How many pilots are back in town?"

He gave me the number where Flair had stopped in Post Falls, Idaho. I thanked Buck and called 'Flair' and connected with my ride. He arrived just as I stuffed the last of my gear into my bags. Now for the four-hour drive back.

What a day it had been. Five pilots had made it to Idaho! Mike Neuman, from Pennsylvania, had flown the farthest and his flight is still the longest ever from Chelan Butte. He landed in horse pasture next to the freeway in the northeastern part of Coeur d'Alene for 157 miles! Gerry Uchytil, from Wisconsin, wound up with 154 miles and 5:05 hours! Doug Johnson (that's me) from Minnesota had 152 miles; this flight is still my longest. John Elliott, from Seattle, flew to just past Post Falls, Idaho for 142 miles and Jim Wilson, who lived in West Virginia at the time, made it to just inside the state line for 140.5 miles. I contacted all of the remaining 'Spudders' for this story.

From Mike Neuman's log: *"Flew conservative to Mansfield. Then burned from one dust devil to the next chasing Dave Demming. Slowed down and flew clouds after 100 miles. Had to stop at the mountains."*

Gerry Uchytil said, *"All of the indicators (of a big day) were automatic. High cloud bases, good drift, good clouds."* He got to 13,500' MSL!

John Elliott said, *"I think I launched at about 11:30 AM (I always liked to launch early; at the same time every day). I bobbed around for about 15 minutes before getting high enough to easily cross the Columbia and get to the flats. The going was pretty slow until I got to Mansfield. At Mansfield I was amazed to find Gerry Uchytil had caught up to me. We shared a thermal. As I slowly tried to top out the thermal I saw Gerry shoot off at high speed leaving at what I thought was much too low an altitude. I was flying a Wills Wing Sport 167, which is not noted for being a real fast glider. There was a 20-knot tail wind so this day was a good one for a slow glider. Just past Banks Lake I saw some other hang gliders and could hear them on my CB. I tried to talk back but no one appeared to hear me. I passed about one mile north of Fairchild Air Force Base and noticed a big jet landing as I went past. I think it was a B52. I realize now that I should not have violated the airspace but at the time I was too excited to worry about it and I wasn't sure exactly where I was anyway. I continued on and followed the freeway through downtown Spokane. It was kind of neat to fly over a major city with large buildings. I remember getting low over the railroad yards but was able to find a good thermal at about 2000' AGL and continue on. I finally landed near Post Falls, Idaho at about 6 pm. This was by far my longest flight, both in distance and time. I remember going up to a house, where apparently a prayer meeting was ready to start, and asking what state this was. The people in the house told me this was Idaho and looked at me a little funny, like I was a crazy person."*

And this from Mike Neuman on Jim Wilson: *"I am sorry to say that the 'Spud Club' is down to four members. Jim Wilson (JW as we called him) died in a car accident about ten years ago. He was on his way to or from work when he rolled his truck down the side of a mountain. He died instantly. We all still miss him very much."*

There is talk in Chelan these days of new goals for XC. The first 200 miler in Washington is what they're after now. I hear there is even prize money involved. It may not be possible by going straight east, but it will be done. I'm sure of that. So, if you're looking for a great place to get some great XC, go to Chelan and let 'er rip! I sure like the place and the people there. There is surely no place finer. Set your glider up, tap your heels together and say, "There's no place like Cloudbase!" Who knows; you may get your trip paid for!

Thanks to Danny Uchytil (mentor) for providing the historical data for this article.

This story is dedicated to John Elliott who is one of the nicest pilots/people I ever met while in Chelan. John always had a smile for everyone. To say he was easy-going would be a major understatement. He was totally unflappable. He basically lived on the Butte, completely self-sufficient, often launching and landing there. He would stash mini-bikes out in the flats so he would not have to impose on anyone for a ride. John crashed his Swift while launching at Chelan several years ago. His injuries were very severe. He no longer flies hang gliders, but when he did, he was damn good. He probably flies his RC the same way! This one's for you John! We all love you.

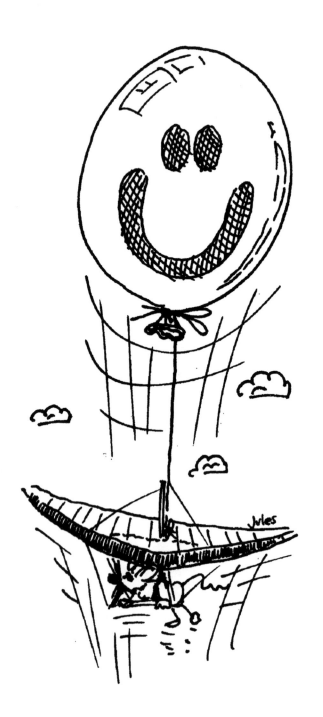

As Low As Can Be

Amir Shalom

I am looking at the G.P.S's screen; 98.9, 99, 99.1, 99.2... I'm excited and satisfied, thought I am only 1000 m' ASL, and the hour is already 17:30 winter time – but Jericho is behind me, Almog junction is underneath me, and the Dead Sea is ahead of me, and within reach. 99.8, 99.9 – 100!

It all started 6 hours before at the Southwest Tavor take off. A clear, continuous, side wind sent us to the upper north takeoff. This takeoff is not necessarily known for its friendly formation to hang gliders in null wind. There is no slope, and right under there are many trees. Still, even in light winds it is OK. The takeoff welcomed us happily as we got there. Nicely developed CUs added to the optimism, and for a while we were rigging and preparing. A while? That was not the thought of those in charge as we are still laboring. (Do I hear PG pilots laugh? Have you never heard of the saying, "He who labors- reaches!") The wind came down to zero, and then with hesitancy but with consistency, started blowing 90 from the right.

Full of faith, I got in the harness and stood at the takeoff. After 25 minutes of waiting, with less faith, some back wind, and a lot of side wind, I got out of the harness and joined the others, under the tree shade. As always, two minutes didn't pass, before I noticed a change in the wind direction. Two consecutive nose-blows longer than two minutes each have swiftly sent me to the takeoff again. I believed that this Friday's flight was going to be short; clouds seemed too far, and the conditions looked promising—promising to send us home quickly. "Well", I thought, "at least we get home early, today".

A steady nose-blow; wild run, airborne!

What a fear!

The immediate terrible sink did not catch me unprepared. Still it had sent me directly to the bushes under the takeoff. I push out a beat before, and barely pass them. I warn the others on the radio. Now, I turn west trying to elongate what seems to be a short flight. Nothing. Not the road, nor the village or the southwest takeoff – none of them give lift. At 70 m' AGL, with the zipper open (of the harness, the harness!) I am busy planning the landing, trying to relate the unclear wind direction and many electric wires. The Vario slightly burps. I lift an eyebrow. My altitude does not give a lot of maneuvering space, one small mistake, and I am out of reach of the LZ. I get a slight and not regular, series of burps and groans, that slowly develops to a light thermic, with a variable drift. At 850 m' AGL, I relax, and take south, to Giv'at-Hamore Hill, pessimistic about the chances of my friends to find and successfully core a random thermic, such as I was lucky enough to find. At 250 m', after infertile wandering in the Dovrat area, the factories, everywhere, I catch a "pip", and take it to 1300 m .

A few minutes later, I hear Yaron, Ilan and Yoram taking off to embracing skies, climbing almost to the second metric millennium. Yaron advises Avi, who is on the ground to coordinate with the army, of his flight plan to Jericho. I smile to myself, *100 km*, Yaron is very ambitious! I am for it! And with three gliders it is easier, and more fun, so I decide to wait for them.

After an irritating wait of an hour and a half (my radio did not transmit, and received occasionally), cruising between 1800-2100, no eye contact with them, I decide to head south alone.

Blue clear skies take me down to 900 m on the eastern side of the Gilboa ridge. In spite of that I find myself, for the first time, over Mehula Junction in 1200 m. This is a point of careful consideration, no landings for almost 20 km; the border with Jordan is just 5 km west. Though I am not in a thermic, due to a light south drift, I decide to keep on. This is a tiring, "Dolphin" flight. I am 150 m over the middle of the ridge near Argaman, but I find something and get up to 700 m', and go on.

Just before the end of the ridge at Adam Junction, 70 km from start, I am again low, only 50 m over the ridge. Determined, I fly to the highest, rockiest peak. I am in save, slow mode, expecting something. And what a thing! A steady strong thermic takes me up… over Sartaba - 1700 m'.

In all my previous flights here, this is the point where the skies die, except for narrow and very weak lift. This time, surprise! Over Uja I get up to 1500 to pass over Jericho at 1350 m', reminding myself that it is 320 m under sea level. I set a *Go To* point on the G.P.S to the Tavor, my start point. No, I do not intend to go back, but the joy of watching the numbers rising consistently to the 100 km line, and crossing it will be exhilarating. The altitude is decreasing as I pass the Almog, then the Dead Sea shoreline and the Kumeran monastery. As I get to the ridge overlooking the Dead sea from the west, with a south west wind, I can feel the fight ending. I pass over the lifeguard station on the beach of Ein Phash'ha , 200 m' above, and decide to look for a landing spot beyond the next hill. After a quick look, I decide to land in Ein Phash'ha. I choose what looks like a wide sandy area, 150 m' from the lifeguarded beach. On final I hit strong northwest wind, and I land beautifully, only 250 m' short of my target. Wow!

110 km, a site and personal record, and after such a beginning!

But that is only the introduction. Here starts the real story.

An excited phone call to the ungrudging Ilan, brings a picture of nice flights; but retrievals, well, not so good:

Ilan landed in Mehula – well done, but 70 km back.

Yaron landed in Argaman, first time to pass Mehula! He is only 40 km back; but he has been arrested by the police. Apparently, Avi did not coordinate a thing.

The car is in the Tavor, 110 km back, alone and unattended

Avi, who is supposed to retrieve us, is in the Golan Heights, flying.

The plan: Avi will finish his flight, land, de-rig, and drive to the Tavor to pick up the car. He will pick up Ilan, and they both will go to the police to rescue Yaron. Finally, they will come to pick me up. I should expect them around 22:00.

17:30. I have time to de-rig and a lot of time to debrief myself, and happily relive my flight. I start de-rigging (PG pilots do not laugh anymore, do they?) The area in which I have landed is a bit muddy, and I clean every sprinkle of it from my glider.

18:00. Glider de-rigged, harness on the back. I lift up the glider. My right leg sinks in the mud over my high shoes, and they are high! Another step. The left leg sinks up to the knee. I look yearningly towards the lifeguards cabin, far 250 m away. 32 kg and 4.5 m' of glider on my shoulder, harness on my back, I make slow progress—mostly on my knees.

18:30. Satisfied at my persistence, I look back and forth and find I have made it no more than 40m, falling, crawling and bubbling. The area ahead looks even worse. A short call to Ilan, and I realize retrieval is still too far off even to think of. A quick consultation between me, the mud and the setting sun; I decide to backtrack, and try to go west, to the road. The western area looks drier as you go farther from the sea.

19:30. A stubborn struggle brings me 100 m' west of the landing spot, in a drier area, but with plenty of spiny bushes and watery wadies. Wild donkeys are not very happy to see me. The moon is bright, allowing me to go on. I have developed a system: first I take the harness 200-300 m, then I go back and take the glider to the harness. Then I start over.

20:30. Dead end. No access to the road, 500 m' to the west, due to dense spiny tall bushes; south and north, 7 m' wide (and too deep) streams are merrily flowing; going back east is too dangerous in the dark, trying to recross the wadies with the chance of sinking in the mud over the knees. Anyhow, who can find me in such an area in the dark? The moon, rapidly moving towards the horizon, does not make things easier. I struggle, determined to find a way to the road through the bushes.

21:00. I realize I'm stuck. It's time to think again (or maybe not, look at the consequences of my previous thoughts). I'm staying for the night. With the last vigour drops of the cellular battery (too many long calls after landing) I call Ilan, and ask him not to come today, but tomorrow. Ilan determinedly refuses, and due to the battery strength, I can't explain too much. I inform him that I intend to sleep where I am, and give him my G.P.S. coordinates, and promise to call tomorrow when I get free.

22:00. Ilan, Yaron and Avi are here! Their obstinate stubbornness is crashing against the walls of reality. So, they are going home, promising to come early next morning. Seeing the lights of their car just 500 m' away on the road and hearing them blowing the horn as they finally headed home was more of an encouragement than despair. They had failed in an attempt to organize a powered paraglider to track a simple way out for me. I decide to move tomorrow to plan B: *In me I trust.*

23:00. I go to sleep. After washing muddy tired legs, straw-like long hair, and my dry mouth in the stream, I take the harness out of its bag, cover myself with it, and then I give in to the determined sucking of the flies. Female flies, if you don't mind. They are so big here, and do they suck! Somehow, after a while, I fall asleep.

24:00. I wake up to the desperate sounds of lost donkeys, some 20 m' from my lie. I honk back and after a frightened pause, they run away. (Later I found out that the area had been designated as a biblical reserve and these donkeys were brought in as part of the historical fauna.)

03:00. I wake up to the yowls of a faraway, gloomy jackal. Actually, not so far away. Only 70-80 m'. And not just one jackal, it sounded more like 20. And I should be the gloomy one, not them. I turn around, and before I fall asleep again, I think how tomorrow in the car, I will be smiling, considering the whole thing a thrilling experience.

05:00. I wake up and wash as best I can. I turn on the G.P.S., set a *mark*, and hit the road. I leave my gear and glider behind. After 45 minutes and many muddy incidents, I get to the lifeguard cabin. No one is there, and as I approach the taps to clean myself, Yaron and Ilan arrive. Seeing how I look, Yaron laughs until his stomach aches. Just wait, Yaron. In ten minutes the three of us look the same, and not because I was cleaner. Using the G.P.S we find our way back to the glider. Carrying the glider to the car was not very easy, but with three of us, it was possible.

07:30. In the car. I lean back and smile. What a thrilling experience!

Many thanks to Avi who bothered and brought the car, and a million thanks to Ilan and Yaron who insisted on coming in the night, and early in the morning; and who helped, and fell and laughed with me in the mud. Thanks!

From Foothills to Sauratown

Brad Gryder

On Sunday April 8th, 2001 Bubba Goodman and Wayne Sayer flew from Foothills Flight Park to the Sauratown Mountain LZ. I was busy chasing the dolly and playing "rope boy" on the flight line as I saw my two buds fly off high, knowing they were headed out on a decent XC. It got me so upset seeing them fly off without being able to join them that I actually had to cancel my tandems for a couple of hours, just to get my head right.

By the time they landed I was in a good mood. But they had plucked one of the cherries from Foothills Flight Park that I had hoped to claim for myself: The first flight to Sauratown from the flight park, a 50 mile jaunt up the Brushy Mountain Range and past Pilot Mountain. In 1999 Vince Furrer had flown beyond Sauratown to end up in Martinsville, VA, but this was the first time anyone had landed at the well-known Sauratown LZ from Foothills Flight Park.

Monday morning Gary Misenheimer called and offered a tow. I had to decide whether to fly or do my taxes. It took me about 2 seconds to decide. I was finally going to get to fly the GhostBuster in soarable air!

I had purchased the GhostBuster a few months back, but since then every time it's been good weather to fly I've been swamped with other duties (tandems, tow pilot, work) or else I couldn't line up a tug pilot. I was scheduled to fly in the Flytec Championships in Florida in less than a week, and I was beginning to wonder whether I should even go down to the meet with the lack of time I'd had on the glider.

I began setting up the glider and getting ready to fly. The day before had been a hectic hot day of towing and tandem flying in the nearby farm field (Beckham's Field) in Stony Point, NC. Bubba Goodman prefers to fly there, but there is no shade nor wind shadow. I was roasted. I was missing 3 radios. Everything was disorganized, and I was a little tired from all the ground crew efforts. I finally gave up trying to find the radios and told Gary I planned on flying 'till about 5PM and fully intended to land back at Gryder Field. I told him to simply tow me up and then go about his daily business. I needed to figure out how to fly this machine and it looked like a good day to do so.

I released at 1000' AGL in good lift, straight up to 6000' AGL. There were decent looking clouds between here and the Brushys, but it was blue in the Piedmont. This was a "check out" flight. No Radio, no GPS, no speed-to-fly computer jazz. I had slapped my Flytec 4005 on the downtube

I spent two hours messing around north of Taylorsville exploring the flap settings and just trying to get tuned in to the machine. There was a slight SW breeze but it was easy to go any direction I wanted. I knew I should stay close to the field if possible so that Gary could see me every now and then and feel more comfortable about going home or taking a nap (he had been working all night at his 3rd shift job). The airfield was just a little too far out in the blue by now to get back there with ease. Ironically this was the kind of practice that I really needed, but I am terrible at upwind tasks. It was so much easier to stay over the Rocky Face Mountain area where lift is always present due to the granite dome with its nice southern exposure. I finally got sucked so far back into the Brushy Mountain range that I couldn't get back to the flight park. I tried twice to return but got down to 800' and 1000' before giving up. There was an obvious convergence taking place behind me on the Brushy Range.

I knew it was unlikely that I'd be landing back at the airfield; I hoped Gary wasn't too worried. I was dribbling farther and farther back into the NE corner of Alexander County. I wasn't high. Sometimes I was only 500' over the ridge tops. I was very cautious; I'd scout out a potential LZ, survey it well while drifting over it, and keep it within gliding range until I could see the next one with potential.

I finally realized that there was really no reason that I should sink out, I was focusing a little too much on the LZ's and not enough on the sky. It had been a good exercise, though, as I was now very comfortable with the wing and was now better able to interpret its language. Mike Wooten (a long time Rigid Wing Pilot from Statesville) had previously described the rigid wing soaring experience as having a different "flavor" from flex wing flying. I'd have to agree. It was a little different, but by now I was really beginning to develop a taste for it. It had started out tasting like unbuttered popcorn, but now I was eating fried chicken and wondering what's for dessert.

I was getting closer to the crest of the Brushy Mountain Range. The clouds had been looking good there all day. I could feel it getting better. I knew I had it licked now and I was able to get a consistent climb in the circles. Oh, yes, please pass the gravy! I decided to just go with it. I now knew I could make Sauratown if I just committed myself and got on top of the mountains.

Cloudbase was at 8200' MSL. As always, I plan my route while I'm a couple of grand below the base where the visibility is better. Check the sun angle and the drift angle, establish the cloud shadows as a guide, and "GO TO CRUISE!" I now had the GB flaps fully retracted into the sail. I had my palms inverted, my elbows tucked, and my chin over the base bar. I was peeking at the vario and making small pitch changes based on my rate of decent. I was really hummin' but loosing very little altitude as I played "connect-the-dots"

(BIG DOTS) over the crest of the mountain range. I flew this way all the way to I-77 just south of Elkin.

As the mountain range came to an end I had to slow down just a little and start working a little harder between I-77 and the Yadkin River. I worked two clouds and then I had to go toward a little wisp that was more on a course-line to goal. The clouds looked better on a line mid-way between Sauratown and Winston-Salem, but it was getting late and I'm also a middle-aged fat guy who's currently out of shape. I was now determined to make "goal" at Sauratown and call it a day.

When I hit the Yadkin River things started getting pretty slow. I got down to 2000' over the river bottom and had to dribble 5 miles in 100 to 200 up. It finally turned on and got me to 3 grand and a little closer to the goal. It looked like I could make it, so I shot for the west finger and hit zero sink to the launch ramps. Of course no one was there on a Monday (not everyone is laid off?) but I still let out a yell as I buzzed launch. With no one in the LZ I thought about going to Denny's airfield, but I decided with the streamers in the LZ I'd be fine. Oops, I did drop the basebar. I just forgot how much weight would be on my shoulders when I finished flying.

This flight lasted 4.5 hours, but I think I could have done it in 3 or even 2.5 had I committed right off. I think Wayne and Bubba did it in about 3 hours on Sunday, but I had not had a chance to talk to them.

I rushed to the YMCA Camp Haynes to use their phone to let Gary know I was OK. The guy in the office said, "Sure, Brad no problem." I wondered how he knew my name as I thought for a minute it might be on my shirt or hat. Turns out I'd given he and his wife each an Intro Tandem Flight in October of '99 during the "October's Best" Fly-In. I couldn't get through to Gary so I called Tommy Thompson so that he could continue to try to get through to him. Tommy called all the right folks and thus avoided an unnecessary search party that evening. He also drove to the LZ with his custom padded "RigidWing Rack", helped me break down, load, and told me supper was waiting for me at his house! His wife, Robbie, had fixed a great tasting meal (sort of reminded me of my flight). Tommy then drove me to my brother's house in Advance, NC and once again helped with rigging a temporary "super-padded" rack, and the loading and unloading of the "Gutbuster". My brother drove me home.

I was in bed by 11:00 with visions of buttered muffins, angel food cake, and hotfudge sundaes suspended below a cool cloud. Man, that stuff really tasted GOOD!

And Robbie's cookin' wasn't bad either! UMM UMMM...

It's going to be a Great Spring in NC!

A Different Sort of Cross Country Flight

Richard E. Cobb

Although I don't get around to doing it very often, I love the thrill of departing the mountain at the beginning of a cross-country flight. There comes a moment when you know you are beyond any chance of returning to your normal LZ. Any doubts about whether or not you should go vanish, and the adventure of trying to stay up as long and as far as you can begins.

Most XC flights are rather 'impersonal' with regards to the landscape you are flying over. The whole goal, after all, is to "get high and go far". At normal XC altitudes you are pretty remote from life on the earth below. You can see the roads, rivers, towns, and mountains to be sure, but none of the personal details of life in any of those places. Nor is it really important to you, as your eye tends to be fixed on the horizon, where you wish to be.

This story is about a very different sort of XC flight. I did not get very high, and at 15 miles it was not very remarkable in terms of distance. But it turned out to be one of my most memorable XC flights.

The flight started in central Pennsylvania, in early May of 1991, at a site known as the Brickyard. It is on a short ridge located on the outskirts of the small town of Alexandria. The take-off is actually from a mound of debris and earth that was discarded at the top of the mountain where a brick manufacturing plant had been many years ago. The mound was rapidly becoming part of the landscape with vegetation now growing on it, but because it was a bulge near the top of the mountain it was very easy to create a launch site there. Ron Dively, a hang glider pilot living just behind the mountain in Alexandria, saw the potential and did the necessary work to establish it as a flying site.

This particular day was warm and sunny, but not very promising for remarkable flights. High cirrus were the only clouds to be seen, and the wind was somewhat cross and variable ranging from 5 to 15. Still, it was a beautiful day with spring firmly established after a long winter, and it was at least marginally soarable. There were four of us flying, myself, Ron, and Dennis and Claire Pagen. Most of the time we were just scratching in the light lift at 500 feet or less above the mountain.

At one point I ventured down to the 'far' end of the ridge (which was not very far, less than a mile) and discovered what might have been the only real thermal that any of us found that day. Although the rate of climb was only several hundred feet a minute, at 1000 over I was still climbing consistently. But I was drifting quite a bit, and I knew if I stayed with that thermal much longer I might not be able to get back to the ridge.

The ridges in this part of Pennsylvania tend to be separated by broad, flat valleys that are often planted in corn or other crops. But when there are no crops growing, as then, all those open fields meant you could land nearly anywhere you wanted. I decided just to stay with the thermal and kept drifting and slowly climbing. I watched Alexandria drift by and eventually topped out at about 2200 over take-off. By this time I was nearly over Petersburg, another small town several miles behind the mountain. Looking back at the mountain it was doubtful that I could have made it back, even on a downwind glide, so it was not a difficult decision to just keep on going.

The thermal dissipated and I drifted downwind over the open fields, searching for more lift. I encountered lift bubbles in the afternoon warmth that would coax little chirps from my vario, but nothing defined. It was not long before I found myself back down at takeoff level, perhaps 800 to 1000 ft above the fields below. I began picking out places to land, as landing seemed imminent. But I kept running into more little bubbles that would let me get perhaps a turn or two in each of them before they disappeared. I kept drifting up the valley in this manner, picking out and then discarding potential LZ's as I went.

The valley is oriented in a SW-NE direction, and a very small ridge, perhaps 100 or 200 feet high, runs up the center of it. The wind was generally WSW, but I discovered that the little ridge, even with the crossing wind and its low height, seemed to be collecting the lift bubbles. I followed the ridge up the valley, slowly drifting and turning, always knowing that I was perhaps only one or two 360's away from landing.

It was really quite magical. The sun was warm at this low altitude, and the afternoon was advancing so that the lowering angle of the sun highlighted the texture of the land and the lush spring colors. The sounds of dogs barking at my passage drifted up to me. I watched and listened to life going on below—a tractor in the field, cows grazing in the pastures, the lawn being mowed, people out working and walking and enjoying the beautiful day. I doubt that I was ever as high as 1000 feet above the valley floor as I drifted. I was flying with a very light touch, just hanging on to every scrap of lift I could find and turning as gently as I could. The intermittent chirps from my vario blended in pleasantly with the sounds of life below.

But all good things must eventually end. At the NE end of the valley the ridges come together, forming a shallow bowl. But before you actually get to the bowl the fields turn to wooded areas without any landing possibilities. I was looking straight out, and maybe even up, at the surrounding ridges. And the lift was getting lighter as the sun sank lower in the sky. I picked out one of the last good LZ's and landed on a small hilltop.

According to the map I was in or near a town called Saulsburg, although I didn't see much more than a farmhouse next to the field I had landed in. The farmer was at home and had watched me land. He was a very friendly guy by the name of Bob Miller. After I tore the glider down he helped me load it on his pickup truck and he took me back to meet the others.

The entire flight only lasted an hour, and I only went 15 miles. But it will be a flight I will remember long after other flights where I flew longer, higher, and farther will have faded away.

Dust-Devil-Hopping 100-Miler

Doug Prather

Normally I'm too busy with my everyday life to take a vacation. I'm the owner of a carpet cleaning business and a hang gliding business in Modesto, California (Dream Weaver Hang Gliding 209-556-0469), and I've been a waiter at a seven-course dinner house for more than 16 years. During the day I clean carpets or give hang gliding lessons and also sell just about anything you may need for hang gliding, new and used. I also have the dealership for all of northern California for the Mosquito powered hang gliding harness. If it happens that I don't have any work scheduled, I go flying. At night I go serve seven course dinners at the best restaurant in town, Hazel's Elegant Dinning, in Modesto, California.

The last time I took a real vacation was six years ago, the summer of 1995. My wife Nancy and our son Alex and our dog Valerie and I packed up and left for a month long vacation.

We first stopped and had a great flight at Wood Rat Mountain near Medford Oregon, then off to Chelan Washington to fly in the nationals. We arrived one day early and decided to take a practice flight and to fly XC as far as possible to get to know the site. This was my first visit to Chelan. A few of my local flying brothers, The Mother Lode Sky Riders, were already there and they had been getting 60-mile flights on the last few days.

We set up our gliders in hopes of a long flight, we launched and quickly worked thermals up to 12,000' asl.

Ken Muscio and Shannon Raby led the way, and I was right with them. We flew downwind across the river gorge for about 10 miles to the flatland desert. We were greeted by a big dust devil; before we even got to it we were climbing 1,500 fpm. In a few minutes we were up to cloudbase at 14,000' asl. The desert floor was 2,000' asl, and flat. There were nothing but landing zones and highways for as far as one could see. This would be my first flat land flying as I normally flew in the mountains.

We were 12,000' above the ground, and as we looked downwind we could see dust devils every 10 miles. They looked like small tornadoes stretching from ground level to cloudbase. The local pilots say that ever since the eruption of Mount St. Helens there has been a fine layer of ash everywhere, which is so light that most thermals can be seen as dust devils. We topped out and flew downwind to the next dust devil and topped out at 14,000' again.

Heading for the next thermal, I saw a bigger dust devil lifting off behind us, upwind. I radioed Ken and Shannon that I was going back for more, but they continued downwind as I backtracked. I worked my way back up to cloudbase, but then I realized my mistake; Ken and Shannon were now a good five or six miles ahead of me. I had to fly extra-fast to try to catch them. I finally did catch them, but by then I was 6,000' lower. I raced along in front of them for an hour, marking the thermals for them as I flew. Then, a couple miles ahead, I could see the biggest dust devil of them all. I thought to myself, this is my chance to catch them! I flew as fast as I could, and I flew right inside to the heart of the dust devil. Nancy was on her radio, and Ken and Shannon were on their radios, saying, "Look out Doug, that big dust devil is right in front of you!" They say that I just disappeared into the dirt. The lift was smooth throughout as I climbed 2,200 fpm. They could hear me on the radio singing *Ride The Snake* (The Doors). After five minutes I emerged at cloudbase, higher than and in front of Ken and Shannon. I had done it; I had caught up to them!

Soon we were at the sixty-mile mark. Shannon was staying high, but Ken and I were getting low, with no dust devil or thermal in sight. Nancy was below us with the retrieval vehicle, and it looked as though we would be landing soon. We were side by side at 500 feet when Ken found a very weak 100 fpm thermal that was drifting fast, but going up. I joined him in his newfound lift, and we drifted and climbed slowly for 15 minutes. At 2,000' agl the lift turned into 200 fpm, then 300 fpm; then it turned on to 600 fpm all the way up to 8,500' agl. We were back! Shannon was nowhere in sight. Ken and I split up, and we were all flying our own flights. We each found a few more thermals before the lift weakened. Three and a half hours into our flights and we were all on final glide.

We were all flying with GPS's, and we all landed along the same highway. (We try to keep our drivers happy!) Ken landed at 99 miles, I landed at 100, and Shannon made it 101 miles to land in the town of Reardan. I had been hoping and praying for my first 100-mile flight; thank you God!

I in no way recommend that anyone fly his glider into a dust devil. A few days into the competition several gliders tumbled trying to fly into dust devils and had to deploy their parachutes!

During the meet we had a couple 60-mile XC days, but the best air by far was the day before the meet.

After the Nationals we flew the Rocky Mountains of Golden Canada; Lake View, Oregon; Slide Mountain near Reno, Nevada; and then on to the Sonora Pass on the east side of the Sierras in California.

Ever since I've been back to the everyday grind. But this year, 2001 we are taking another six-week vacation. Hope to see you in the skies.

A Newbie to the Owens Valley

Steve Rudy

I moved from Texas to California in 1985 with visions of big miles and incredible flying in the Owens Valley. I made several trips up there in 1985, but, because I didn't know the area, my longest flight was only 40 miles. I was a serious XC pilot. I'd been flying XC for seven years, however my personal distance record was still only 46 miles.

I had assumed that I would be able to tag along with some of the other pilots—about 40 pilots launch soon after the first thermals kick loose. Many of the pilots use CB radios to communicate. It surprised me to find that, as soon as I left the launch area, I might as well have been by myself. Some pilots work lift off the foothills down to about 7,000' while others are topping out at 14,000'. The fastest pilots might be 25 miles down the range while a gaggle is still climbing from takeoff. Twenty minutes into my flight, I couldn't spot another glider. The information coming over the radio didn't help. "This is Jim at 12.5 over Lone Pine Peak," or "This is Mike approaching Williamson at 13," are not much use when you don't know any of the landmarks.

Then there was my Texas perspective. Lots of articles in the magazine talked about desert conditions down in the Owens Valley, with monster thermals and big air. They didn't say much about high alpine meadows. Texas is hot in the summer; it is hot day or night. After my short flight, I drove back up the mountain and past the takeoff to the camping area at the end of the road. I was busy setting up my hammock between two trees and spreading out my only bedding, a sheet, when the campers next to me asked if I planned to sleep there. They mentioned that it gets kind of cool overnight at 9,000'. Their water jug had frozen solid the previous night. I spent a cold night in my car wrapped in my harness and everything else I owned.

The following June, 1986, I was excited to be making my first trip of the new season with a group of pilots (Herb Sidenburg, Tom Oeftering, and Dennis Sharp) who had lots of experience and big miles flying in the Owens. Herb's group always leaves the campsite in the Valley by 7:00 am to claim prime set-up spots for the Horseshoe launch. Before pilots started launching we had 47 gliders set up in an area that should hold 20. Everyone wants to launch as soon as the thermals start working, usually between 9 and 10 am.

The earlier you start, the longer you have to accumulate XC miles, and pilots not along the front edge are at the mercy of those in front.

Since my group had prime set-up positions and Herb is always willing to wind dummy, all four of us were flying before most of the rest of the lemmings poured off the hill. Lift was weak and many pilots wound up with extended sled runs. My mentors had coached me about 'house thermals' going north along the primary route. I found enough lift at the first couple of spots they had identified, and then Tom Oeftering coached me along as we worked our way north from ridge to ridge.

The west winds picked up quickly, leaving us in leeside conditions down the eastern Sierras. I climbed to 12,500' at Whitney Portal, about 12 miles north of Horseshoe, and got hit by strong turbulence. Wave clouds were beginning to form out in the valley, and Tom recommended heading out. We found lift in the valley and at lower altitudes the wind was southwest instead of the due west. We crabbed our way north above highway 395 in the middle of the valley.

I was very low near Tehachapi Lake, about 45 miles from launch, but finally climbed to 8,500'. I crossed the lake and headed for the Inyo foothills, the west facing mountains across from the Sierras, into an area without retrieval roads. I was willing to risk miles of walking out, since this put me beyond my personal distance record.

There was enough lift to scratch low along the base of the Inyos and into Westgard pass. Tom had talked about a ridge on Black Mountain that he would normally follow to climb out of Westgard Pass. I found lift on a ridge leading up Black Mountain and climbed to the peak. Unfortunately, the ridge I had picked lead to a secondary peak about a half-mile behind the main peak. From 1,500' over, I tried to penetrate directly into the strong west wind to get back in front of the mountain. I found myself thrashed around and then back working the same ridge out of Westgard Pass, from several thousand feet lower. There is no place to land without getting around Black Mountain and into the Owens Valley. Westgard Pass in high winds is a horrible place to get stuck. I made four attempts climbing out over the back peak, diving towards the forward peak, and getting thrashed back down into Westgard Pass before arriving on valley side of the mountain after about an hour.

Tom was far ahead of me by the time I left Black Mountain. I knew Herb had been ahead of Tom, and I hadn't seen or heard from anyone else for hours. From all previous experience I expected the best lift to be near the top of the range. I kept positioning myself too deep into the mountains. Even though the thermals were very strong I would be drifting away from the potential landing areas at about 30 miles an hour every time I circled in a thermal. With strong winds perpendicular to the direction I wanted to fly, it was very tough going. The sink between thermals was often strong. As I would dive the glider for penetration I would put myself below the ridges, deep in jagged canyons, and praying for divine intervention. The batteries for the CB had given out so

I had no communication with the rest of my group. I knew Owens Valley offered the potential for major distance in often-violent conditions, but it was kicking my butt.

I eventually got to Boundary Peak at the end of the range and found Janey's – the whorehouse with a landing strip. Janey's is the usual goal (just over 100 miles from Horseshoe) if conditions are not good enough to make the next pass. Since I had shut the radio down for the last couple of hours, the batteries had recovered enough for me to reach them for a few seconds. Herb and Tom had landed at Janey's much earlier. They had packed up and discussed where I might be. They eventually decided that I must have gone down somewhere north of Black Mountain. The car was loaded and they had just started the drive south hoping to find me somewhere along that 50-mile stretch. The radio worked enough for me to report in at 13,000' over Janey's. They came back and waited while I burned altitude.

I whacked it pretty good on landing. I was surprised that my landing was so poor until I realized that I could barely stand up. I had been in the air eight and a half hours. My longest duration flight prior to that had been less than 4 hours, and I had never worked as hard in the air as I did this day. Even though I was wearing a down jacket and heavy gloves, much of the flight was over 11,000' and cold. Without any goggles or sunglasses, my eyes were sun and wind burned. I don't think I had ever been that exhausted. Luckily my friends helped me pack up and they loaded my gear.

My euphoria at more than doubling both my personal distance and duration records superceded my stupor and pain. It didn't matter that Larry Tudor had flown 224 miles years before, or that I would have been on the ground close to launch without help from the group, or even that I had made lots of decisions that had put me on the wrong side of the reasonable risk line. I had just won entrance to the elite club of XC pilots with flights over 100 miles. I couldn't have been happier. Luckily we stopped at Keogh Hot Springs on the drive back to our campsite. Soaking in the hot water reduced the pain to the point I was ready to take on the Owens again the next day.

I have flown to Janey's and beyond often since that first 100-miler, but no other flight has provided as much joy or challenge. I know now that it is easier to fly major distances from various flatland sites, but I continue to be addicted to the big air in the Owens Valley. The record I still pursue is beating the level of euphoria I got from that first 100-mile flight.

97 Miles as the Crow Flies

Patti Cameron

It was a day or two after the Nationals at Quest Air. We were all a bit tired and in a casual mood down at the Wallaby Ranch in Florida. I launched late, around 1:30, and beamed up to six grand with a light north to northwest wind. No radio, no GPS, no map, no retrieve, no money, no company. I wasn't even planning on leaving the flight park.

The streets set up lengthwise through the state and I jumped towards the east as I proceeded south. About five hours later I came upon a rather large body of water. The street just touched the northwest side of the lake and arced back south and to the west. I could have gone on, however it was getting late and I knew I was in for a bit of a sticky retrieve. I had no idea where I was.

I landed and broke down; this is where the real adventure always begins. I walked down the road to the local hotel and pub. I was on the bountiful fishing shores of Lake Okeechobee. I was also in sugarcane-field-central. After calling the Ranch and begging Mike Barber to drive three and a half hours to pick me up, I arrived at the bar to find all of the locals sitting in a row. Having knocked out my front tooth the week before at the Wallaby Open, I fit in perfectly. Soon I had a Bud and a meal in front of me, and a dance with the local bachelor (his name was Bud, too) that they were all trying to marry off. Three hours later when Mike arrived, I had to bid goodbye to all my newfound friends to begin the long journey home. It was 97 miles as the crow flies. If I had known, I would have gone the extra three miles to break 100.

East Coast Record

Mark Poustinchian

As a wind dummy during the competitions, on Thursday I took two early flights after 11am, and both times was able to climb in the first thermal to about 3600' agl and then sink all the way to the ground. It was not going to be an early day. I had enough for the day and I was looking forward to Friday. I ran into Russell Brown, one of the co-owners of Quest Air, and told him that tomorrow would be a great day and that I was going to set a new record. I had this feeling that it was going to be a great day. Cold night about 55 degrees Fahrenheit and then a forecast high of 85 for Friday and a SE wind about 10 mph. It was perfect and a day that I had been looking for a long time.

On Friday morning, April 20th, I was trying to kill some time before the conditions were good. I started playing the *Age of Empire* on the computer and before I knew it I was in trouble, the enemy was attacking me from all directions. I lost track of time trying to save my Empire. My girlfriend, Samantha walked in and said, "The sky is full of cumies." I almost fell out of my chair; this damn computer game was going to cost me a great day. It was about 10:45 am and a glance at the sky showed that I was already about an hour late.

I quickly moved my glider to the takeoff area as Samantha helped me with my gear. I quickly hooked in and got on a tow dolly. I saw Bobby Bailey and asked him if he could give me a tow. "We are going to have a meeting right now, maybe I could get someone to tow you up," he replied. Oh no, this was not good; every minute was going to cost me at least a mile. I quickly unhooked and started running around to see if I could find a tug pilot to get me out of there. I was very lucky to find Mike Tomzack in a hanger. I asked him if he could give me a tow and he responded with a big smile and grabbed his hardhat. All right, I was finally going to get going. At the same time Davis, in the pilot's meeting, had made a comment that if I was not in air and gone by now, I was not going to break any records.

The air was full of activity and as much as I tried to stay on tow until I reached 2500', it didn't happen. At 1900' agl I released in a good thermal, about 11:15 am, and was on my way. Wow, these clouds were awesome looking, a great fast start was in order, I was about an hour behind and the conditions were so good that I needed to quickly make up for the lost miles. I lined up the glider under a nice cloud street and ignored any thermal less than 400 fpm. I kept on gliding while I was getting close to the cloud base at 4500' agl. There wasn't any need to make any turns. Gliding from one cloud to the next was only putting me down about 1000' to 1500' below the base and I quickly gained all the lost altitude back just by slowing down.

Before 1:00 pm, I was 75 miles away and over 5000' agl. This was too good to last and too good to be true. However, I could see that the hard time was ahead of me. The sky turned completely blue ahead of me without any sign of any clouds. I couldn't believe my eyes, how could this happen? I had no choice but to take a chance and hit the blue hole. About 80 miles out and I was down to about 1500' and thinking I may be landing soon. No thermals to be found anywhere.

Desperately, I flew towards some dry fields with a lot of contrast. I hit some broken bubbles and start working very light lift. I really appreciated my new Flytec instrument. The new excitement level, which I had customized to my liking, came in very handy. I had increased the excitement level by two notches from the original factory setting. I was feeling good, maintaining zero sink, and looking for any new sign of cumies. But no luck. However, the lift started to get better. My averager was showing 200 fpm climb rate. All right! An hour ago I wouldn't even have slowed down for this, but I could sure appreciate it now. Things can change so quickly.

I was over 4000' agl again before the thermal fell apart. Carefully, with fingers crossed, I started gliding again in the blue hole; there was still no sign of any clouds. My average ground speed had slowed down and I was in survival mode, trying to maintain altitude and waiting for the cumies to start popping. After a few miles of gliding I hit a stronger thermal and got back close to 5000' agl. There were still no clouds over my head. Blue thermals were present, but the cumies were missing. The visual assurance of lift makes all the difference when it comes to getting the miles the fast way. I still was working 100 fpm average climb at the top of the lift and milking it, as if it was my last lift. An hour passed. I was 20 miles into the blue hole and had been able to stay above 3500' agl. The blue thermals were actually getting stronger.

It was time to release the brakes and go for it. I was only stopping for 300 fpm or better. Soon I was rewarded with a boomer which took me over 6000' agl; the vario was pegged at times. Still there were no clouds. I was feeling good and took a direct line downwind to the northwest. My GPS was showing 40 mph with a 7 to 10 mph tail wind. I was getting over 6000' agl. The air was so cold. What with the altitude and all the water that I drank when I got to the blue hole, it seemed the right time to relieve myself. The bladder pressure was building. I unzipped my harness, moved four layers of clothing out of the way, and tried to go. But the air was cold and I could do nothing. Damn it, after five minutes of trying I closed the zipper before I froze my little buddy.

I passed 100 miles and my groundspeed was increasing. At 130 miles I was over 7000' agl in the blue thermals. Wow this was cool. No, as a matter of fact, it was too damn cold! Samantha had a late start and was too far behind for my radio to reach her. I could hear her but she couldn't hear me. Bo was in the air doing the 92-mile comp task to the north. He was between us and came to the rescue by transmitting my location to Samantha.

Clouds started to appear in the far distance to the north. What a welcome sight. It looked as I if could make it. 150 miles away and I was under cumies again. And freezing my butt. Four layers of clothing and I was still cold and shivering at 7000' agl.

At 165 miles I crossed the Georgia border, the sixth time since last year. I felt wonderful; I was flying over familiar ground. All I had to do was to stay west of restricted air space around Valdosta, Georgia, and I would be in good shape. I asked Bo to tell Samantha that I had passed Valdosta. I was 185 miles away and going for a new record. He cheered me on. He was also getting close to goal and happy. Thanks Bo, may you go 224 miles.

I had jumped to a cloud street to my west about 5 miles away and was in a good position. But the clouds were dissipating and the lift was diminishing. I kept on gliding, excited about the upcoming 200-mile mark. It would to be my first. My eyes were glued to the GPS: 197, 198, 199... Damn it, it took forever. Finally, 200 miles! Celebration! What a great feeling. With all the excitement, though, I was getting low. At 204 miles, just nine miles short of a new East Coast record, I found myself at only 2600' agl. Damn it, I may not make it. I altered my path a little to the west and got downwind of some dry fields. I could feel a bubble of lift and started to pay attention to the glider's drift and speed near the thermal.

A few seconds later I gladly started to work 100 fpm lift as if it were my last thermal. As it turned out, it was my last thermal. After about 20 minutes of turning I was back at 5500' agl and 206 miles away. What a fantastic, wonderful feeling! I went on the final glide; the air was great with minimal sink. At 212 miles I got on the radio and announced that Davis's East Coast record is broken and asked Samantha, now about 40 miles behind, to call Quest Air and let them know that I was passed 212 miles and was still going. A few minutes later she was back on the radio and said that she called Russell Brown and gave him the message. Russell loudly announced to a large crowd that I had passed 212 miles and was still going. They were cheering loudly for me. It is great to get support like that; I couldn't have been happier.

I picked a big brown field next to highway 75 and went for it. The fields were not as plentiful in this area, lots of trees and buildings. As I got closer I noticed a dark object at the middle of the field. I didn't have any other good choice for landing. A few minutes later I realized that the dark object was a major electrical tower, with the power lines running north and south. Not good! I hate power lines, especially when there are a bunch of them.

I looked at another, much smaller, field about ½ mile north on the other side of the highway. I was high enough to go check it. It seemed as it had streets in the middle of it. I got a little closer and saw large white things sticking out of the ground, I'll be damned; it was a cemetery. I was getting low and thinking that I may not have enough altitude to go back to the power line filed. I could just see the headlines; *Hang Glider Pilot Crashes In Cemetery, Hits Tombstone, Buried At Crash Site.* That was enough to turn the glider around and try to go for the power line field. I decided I'd have to take my chances there.

Thanks to minimal wind and good late afternoon air, I barely made it back over the power line field. Oh no, another small power line running east to west. Crashing in this field was not what I had in mind to end a great flight. I fly with a drogue chute just in case of emergency and landing in very small fields. This was definitely an emergency situation. As soon as I saw the other power line, I ripped the chute out of its container. I held it in my hand until I was 20 feet over the power lines, and as I turned to go on final I threw it into the air behind me and quickly glanced to see if it was open. What a great sight that was, thanks GW from US AEROS for a great drogue chute.

It felt as if I was on the final glide in a smooth, 10 mph head wind, even though there was no wind. I was coming down fast; I was on the ground well before I hit the trees. I had a great landing. I thanked God for a great flight and a good landing, and I was the happiest man alive.

I called Samantha on the cell phone and a few kids showed up to talk to me. They said I landed in Tifton, Georgia. The GPS was showing 225 miles away from Quest Air at 6:40 pm. Samantha was 25 miles away, and before the glider was in the bag she was there with cold drinks. Life is good. We loaded up the glider and headed back to Quest Air.

On the way back, I watched *Brave Heart* on the DVD on my laptop with the car sound system attached. It just couldn't be any better. I have the most perfect retrieval car and driver. The movie, which Samantha bought for my birthday, was great and I watched the 3-hour movie on the way back. With all the emotions of the record-breaking flight, the sad ending of the movie got me emotional and crying. That was a damn good movie, however the ending was so sad.

We got back about 1:00 am. As we entered Quest Air's parking lot we saw this big sign that read, *"Congratulations Pistachio, 225 miles, new East Coast Record."* There was a little pistachio cartoon drawn next to it. Thanks everyone, that was a great sight to see. The next day in the pilot meeting I was asked to tell about my flight and the support from the comp pilots was great, thank you everyone.

On Saturday night, which was the last night of the Flytec Championship, during the award ceremony I was awarded a great gift from Flytec. It was a complete instrument deck with full instrument pod containing a Flytec 4030, airspeed indicator and a Garmin 12 map, along with $225 for all the miles. I'd like to thank Steve Kroop, the US distributor for Flytec Instruments, for his great support. It just adds so much to the pleasure of flying when you get wonderful support like that. I was also awarded a great sweatshirt from Mike Eberly from Flight Design, who is the US distributor for my great glider, my very wonderful GhostBuster. Thanks Flight Design, I can't wait to fly your new glider and set the new World Record with it. Last, but definitely not the least, I want to thank Quest Air and their crew for great support and for providing a wonderful atmosphere for great flying.

As I was writing this story I noticed that the skin at the bottom of my nose was dark and itching like crazy. As I started rubbing it with a wet towel, a layer of skin came off. Sounds like frostbite to me. With the running nose and the freezing cold temperatures, my nose paid the price. It may take a week to recover. However, it was well worth it.

Hang Gliding

Ernie Antinori

At the instant I leave the ground,
An unbelievable feeling I've suddenly found.
Unlike anything I've ever known,
The entire sky I now briefly own.
All the worries and problems of today,
Are left below, as it's my time to play.
As the clean crisp air blows into my face,
I pull in on the bar and find a new place.
The lift of the air brings me to heaven above,
My senses are peaked, it's a feeling I love.
The ability to fly, like my new feathered friends,
To fly as high and as far, I hope this joy never ends.

©skyout
Jules Makk 2001

Afterword

The Editors and contributors of Hang Gliding Spectacular hope you have enjoyed reading the stories in this book. The heritage and culture of our sport is shaped by the many stories, which are passed from pilot to pilot in the LZ, over your favorite cold beverage or among friends at the dinner table. Please make it your responsibility to pass on the torch by writing and recording your most memorable flying experiences either in writing or on the computer so they will be there at a later time to share with others.

➢ Remember, never whack in front of other pilots, always save the whack for when no one is looking.

➢ If you do whack, always practice your excuse ahead of time so that it sounds realistic.

➢ Always return to Hang Gliding more than you take from it.

➢ Support your local Club, Flight Park, National Organization and local dealers because the health of our sport so depends upon them.

➢ Always say Thank You to your wire crew, your driver and the land owners, a small thank you can go a long way.

➢ Lastly, always fly safely and watch out for the safety of fellow pilots no matter what shape of wing they fly.

About the Contributors

Rick Agudelo, USA

Rick Agudelo and his wife decided to take hang gliding lessons from Tracy and Lisa Tillman at Cloud-9 in Michigan. After soloing that summer and spending the next winter "hang waiting" they packed up and went to Quest Air in Florida to absorb themselves in the world of flight. Steve Croop trained Rick to fly the Dragon Fly so that he could be a back-up pilot at the Flytec Championships during April 2001. By the time the competitions started, Rick had accumulated over a hundred hours in the tug and had made his Hang-4 rating, USUAL pilot rating, his ATP from USHGA and is to take the written test for his BFI. Rick states that Florida has been good to him.

Lori Allen, USA

Lori Allen is an excellent Hang 4 pilot in her mid-40s who has been flying since the spring of 1993. Lori has spent the past 6 years living at Lookout Mountain Flight Park in Rising Fawn, Georgia. There are few pilots who pass through Lookout who do not know Lori. She is now living in Salt Lake City, Utah and attending the Utah School of Massage Therapy. She enjoys snow skiing, hiking, bicycling and scuba diving. She is a single parent of two children, Krissi and John.

Ernie Antinori, USA

Ernie Antinori became interested in flying hang gliders one summer evening while flying an RC plane at Torrey Pines. As he watched pilots step off the 300' cliff and soar until the sun went down, he knew he had to sign up for lessons. Ernie still recalls running with the glider on a small slope during his first flight; his feet came off the ground and he floated about 75 feet. From that point, Ernie was hooked. Ernie Antinori is a Tandem rated pilot with many years of mountain flying experience. Hang gliding remains a major part of life.

Peter Birren, USA

Peter Birren is an advanced pilot, flying since 1977 He is president of the Reel Hang Glider Pilots towing club. He invented the Linknife Tow Release system which is being used by NASA as well many hang glider pilots (http://www.birrendesign.com). By day he's a mild-mannered graphic designer who's been married to the same woman, Krissy, for 30 years. Peter is not only a great pilot but also a great person, one who is true blue and always looking for altitude.

Mark Bolt, USA

Mark Bolt is a 46 year old pilot who has been married for 25 years. Mark loves to fly hang gliders, and after 21 years just recently learned how to fly a Dragon Fly at Cloud 9 Air Field in Michigan. Mark started flying hang gliders at a gravel pit in April of 1979, with a half hour ground school and one demo off the hill. Mark and friends would run off the hill, with no help from the instructor, until they broke the glider. Mark fell in love with the flying experience and was self-taught from then on. Mark has a 26-year-old daughter, a 17-year-old son and a 5-year-old grandson. Mark has lived in Michigan all his life. Mark has worked for General Motors for 25 years as a tool and die maker.

Patti Cameron, USA

Patti Cameron became interested in hang gliding in the spring of 1991 while flipping through Outside Magazine. As a schoolteacher, Patti had the summer off and was looking to learn something new. The ad said, "Come to Lookout Mountain Flight Park and learn to fly." From that first day on the training hill she has been addicted to hang gliding. After 99 flights on the training hill, Patti was ready for her first mountain flight. She has since progressed to become a member of the Woman's World Team and has become one of the Ladies of hang gliding.

Richard Cobb, USA

Richard Cobb took his first training hill flight over 20 years ago, and has been in love with hang gliding ever since. He has been a USHGA Advanced Instructor and Examiner, and he recently added a paraglider and a Mosquito power harness to his pile of flying toys. In his other life he earned a PhD in Mechanical Engineering and works as a Defense Industry consultant, specializing in shock and vibration. In Virginia, he is known as the Grand-Daddy of hang gliding, having taught and influenced most of the top pilots in the region. When not flying hang gliders, he can be seen in the air with his lovely wife, Jean, under the canopy of a paraglider.

Francois Dussault, Canada

Francois Dussault, known as the SensorMan among his Canadian friends, lives in Thetford Mines, Quebec. Francois has been flying since1988. Francois was born in 1967 and has lived in Thetford Mines his whole life because the area has both great mountains and lakes for recreation. His favorite passion is for hang gliding. Francois says he needs hang gliding to stay alert in every aspect of his life; it helps him keep a competitive edge in all that he does.

Larry Flemming, USA

Larry Fleming is 45 years old; he began hang-gliding in1974, which adds up to 27 years and 2,000 hours of experience. He lives in Fresno, California. His favorite vacation area is the Owens Valley. Good friends, great flying, and new, improved gliders keep Larry in the air. Besides being an excellent pilot and model pilot for the sport of hang gliding, he is also the author of the famous hang gliding book, Downwind, still available through the USHGA.

Kevin Frost, USA

Kevin Frost was born in 1960 and enjoyed an idyllic childhood in a small mountain town in Idaho were all the men are enthusiastic outdoorsmen and all the women are good cooks. Kevin learned to fly hang gliders when he lived on Oahu in the early 1980s. Kevin has done commercial fishing in Homer Alaska, carpentry in Phoenix and Seattle, driven a rickshaw in Hawaii, and horse logged in Oregon. Presently, Kevin is a penniless glider bum in Idaho where we continuously hunts for hundred-milers.

Roy Garden, United Kingdom

Roy Garden has been a hang glider pilot for 13 years. At 36, Roy describes himself as being married, mortgaged, and involved with his two "ankle biters." He can be occasionally seen skateboarding. Roy works in the oil business as a coiled tubing supervisor, while living in a lovely flat in Stonehaven, Scotland, with his wife, brats and cats.

David Giles, USA

David Giles lives in Alabama with his beautiful wife Rachel, and his wonderful son Carter. David learned to hang glide in 1992 at his home site, Rudy's Ridge, near Huntsville, Alabama. He currently holds the Alabama XC record with a 102 mile flight made from Rudy's Ridge in 1997.

Bob Grant, Canada

Bob Grant has been hang gliding since 1972 and now, at a young 58 years old, he still enjoys free flight. Bob Lives in London, Ontario, Canada and enjoys flying the Finger Lakes of New York and aerotowing with Tracy Tillman at Cloud 9 Aerotow Flight Park in Michigan. Bob usually travels to the west coast in July to enjoy great flying and windsurfing.

Daniel Gravach, USA

Daniel Gravage was born and raised in Montana where the men are men and the mountains are high. Dan made his first hang glider flight in the late summer of 1976 at age 20. Encouraged by his wife and three sons, he has flown many sites throughout the western U.S., and Canada, and he hopes to return to enjoy the Venezuelan skies again someday.

Gilbert Griffith, Australia

Gilbert (Chainsaw) Griffith, born September 1951 in Melbourne, Australia, is a young 50-year-old pilot. Gilbert achieved his Private Pilot's License (restricted) in1968. He visited England in July 1972, left February 1976 and married 31st December 1974. Gilbert settled in Bright, N.E.Victoria in late 1976 and started hang gliding November 1976 at the "teach yourself" school of standard hang gliders. He now is flying an ATOS. He received his trike License January 1997; his Ultralite license (in Skyfox) in 1997; and paragliding license in January 1998. Gilbert's home flying site is Mystic in Bright, only 15 minutes away from home. All his flying has been mountain flying with only two coastal flying experiences. Both his sons also fly.

Mark Grubbs, USA

Mark Grubbs took his first hang gliding lessons on the sand dunes of Marina Beach, near Monterey, California. He quickly began pursuit of his healthy obsession with hang-gliding. Mark cut his teeth flying the coastal ridge-lift of Fort Funston, the thermals of Dunlap, CA in the Sierra foothills, and acquired his passion for cross-country flying during his first flight from Lake McClure, CA. Mark was awarded his Advanced Rating just in time to assist in the opening of Mt. Diablo, and was privileged to be one of the first pilots to fly from Diablo's North Launch. Hang gliding is an addiction, says Mark. "I'm glad that there's no 12-step program to help me kick the habit. I will always treasure the surging, soaring feeling in my heart when I hear the happy screech of a red-tail hawk as it banks it's wings into a 1,000 fpm core; knowing that we've shared the same experiences."

Bradley Gryder, USA

Bradley Gryder was born in 1960. He grew up the son of a cattle farmer who converted his farm into an airstrip around 1970. Bradley learned to fly an Aeronca Champ and also a Champion Citabria. He attended the Stewart Smith Memorial Fly-In at Moore Mtn, NC and saw hang gliders soaring above the mountain for the first time above; He knew he had to learn to hang glide! Bradley went on to learn hang gliding and acquired a Seagull Seahawk and a spaghetti harness. Bradley is now an advanced hang glider pilot, an owner of a Dragonfly tow plane, and a Flight Park Operator. His personal soaring machine of choice is now a Flight Design GhostBuster, although he also like to fly his friend's Millennium whenever possible. Bradley loves to teach people to soar using the tandem Pacific Airwave Fly2 and the Exxtacy-Bi.

John Hamelin, USA

John Hamelin has been flying for the past 26 years. John enjoys the relationships that he shares with his flying buddies and consider them to be the best friends that a man could ask for. John shares his flying passion with his wife, Maureen, with whom he has raised two boys. Over the years, the family has traveled to many hang gliding sites throughout the country. John hopes to be flying for many years to come.

Lyman Hart, USA

Lyman Hart was born in Chattanooga, TN, in 1961 and has since lived in 10 different states and two countries. Lyman became fascinated with flight at the age of three. Birds, kites, planes, almost anything that files holds some fascination for him. Lyman is often seen flying hang gliders and three axis ultralight aircraft along the beautiful mountains of Virginia. Lyman is a veteran of aerotowing and is one of the top pilots presently flying in Virginia.

Grant Hoag, USA

Grant (Groundhog) Hoag has been hang gliding in California and the southwest United States for 13 years. Currently, as a graying 46 years old, he confesses to associating with members of the Sylmar Hang Gliding Association in Los Angeles, which he calls home. While most of his flying is in the LA area, Grant's favorite hang-lies have originated from flights in the Owens Valley.

Karen Holbrook, USA

Karen L. Holbrook was born in North Wilkesboro, NC in 1958. When she was young, she was watching a television program about hang gliding with her brother and knew from that point on that she wanted to learn how to fly. After graduating from College she joined the US Army, earning the rank of E-6/SSG. Karen enjoyed being able to fly in numerous helicopters and airplanes during her tour of duty. One day Karen met Brad Gryder, USHGA Instructor and soon after she began hang gliding instructions on the tandem Pacific Airwave Fly2 with Brad. She made her first aero-tow solo flight August 5, 2000 on a Target; and now owns a Saturn 147. Karen loves the sport of hang gliding, and the hang glider pilots that she has met.

Ralph Hyde, USA

Ralph Hyde began hang gliding at Dillon Beach in 1977. During 1980, Ralph was instrumental in forming the world famous Sonoma Wings. Ralph spent much of his flying career at Hull Mountain and Elk Mountain in the Mendocino National Forest. Ralph has competed in most Regional events from 1984-2000, and in six National Championships from 1989-1996. Ralph retired to Lakeview, OR in 1995, where he met his wife Julie on a mountaintop in 1996.

Scott Jewell, USA

Scott Jewell is a Hang V Tandem instructor and tug pilot. Because of a lack of instructors where he started flying, he taught myself hang gliding under the supervision of two local clubs. Scott has given up a career in emergency medicine to teach others hang gliding. Together with his close friend Jan Johnson, they created Adventures Unlimited; bringing hang gliding to developmentally and physically disabled people. Scott is best known for his playful antics both in the air and on the ground. He considers himself just an average pilot, but believes, as selfish as it sounds, that there are few people who enjoy hang gliding more than he does.

Doug Johnson, USA

Doug Johnson is a young 49 years old from Duluth Minnesota. His hang gliding ratings and appointments include: Master (Hang V) Pilot, Tandem Instructor, Observer (Region 7), Basic Instructor. Doug first flew in September 1979 and became one of the famous "Skyline Skydogs" on June 6, 1980 by flying "The Rock" located in Duluth, a requirement to becoming a true Skydog. His mentors include "Skyline Skydogs" Gerry Uchytil, Danny Uchytil, Buck McMinn, Dan O'Hara, Larry Majchrzak, Jerry House, Lee Fisher, Jon Solon, Pat Boyechuck, Joe Baron, Skip Waterhouse, Larry Smith. "I learned something from every one of them. They showed me the way!"

Mark Jones, USA

Mark Jones, known as "Mark the Shark" to his pilot friends, is a 27-year old pilot from northwest Ohio. His first tandem lesson was on May 21st, 2000, at Cloud 9 Sports Aviation in Michigan, where he continues to hone his flying skills. Mark plans on spending the next few years experiencing flight at many different sites. The beautiful Colorado mountain ranges are at the top of his list.

Wayne Kerr, USA

Wayne Kerr presently lives in Ithaca, New York with his wife Rachel and daughter Carmen. Together Wayne and Carmine run First Light Aviation, their flying business. Originally from Ontario, Canada, Wayne chose to come to Ithaca for Rachel's PhD, which she is pursuing at Cornell. Upstate New York has been wonderful, especially the almost supernaturally beautiful fall colors and spectacular flying conditions. Wayne can't remember a time when he wasn't thinking about flight, flying, and things that had the ability to fly. He used to dream about gliding and spent hundreds of hours drawing airplanes and gliders as a kid. Wayne considers himself lucky that people actually pay him to combine two things he loves very much; flying and wild life research.

Chad Koester, USA

Chad Koester is originally from Indiana. After attending college he moved to Arizona where he learned to fly. Chad's formal education is as a classically trained musician and studio engineer, but upon realizing the starving process that goes with music, he moved into computer support and computer programming. Chad spends all available free time with his true love, flying hang gliders and instructing others to fly them.

Marc Laferriere, Canada

Marc Laferrière was born in Thetford Mines, Quebec He began hang gliding in 1981. Since then he has savored each moment he spends soaring with his pilot friends and the members of the Thetford Mines HG Club. Not knowing the meaning of the term "sled run," Marc is presently considered to be the top pilot in Quebec. He often soars while others are on the ground watching. As an artist for over 20 years, Marc uses his talents to capture and express all the emotions and passion of flight. He uses his paintings and stained glass reproductions to allow pilots to share their most unforgettable flying moments with others and to excite pilots with moments which will keep them soaring year-round.

Steve Lantz, USA

As a Master Rated Hang Glider pilot, Steve Lantz has been flying since 1974. Currently flying a Millennium and a Super Floater, Steve is the owner and president of Crystal Bay Aviation at Carson City, NV. Steve is also an Advanced Rated Paraglider pilot and has been skydiving since 1959. Steve is the current founder of Second Chantz recovery systems. Beginning 1980, Steve was flying his personal aircraft on a daily basis, and his flying experiences include a Romaian IAR 823, Super Cub, 1941 Navy N3N, British Provost Mk. 5 Jet, which was formerly the #6 slot plane for the Red Arrows Demo Team.

Roger Lennard, United Kingdom

Roger Lennard is a 36 year old, happily married dad with two young children. During the day he teaches biology at a school in Bakewell, a town set in the beautiful English Peak District. Having only just qualified as a pilot, Roger looks forward to many hours of soaring the English countryside.

Mark Lukey, USA

Mark Lukey is a Civil Engineer for the US Air Force at Dayton Ohio. He retired last year from the US Navy Reserve. He lives with his wife Martha, four children, his WW Sport 180 (Marsha) and his Mistral (Jennifer). Mark enjoys flying, playing music with the family, good puns, and red meat.

Jules Makk, Australia

Jules Makk , 40, lives in sunny sub-tropical Brisbane in Queensland, Australia. John began flying in 1983 and has been an avid flyer and competitor ever since. John started scribbling cartoons for the hang gliding magazines after being so inspired by free flight and the antics of his fellow flyers. His first cartoon compilation, "SKYOUT", is a collection of 12 years of hang gliding cartoons, a few of which are reproduced in this book. John's best flights have involved spectacular scenic views of the Outback of Australia from great heights. John describes himself as a Sky Tourist. His longest flight, in1987, was 252 kms, 6.5 hours, and 14,500 ft. altitude gain. John describes himself as a cartoonist , musician, songwriter, poet , artist , hang glider pilot and generally nice guy who , on regular occasions , is compelled to go COMPLETELY LOONY !!

Tiki Mashy, USA

Tiki Mashy is one of those rare pilots who will impact each person she meets. Tiki has been flying hang gliders for many years and is presently a tug pilot at Wallaby Ranch. The dedication of this book was written b Tiki Mashy and the very best way to know her is to read the words she wrote about Michael Champlin. The words are from her heart as are all her actions. Tiki is just the very best of the best. Details of her autobiography can be found in the Dedication of this book.

Shane Moreland, USA

Shane Moreland began hang gliding in 1984 when he taught myself how to fly off the hills in Oklahoma and West Virginia. Shane gave up hang gliding for 15 years and then rejuvenated his passion for real flying when he moved to the beautiful mountains of southwestern Virginia. Shane has a lovely wife, Lucia, and 9 children. Shane is the news director at the NBC affiliate in Roanoke, VA. Shane has moved to the forefront as one of the most skilled pilots in the region. Armed with his new Airborne Shark 144, Shane is often seen soaring the mountain range surrounding his home in Montvale, VA, and has recently been named President of the SWVHGA.

James Palmieri, USA

Jim (SkyDog) Palmieri has been flying hang gliders since 1992. Having been introduced to hang gliding by his lovely wife Maggie, Jim has combined his love for science with his love of flying. As a member of the editorial staff of Hang Gliding Magazine, Jim has contributed many articles. In addition, Jim and Maggie have edited three books on hang gliding and run their own publishing company, SKY DOG PUBLICATIONS. Jim has towed hang gliders behind trucks, boats, trikes and ultralights and he combines these skills with his love for flying the mountains of Virginia and Tennessee.

Maggie Palmieri, USA

Maggie Palmieri began flying hang gliders on the dunes of Kitty Hawk during 1991. Maggie's true love is aerotowing at Wallaby Ranch in Orlando, Florida, but has spent a fair share of time flying the mountains of Virginia and Tennessee. Maggie is the true brains behind the publishing of the two Sky Adventure books and This Hang Gliding Spectacular book. Presently working as a network computer specialist, she combines her computer skills with her flying knowledge to make SKY DOG PUBLISHING successful.

Adam Parer, Australia

Adam Parer was born April 1967 in Newcastle, New South Wales, Australia. As the son of an RAAF fighter pilot, he developed an interest in aviation at a young age. Adam lives close to the shore, so most of his 902 logged hours are coastal flying. Adam is now flying an Airborne Climax 13 and lives just 15 minutes from the Airborne Windsports factory. Known locally as a great pilot, Adam is one of the top coastal pilots in Australia. Adam is employed as a fireman with the N.S.W. Fire Brigades. His other interests include surfing, rock climbing and flying model airplanes.

Mark Poustinchian, USA

Mark Poustinchian was born in Iran and moved to the US after high school in 1975. In 1980 Mark received his Structural Engineering degree from the University of Illinois. Mark started hang gliding in 1990 in Arkansas. As of May, 2001, Mark has logged about 1790 flights, over 1900 hours, close to 14000 miles of XC flying and holds the Arkansas and East Coast XC records. Mark Poustinchian is a master rated hang gliding pilot and a tandem instructor. At the end of 1999 Mark gave up his position as a Senior Structural Engineer at a nuclear power plant to follow his dreams of flying. His life since then has been very simple but full of joy and pleasure. He is having a great time meeting and making new flying friends. Presently, many consider Mark to be one of the finest hang glider pilots in the USA and the world.

Doug Prather, USA

Doug Prather, 35 years young, was born and raised in Modesto, California. He is very happily married to his wonderful wife Nancy, who is also a hang glider pilot and understands his commitment and passion for hang gliding. They have a son Alex, 15, who took up the sport, as well as dog, Valerie Ashley Prather, who they treat as their daughter. She is a 15-year-old Yorkshire terrier who also loves to fly! Doug and family had plans on moving to a lush mountainous area to live and fly but he started a hang gliding business, Dream Weaver Hang Gliding in 1996, and it has taken flight. Doug also maintains an extensive collection of hang gliding books and memorabilia.

Daniel Redick, Canada

Daniel Redick was born on a farm a few kilometers from the hamlet of Wyoming, Ontario, in May 1948. He is one of the last generation to have attended a one-room country school. Daniel has always been fascinated by flight, but the love in his life is fully endowed upon his wife, his two children, and his two grandchildren.

John Reynoldson, Australia

After a quarter century of hang gliding, John Reynoldson can still be seen regularly floating around the skies of his native Victoria, Australia. John spends much of his time with communications gear for light sport aviation (www.aerialpursuits.com) or being the all-around family guy. Lately, he's been flying his homebuilt soaring trike/hang glider; and he is working on constructing an ultralight sailplane.

Michael Robertson, Canada

Michael Robertson, often referred to as the "Bald Eagle," due more to his hair style than his flying ability, has been flying hang gliders for over 30 years and has logged over 15,000 flights. He has flown almost everything that has wings. Michael is probably one of the most well known pilots in the world with so many achievements under his belt, some of which include: Senior Flight Instructor; creator of RCR Risk Management Charts; USHGA 4th Diamond Safety award; Flew from CN Tower for Diet Pepsi in 1988; Film work: "Fly Away Home" & "When Night is Falling", various TV spots including Outdoor Life Network; 1972 World Flat Kite Champion; invented the wheel for hang gliding; and maybe even taught Otto Lillienthal how to fly.

Scott Rowe, USA

Scott Rowe is a 46 year old Advanced Rated hang glider pilot from Penfield, New York. Scott began flying in 1979 at the local training site, which is a small glacial drumlin that can be launched from numerous wind directions. Hang gliding has been his passion for many years and has significantly influenced his life, allowing Scott many great experiences and friendships.

Steve Rudy, USA

Steve Rudy first learned of hang gliding in 1972 while perusing some sleazy magazine along the lines of "Big Jugs". Incongruously, they had included a short article on hang gliding. Steve soon tracked down a glider manufacturer, bought a glider, and started learning to fly by trial and error. He has been obsessed with the sport ever since. Although he lives in Reno, for 16 years the majority of his flying has been in the Owens Valley.

Jim Ryan, USA

Jim Ryan first joined the USHGA in 1975 when he was ten years old and had built his first flat hang glider out of cardboard. Needless to say, he was yet to experience flight. He first ground skimmed in a standard Rogallo and an SST in 1980 when still in high school, but then he stopped flying. In the mid-1990's he was sick for a week and lost 11 pounds. As he lay in bed he could think of nothing but flying, so he got back into the sport. Shortly thereafter he flew his most memorable flight (see story in this book).

Terry Ryan, Canada

Terry Ryan was born in 1945, a time when, if an airplane flew over, everyone ran outside to have a look. His love of physics and 'phreedom' led him to both motorcycling and wind surfing. Terry lives just north or Toronto, Canada. Flying always fascinated Terry and he has followed hang gliding from its inception. Family and career took their toll, but his dream was finally realized in 1993 when he took his first step into the air under the tutelage of Michael Robertson. Terry feels so fortunate to have a passion of any sort at his age. In 1998 Terry met a 73-year-old pilot, Otto, at Quest Air. Otto was, and still is, his inspiration. Terry has tried powered flight, but believes there's nothing like hang gliding for flying at its purest.

John Scott, USA

John Scott started hang gliding in 1984 after spotting a glider in the air on a weekend getaway in Santa Barbara. Like everyone else, hang gliding was something that he always wanted to do, and so after making a few phone calls John started taking lessons the very next weekend. John liked the idea of getting out of town so he decided to take his first lessons from Ken de Russy in Santa Barbara. And even to this day John still does most of his flying in the Santa Barbara area. The highlights of John's flying career include, a top twenty finish (top ten among US pilots) at the 1996 Nationals, his first and only major contest, and his involvement in the Michael Champlin World XC Challenge. Lowlights include surviving flying off the Alternator launch in Santa Barbara without hooking in and the Golden Hammer award at the 1987 Telluride Festival for landing in the trees near "Seizure Park."

Amir Shalom, Israel

Amir Shalom learned to hang glide in 1991 and began serious flying at 1996. Amir has been the Israeli XC champion for 1999 and 2000 and has been a member of the Israeli International Team since 1997. His personal record includes a 175 km XC flight in the southern region of Israel. Amir's currently flies a La-Mouette topless. He also enjoys flying and teaching flight by both paraglider and powered parachute. Amir flies paragliding competitions with his dog, Kai. Amir practices law and enjoys acting and being single.

Daniel Shell, USA

Dan Shell been hang gliding since 1987 using his Wills Wing Sport Euro 167 for most of that time. Dan teaches band at Sequatchie County High School in Dunlap, Tennessee, Hang Gliding Capital of the East. Few ever visit the famous Henson's ramp without meeting Dan Shell and few forget the Van From Hell he has been known to drive. There are few pilots who can better represent the finest aspects of hang gliding than Dan. Dan has been married to Cindy for six years and has a two year old son, Jackson.

Terry Spencers, USA

Terry Spencers learned to fly at Kitty Hawk Kites in the spring of 1998. Terry then started truck towing at Manquin Flight Park under the direction and instruction of Steve Wendt. It was Steve's instruction, which changed the way Terry flew, refining his flatland thermalling skills. When Terry flew in the mountains of Virginia, all the past skills came together. Terry feels he is lucky to have shared the sky with some very experienced and skilled pilots. As a Hang 4 pilot, Terry realizes that there is still so much to learn.

EJ Steele, USA

EJ Steele is a hang glider pilot with strong California roots. His only fear is a fear of heights, standing on a cliff and wanting to jump. His college afforded him a degree to enlist as an Officer (passion deep - answer elusive). When young, EJ was sifting through the phone book looking for barbers under "H" and found hang gliding... BOOM! He made the decision not to fly F-16s, but to fly hang gliders. The rest is history. If the week has a weekend, EJ will be flying.

John Stokes, USA

John Stokes is a 44 years old hang glider pilot who has been flying for over 26 years. John works for the American Eagle Foundation, a non-profit organization sponsored, in part, by Dolly Parton's theme park, Dollywood. John's first exposure to hang gliding came in 1974 when he was attending Memphis State. He saw an article in Reader's Digest, "The Flyingest Flying," an article describing people in California flying off hills with giant kites. The flying described in the article sounded like the dream flying he was hoping for. John's first hang glider was a 16-foot standard Rogallo kit costing $350. John's passion is to soar freely with nature's birds.

Davis Straub, USA

Davis Straub, a young 53-year-old pilot has been flying since 1984, the year he married Belinda. Davis started flying outside of Seattle and at Chelan Butte but now he spends most of his airtime in Australia, Florida, Texas, and Chelan. Davis is known by most pilots in the world either by the outstanding flights and records he has attained, which includes two Worlds Records - Longest hang gliding flight - 348 miles; Fastest around a 100 km triangle - 22 mph, or by the outstanding OZ reports he publishes on the Internet. Davis averages about eight major competitions every year. There are few pilots who demonstrate the quality that Davis Straub puts into all he does, whether flying, reporting or publishing. They just don't come any finer.

Tracy Tillman, USA

Tracy Tillman and Lisa Colletti are husband and wife and work as partners in Cloud 9 Sport Aviation. Tracy is an Ultralight Basic Flight Instructor, Observer, and rated Aerotow Pilot. In addition, Tracy is a certified hang gliding Tandem Instructor and Aerotow Administrator with hang gliding experience since 1977. Tracy is a master innovator, having developed structurally and aerodynamically superior light wheel mounts for hang gliders. Tracy is a major force in the training of pilots of excellent quality at Cloud 9. His aerotowing flight training is a model for others to follow. Besides being an excellent instructor, Tracy is an exceptional pilot.

Scott Trueblood, USA
Michael Scot Trueblood is a 43 years old, divorced, pilot, gifted with three children. Scott is a self employed woodworker and building contractor in Jackson, Wyoming. Scott started hang gliding in 1978 and earned his Hang 4 in 1981. Scott currently can be seen flying a Moyes Litespeed 5 with a Woody Valley Nailer harness. When in Jackson, Wyoming, look up high, you will see Scott well above the paraglider pilots.

Mark Vaughn, USA
Mark Vaughn has been flying since 1983 when he received his Private Pilot license. He flew power planes throughout the Valleys and foothills of central CA until 1984. Mark then moved to New England to attend school and study commercial photography. He lives west of Boston Massachusetts. Mark was exposed to hang gliding in 1986 and took his first lessons at Aeolus in Groton MA. From that point on, Mark never looked back to powered flight. Through hang gliding he has fallen in love with flight all over again. Mark received his Hang One at Aeolus. Flying at Morningside Flight Park in NH over the next three years, he combing his two true loves, hang gliding and photography. As a young pilot Mark enjoyed the artistic work of John Hiney, but freestyle just wasn't for him. He developed a more technical approach, instead of the dramatic flying attitudes, to hold his viewers' attention. Mark has developed special camera mounts for his hang gliders to capture different camera angles. With the use of different camera perspectives, colors, composition and the computer, he has been able to make images that are both interesting and pleasing to the eye. Many consider Mark's hang gliding photography to be some of the very best in the world. The editors of this book certainly agree.

John Wiseman, USA
John Wiseman is a 43 years old pilot who has been flying hang gliders for about 3 years. John lives in eastern Pennsylvania, 45 minutes north of Philadelphia. Although fairly good mountain sites are within a reasonable driving distance, he mostly aerotows, either from Highland Aerosports in Ridgely, Maryland, or from a private towing operation at a small airport in central New Jersey. Nevertheless, his favorite flying site is the mountain at Ellenville, New York. John is a member of the Wind Riders Hang Gliding Club based in Valley Forge.

HANG GLIDING VIDEOS
by
BOB GRANT PRODUCTIONS

The Best In
Hang Gliding Videos

Visit us at

www.skynet.ca/~skydog
For a complete listing of videos available

Or email us at
skydog@skynet.ca

Custom Made
Stained Glass Hang Gliders

by
LANCE LARSON

Any Size, Shape or Color Combination

lancesglass@aol.com

Lance Larson
10214 11th street S.W.
Seattle, WA 98146

SKY DOG PUBLICATIONS

Sky Dog Publications is a publishing house dedicated to the production of books and magazine articles about soaring flight.

We take your ideas and flying experiences and put them into print.

Sky Dog Publications
6511 Deepwoods Drive
Roanoke, VA 24018-7645
USA

540 772-4262
Skydog@rev.net
Skydogpublishing@home.com

Order Form

HANG GLIDING SPECTACULAR

Please send me _____ copies of HANG GLIDING SPECTACULAR including the interactive CD with Hang Gliding Videos, computer wallpaper, Hang Gliding cartoons & illustrations by Jules (Sky Out) Makk as well as contributor profiles@ $24.95 per copy or 5 copies for $100 (individual or club prices). Dealers, contact SKY DOG PUBLICATIONS for special dealer pricing.

Send All Check Orders To:
SKY DOG PUBLICATIONS
6511 Deepwoods Drive
Roanoke, VA 24018-7645
540-772-4262
skydog@rev.net

Or order on line at:
http://www.skydog.net

Name: _____

Address: _____

City: _____State: _____ Zip: _____

Country: _____ Telephone: (_____) _____

E-mail address: _____Amount Enclosed:_____

Comments or Special Instructions

_____
_____
_____

- Shipping: $5.00 for the first book and $2.00 for each additional book. Orders of $100 or more, shipping is FREE.
- Sales Tax: Please add $0.68 per book for books shipped to Virginia addresses.
- Payment: Please enclose check or money order.
- I understand that I may return any books for a full refund, for any reason, no questions asked.